MY AUDIENCE SHALL BE MY READER,

MY STAGE THIS BOOK.

—JEAN-EUGÈNE ROBERT-HOUDIN

HOW MAGICIANS THINK

MISDIRECTION

DECEPTION

AND WHY MAGIC MATTERS

JOSHUA JAY

WORKMAN PUBLISHING * NEW YORK

Library of Congress Cataloging-in-Publication Data is available.
ISBN 978-1-5235-0743-6

Design by Lisa Hollander
Jacket and interior illustrations by Kass Copeland

Workman books are available at special discounts when purchased in
bulk for premiums and sales promotions as well as for fundraising or
educational use. Special editions or book excerpts can also be created
to specification. For details, contact the Special Sales Director at
specialmarkets@workman.com.

Workman Publishing Co., Inc.
225 Varick Street
New York, NY 10014-4381
workman.com

WORKMAN is a registered trademark of Workman Publishing Co., Inc.

Printed in China
First printing August 2021

10 9 8 7 6 5 4 3 2 1

CONTENTS

• • • ━━━━━━━━━━━━━━━━━━━━━━━━━━━━━━━━ • • •

THE DOOR TO MAGIC IS CLOSED,
BUT IT'S NOT LOCKED.
—JACK DELVIN, MAGICIAN

INTRODUCTION

I spend three hundred days a year on the road, performing magic. I spend a lot of time on the other side of the stage, too, watching magicians. One night, I was in the audience for a performance by Yann Frisch. His act looks like nothing you've ever seen: A little red ball torments Yann by disappearing and appearing where it's least expected, driving him mad. At one point, it even leaps off the table and hits him on the forehead. And though the show is as funny as it is skillful, what happened at the end of his act that night was something nobody in the audience will ever forget.

I had seen Yann's act a dozen times and knew all my favorite moments by heart. But when he finished his act that night, Yann bowed for applause and a thick stream of water poured down from the top of the stage, soaking him and his signature white T-shirt. As the water drenched him, he extended his empty hand into the spray . . . and a bright red ball appeared. *Blackout.*

That wasn't how his act was supposed to end. But the previous act in the show used water, and this was Yann's way of winking at the audience to let them know that he'd been watching the show, too. He adapted his magic to the venue, scrambling the audience's expectations while pulling off the perfect trick for that evening.

As a magician watching a magician, I'm looking for two things: seamlessness and context. Seamlessness means that the illusion is airtight, that the magic flows naturally. If the technique is poor or the material choice is ugly, there's no illusion—so the first step for any magician is to attain fluidity, to become seamless.

The other thing I'm watching for is context. Suppose I *borrow* a dollar from a child and change it into a one-hundred-dollar bill, and then *give it back to her*. There is context, since I'm using money that belongs to someone else. There's a story line—causing money to multiply. And there's an emotional hook, since I give her back something far more valuable than what she gave me. The "magic" money feels real to the child because she can touch and remember it—and spend it!

My hope is that after reading *How Magicians Think*, you'll watch magic shows differently—not less critically, but in a more enlightened way. Too many of us watch magic shows to figure out how the tricks are done. As you'll learn, that mindset is a trap. While you're busy trying to find the solution to an illusion, you miss what is in plain sight: artistry. You miss the staging of the illusion, the carefully considered script, and a perfectly timed observation that distracts your mind or makes you laugh. You ignore the aesthetics of the show, the grace with which the objects appear and disappear, and the way the lighting, the costumes, and the props are thematically linked. You fail to grasp the metaphor of what the magician is doing and the interplay between their work and what's going on in the world around them. Magic tricks aren't puzzles, but most of us see them that way.

At its very best, magic reminds us of the thrill of the unknown. Many of the performing arts can take our breath away, but only magic makes you question whether you saw what you just saw. Most other performing arts are about understanding and experience. Magic puts front and center what we *don't* understand, so we can marvel at the mystery.

People often conflate being fooled with feeling foolish. I want to help people see that although being fooled is magic's baseline for success, it can be—and *ought* to be—much more. Magicians do things beyond our comprehension. When done well, those things should instill in us a unique cocktail of feelings that no other performing art can deliver: escape, awe, and—in the best cases—pure wonder.

I would further argue that there *is* a place where we can appreciate magic without knowing how it works. This book is a road map to that place. You'll still be fooled by the magician, but you'll notice and appreciate her choices. Magic shows make for great stories, but the better stories are about the formation of illusions, the characters who create them, and the psychology behind the tricks. Houdini observed, "Many things that seem wonderful to most men are the everyday commonplaces of my business." I'll share some of the remarkable ideas and people who are changing the way we think about magic, and even the world.

The performance of magic is necessarily shrouded in secrecy. Most magic performances are elusive by design—you get glimpses of a magician's interests and origins, but only enough to serve the illusion. My show, and the shows of my colleagues, are meant to make you perk up and ask: "Where did that go?" "How did he know that?" "Can I see that again?" Secrecy breeds curiosity. People want to *know*—they want the gaps filled in. Each of the fifty-two essays that follow is set up as an answer to one of the many questions I'm asked after shows by people who are fascinated with magic. The questions vary, but they tend to come from the same core curiosity: People are trying to better understand the power of magic beyond a particular trick. And because I've dedicated my life to creating and performing magic, they think perhaps I might have some insight to offer. Each essay stands alone, so feel free to skip around to what interests you most. I hope that, taken together, they'll give you a deeper appreciation for how magicians think.

I wrote this book on tour, in the days and hours between shows. These words brought me face-to-face with my subject every night, an endless supply of the ups and downs experienced by a performer in the trenches. The secrets shared here can't be found in YouTube tutorials or Google searches. They are psychological in nature, developed over centuries of deceiving the public. My answers are part essay, part memoir, and with one exception, I reveal everything but how tricks are done. I've been careful not to reveal too many of the actual secrets to magic tricks, yet still some magicians will inevitably be upset about the concepts I explore in these pages. But if I deepen your interest and respect for the art of magic even a little, it's worth bending the rules.

Showtime.

✦ ✦ ✦

1

WHY MAGIC?

(PART 1)

ANY LIFE IS MADE UP OF A SINGLE MOMENT, THE MOMENT IN WHICH A MAN FINDS OUT, ONCE AND FOR ALL, WHO HE IS.

—JORGE LUIS BORGES, WRITER, POET

✦ ✦ ✦

Werner Reich, a ninety-one-year-old Holocaust survivor, has a fascinating answer to why he does magic. Orphaned during the war, he endured two different concentration camps before being transferred to Auschwitz. His bunkmate there was a magician who showed Werner a simple trick, along with its secret. The two used magic to assuage hostile guards. Werner remained a performing magician his entire life. He spoke to me about the importance of jokes and magic in the camps. "They took us away from reality," he said. "They engaged your imagination and moved you away from the dismal surroundings. It is there that I learned the true value of imagination."

I asked the same question of magician Abbey Lynn Albani. Abbey was floating ten feet above a stage, rehearsing an illusion with her husband, David Goldrake, when she unexpectedly fell to the stage floor and broke her neck. The fall also damaged her spinal cord. She was flown to Luxembourg and Germany for lifesaving procedures, and for a time used a wheelchair. "After being told I would never breathe alone, walk, or move, I am now able to breathe without support, sit up, and stand," Abbey said. I shared the stage with her at a magic conference in Las Vegas and watched from the wings as she recounted her harrowing accident, then rose out of her chair and *walked* across the stage.

When I asked Abbey what drew her back to magic, she recounted the anguish she still feels about her injury. "Before the accident," she told me, "going a day not performing would drive me insane. Now it's been almost four years, and I don't know if being on a stage is even in the cards for me. I battle these thoughts every day. It honestly kills me to even think that I may never perform again. It's all I ever wanted in life."

I asked David Copperfield this same question. He's worth just south of a billion dollars, and yet he does more than five hundred shows a year in Las Vegas. He owns his own private island in the Bahamas—and a private jet to get there—yet almost never takes vacations. What draws him back to magic? An impulse to push the craft forward, it turns out. "I'm trying to change theater in my own way—not just magic. I say that humbly because I'm learning every single day. I do fifteen shows a week, and every single audience I have is like a test screening."

Werner Reich used magic to momentarily escape Auschwitz. Abbey Albani still feels a call back to the magic show stage, despite a trick almost ending her life. David Copperfield performs a back-breaking fifteen shows a week in pursuit of perfecting new material. What do these magicians have in common? Nothing, except being uncontrollably drawn to magic—and that's the point. Critics paint magicians with the same broad brush. But magic means something different to every magician I interviewed for this book, and while each was powerfully attracted to magic, they all came to magic for a different reason. What's more, the reason someone gets into magic is almost never the reason they stay with it.

Esteemed magic historian and mentalist Max Maven observed that we have to evolve beyond whatever got us into magic in the first place. Everyone goes through a magic phase, but loving magic comes from a place of wanting to figure out how things work, to know something others don't. I got my start in magic when my dad did a card trick for me and *didn't tell me how it was done*. I had to figure it out for myself. And the act of solving the trick and performing it for him hooked me. I couldn't wait to show off my new skill to anyone at school who would watch. That's what magic is about for most of us when we start. We want to fool our friends, but for me that wore off by the time I was ten.

Around that age, I became attracted to something else in magic, something subtler and harder to define: the chase. I had an idea for a trick that wasn't in the magic catalogues or in my small collection of magic books. The daydream was this: I wanted to show a handful of beads, wave a wand, and show that all the beads were now connected by a string. Not miracle material, but I was *ten*. Since the trick didn't exist, I had to invent it. So I did.

That trick—that silly stunt with the beads—would be my moment. I started to understand how little I understood, and how much more magic could be. It isn't just about fooling people. It's about *transporting* them.

✦ ✦ ✦

2

WHEN DID YOU KNOW MAGIC WOULD BE YOUR LIFE?

THE SECRET OF HAPPINESS IS:
FIND SOMETHING MORE IMPORTANT
THAN YOU ARE AND
DEDICATE YOUR LIFE TO IT.

—DANIEL DENNETT, PHILOSOPHER

✦ ✦ ✦

I can't say that I wanted to be a magician my whole life, because I've *been* a magician my whole life. I have no memory of my life without magic. In my earliest photos, I'm top hatted and caped. Dai Vernon, the most influential magician of the twentieth century, used to say that he got into magic at age seven. Then he added, "I wasted the first six years of my life."

Me too. I already mentioned that my father—a dentist by day, magician by night—kindled my interest in magic by showing me a card trick. It wasn't the trick itself that sparked my interest. It was that, no matter how I begged, he wouldn't tell me how it was done (the magician's code is strong in my family). I locked myself in my room with a deck of cards and a notepad. Four tormented hours later, I figured it out. And in that process, I was hooked forever. Writer Graham Greene observed, "There is always one moment in childhood when the door opens and lets the future in." This was mine.

I did my first show ten months later for the Wilkof family next door and charged the princely sum of $25. I've never held another job. I have toured the world more or less nonstop since the age of twenty. I have performed magic for the president of the United States (for Bill Clinton and at one of Obama's official inaugural balls). I have also performed magic at 11:00 a.m. at a strip club buffet.

I have entertained crowds of twenty thousand people. I recently did a show in North Dakota and absolutely nobody showed up—not one person. I performed for Michael Jackson when I was a teenager. I was the youngest person to win the World Magic Seminar. I fooled Penn & Teller on their hit show *Fool Us*, and I was told by producers of *America's Got Talent* that I didn't have the "it" factor they were looking for in a magician but that I should work on a new act and try out again next year. I have read minds with Jimmy Fallon on *The Tonight Show*, and I hold the Guinness World Record for most selected cards found from a shuffled deck in less than a minute. Still, more often than not when I tell someone I'm a professional magician, their response is, "You can make a living doing that?"

I have given magic my sole focus at the cost of much of my social life. Glen David Gold captures the professional magician's plight in *Carter Beats the Devil*: "With age, the world falls into two camps: those who have seen much of the world, and those who have seen *too* much." I have scarcely slept in the same bed for more than two weeks in a row in the last decade. I miss all the important stuff: birthdays, big games, holidays, weddings.

Is it worth it? When I'm onstage doing my best material, and the show happens to be going well, I experience the sensation of what it's like to actually have magic powers. It doesn't feel like sleight of hand or theater—it feels *real*. Yes, it's worth it to experience that thrill.

We teach our children that their self-worth is not determined by how fast they can run or how much money they will someday earn. Yet a magician's self-worth is almost entirely dependent on his relationship to his work. This obsessive drive has left me with few friends, but it's also pushed me beyond what I thought possible for myself. I suppose, in this way, magic has helped me understand my own peculiar paths to happiness.

Every country, every show, every trick brought me closer to this page. A heckler in Fort Lauderdale took a swing at me and taught me something about how to perform for drunk people. At a show in Wichita, an eight-year-old boy shouted something funnier than anything in my show. Every show since, I've used the line as my own, and it brings down the house. Each experience—successes and failures—is a lesson about the vital role magic plays in our lives.

How we explain ourselves to ourselves is who we really are. Writer and illustrator David Macaulay says that he "draws to understand." But understand what? For me, I write to understand magic. But I perform to understand myself.

3

WHAT IS MAGIC?

THE PROFESSION OF MAGICIAN
IS ONE OF THE MOST PERILOUS
AND ARDUOUS SPECIALIZATIONS
OF THE IMAGINATION.

—WILLIAM BOLITHO, AUTHOR

✦ ✦ ✦

Magic is about time. The moment the ace of spades changes into your card. When your signed dollar bill appears *inside* a lemon. That night the mentalist reveals a secret you've never told *anyone*. These moments—collectively less than a few precious seconds—are pure astonishment. Magicians spend their lives in pursuit of these moments. Our tricks take minutes to perform, months to learn, and decades to develop. In very good tricks, those seconds become memories. In the best tricks, those memories create wonder that lasts a lifetime.

But astonishment is fleeting. As soon as the moment is over, your rational mind steps in to try to make sense of what you saw. You're no longer astonished—you're curious. Our job as magicians is to keep you in a state of astonishment for as long as possible. Charles Reynolds, my late friend and a magic scholar, wrote, "The true magical experience should be more about wonder and less about wondering." Which, of course, is easier said than done.

For me, the joy of a standing ovation is short-lived. The audience can't take with them what they feel during my show. When you hear a great album over and over again, singing along to your favorite parts, the music accumulates meaning with every listen.

But a magic show is meant to be enjoyed *once*. The role of surprise is key to the experience—you get exactly one first time. When you watch a magic show a second time, you might laugh as hard and appreciate aspects you didn't notice before, but you won't feel pure astonishment in quite the same way. Wonder decays with repetition, which is why magicians don't repeat their tricks (see page 19).

Pure astonishment is something most of us rarely experience, but we never forget it. There's a Tom Petty lyric about getting high that perfectly encapsulates the first blush of astonishment, about where magic exists in our minds. It's at the intersection, he points out, between a memory and a dream.

Magic can be aesthetic, but it is really a thinking person's performance art. Teller, the silent half of Penn & Teller, captured this notion well: "A romantic novel can make you cry. A horror movie can make you shiver. A symphony can carry you away on an emotional storm; it can go straight to the heart or the feet. But magic goes straight to the brain; its essence is intellectual."

The problem is that good magic—I mean world-class magic—is hard to come by. Most of us have rarely seen magic of that caliber. I hope someday you will. Even most magicians themselves have seen mostly mediocre magic—the kind that amuses as it amazes but rarely does more. It's human nature to mimic what we see, which is why there are so many middling magicians.

The very best magic brings together two conditions in perfect alignment. You need spectators ready to accept that magic can be artistic, even transformational, and a skillful magician who believes that magic can have a profound effect on people. Most magicians don't believe this, and in my experience, most audiences don't, either. But occasionally, on lucky nights, an audience gets to experience true astonishment.

This interplay between magician and audience isn't simply just the most important part of a magic show; it's also what makes magic unique in the performing arts. Juliet always dies by her own hand. Sherlock Holmes always catches the culprit. But the way a good magic show unfolds depends on the audience. What if you chose a different card? What if you thought of something else? We all know it's theater, but it feels real. "Both the viewer and the view are part of the same field," wrote Robert Hughes in *The Spectacle of Skill*. "Reality, in short, is interaction."

There isn't a magic effect unless someone is there to experience it. If you're doing magic alone, you're just practicing.

4
WHAT DOES IT *FEEL* LIKE TO PERFORM MAGIC?

IT'S STILL MAGIC
EVEN IF YOU KNOW
HOW IT'S DONE.

—TERRY PRATCHETT, HUMORIST

✦ ✦ ✦

I'll never forget the first time I cut off my dad's head. I was eight, and my dad lent me the money to buy the gimmicked guillotine collecting dust at our local magic shop (I dutifully paid him back in installments of $10). The prop is one of our craft's endless examples of ingenious engineering. You lock a volunteer into the contraption, load the blade above his neck, and push down. The illusion is perfect, and the prop takes care of all the work. The hard part is learning to trust the method.

The first time is always the hardest. I bolted my dad's neck between two wooden panels and placed carrots through the two tiny holes (the blade actually slices the carrots without harming the assistant, a beautiful feature of the design). Dad was on all fours, face to the floor, as I loaded the heavy blade onto the track. I let go, and the blade slammed down "through" his neck and out the other side. I watched in disbelief, a combination of fascination and fear. *I just cut off my dad's head*, I thought. *I am now a magician.*

For me it was the right lesson at the right time. It's the rare magic effect in which you can forget about technique and focus on presentation. I learned quickly to lose myself in the routine, to believe that I could decapitate someone without harming them. I don't mean that figuratively—I coaxed myself, however briefly, into *actually* believing I had magical powers. This belief made for a convincing finale to my first magic shows.

A couple of years later, I was hired to perform at a retirees union luncheon where a US senator was speaking. In a moment of incredibly poor judgment—even for a ten-year-old—I thought it would be funny to call the senator onstage for my last illusion. I remember loading the senator into the guillotine and glancing stage left into the wing. Only then did I notice my dad jumping up and down, silently begging me not to publicly decapitate an elected official. But it was too late—the senator was on all fours, awaiting a large blade being loaded into place by a ten-year-old. To his credit, the humiliated senator smiled and played along. Nobody lost a head.

I can't overstate the importance of conviction during a show. You may not be able to observe the difference between a magician who is just hitting his marks and one who is *doing magic in his mind*, but you can feel the difference. Rob Zabrecky, one of the oddest and funniest characters in magic, opens his magicians' workshop with the line "Actors and magicians must live truthfully in untruthful circumstances." The quote is adapted from Sanford Meisner, the legendary acting coach. For magicians, this means a complete belief in your own powers.

Performing "real" magic is a peculiar sensation that comes only with complete conviction. When a magician practices so much that muscle memory takes over, the trick unfolds automatically. It's like the last minute of your drive home. You've done it so many times that it feels like the car is driving itself. When I pretend to put a coin into my left hand, even if my right hand secretly retains the coin, I myself am *convinced* that I took the coin into my left hand. With enough practice, nothing starts to feel like something. I feel its weight. I open my fingers a little to check the date. I am looking into an empty fist, but I *see* the coin there. And then I concentrate, I squeeze, and I make magic. Artifice is the enemy of magic; it has to *feel* real.

But how does it actually *feel*? Powerful. Being fully in the zone is unquestionably the best part of being a magician. I envy rock stars during the last refrain of their final song, when the packed stadium sings along. For basketball players, it must be amazing to leave the ground at the end of a fast break, peer over the top of the rim, and then slam the ball through. I'll never know these moments. But several times a week, I get to walk onstage and convince myself that my magic is real. And in doing so, I make it real for someone else. And that feels amazing.

✦ ✦ ✦

5

HOW DO YOU SAW SOMEONE IN HALF?

✦ ✦ ✦

I can't tell you that.
Not yet.

✦ ✦ ✦

6

WHY DON'T MAGICIANS REPEAT THEIR TRICKS?

> ## THEY'RE NOT REAL SURPRISES, IN THE SENSE THAT THEY ARE NOT FULLY UNFORESEEN, NOT SHOCKING. THEY'RE DESIGNED TO DELIVER ON THE PROMISE, TO PLEASE AN AUDIENCE BY COMPLETELY SATISFYING THEM.
>
> —JIM STEINMEYER, ILLUSION DESIGNER

The closer you look, the less you see. That's an old hack line magicians like to use to punctuate the end of a trick. We have confidence in our material because much of the time there's simply too much to take in. And so there's little risk of anyone figuring out the solution, even when they're laser focused. When you're fooled by an illusion, it's usually because you're zoomed in too close or focused on the wrong thing. You're watching hands when you should be watching the table. You're focused on the magician when you should be paying attention to the assistant. By the time the magic happens, it's too late to figure out *how* it happened.

The golden rule of magic, or so the elders say, is to never repeat a trick. Magicians follow this rule because we're worried we'll get caught the second time around. But it's more than that; you can be surprised by something only the first time you see it.

Think back to the last time you experienced true wonder—a film's shock ending, an exhilarating something whispered in your ear, a blazing sunset that seemed to emerge just as you looked up. Wonder is rooted in surprise, in *new* experiences. It's incredibly hard to instill wonder when someone knows what to expect.

Experiences are less impressive the more they happen. Psychologists call this habituation. If I pull a coin from someone's ear, I'll likely get an impressed reaction. If I pull a coin from everyone's ear, I quickly become the uncle who does the annoying coin-from-the-ear shtick every Thanksgiving. And it's not just tricks that get repetitive. Themes, presentations, even emotions can fall victim to habituation. This is why film sequels so rarely outshine the originals. They seek to deliver the same emotional experience when what the audience craves is profound surprise.

All wonder has an element of surprise. But not every surprise has the element of wonder. There are degrees of surprises. Suppose, for example, a magician changes a banana into a bowling pin. There will be surprise, but it will be unsatisfying because it's illogical. You're surprised—perhaps even amazed—but the path leads to a dead end. Why a banana? Why a bowling pin? Without foreshadowing or meaning or context, there is no wonder. The surprise may be impressive, but it's artless.

Building artistic surprise in a magic show is the magician's greatest struggle. Audiences *expect* surprise. So if we expect a surprise, and we get one, is it still a surprise? The ultimate surprise is one that's logical in hindsight. If I change a coin into a key, it's surprising but just as random as turning the banana into a bowling pin. If that key unlocks the handcuffs that bind my hands, however, you'll remember the coin-to-key trick because, in hindsight, it *had* to change into a key. And above all you must see the trick only once, because if you see it a second time, there will be no surprise and therefore no magic.

In 2010, Penn & Teller fooled me so completely with an illusion that as soon as their show was over, I changed my flight and bought a ticket for the next night's performance. I *had* to see it again.

The piece starts with Penn, the taller, talking member of the duo, seated alone at a table onstage. He invites someone from the audience to sit opposite him. The night I was there, he picked a guy in a NASCAR hat, with an impressive mullet peeking out of the back.

Penn handed the man a video camera that was hooked up to a live feed on large monitors, so we could see on the screen what the guy filmed. He aimed the camera at Penn, and from a distance of just a few inches, Penn started doing amazing things. Objects changed and floated, then the tablecloth itself changed color—all under the unblinking eye of the camera, operated by an audience volunteer. What the guy couldn't see while he looked into the camera was that Teller had sneaked onstage, behind him, and was assisting Penn, pulling the tablecloth out from under Penn's hands. We, the audience, could see how these feats were done, but the volunteer was clueless as he filmed apparent miracles. It starts off as a silly piece, in which Penn & Teller pull one over on a volunteer while we watch the interplay of his viewpoint (via the screen), and what's really going on as Teller waves and winks between feats.

But then Penn took the camera from the spectator and aimed it back at him . . . and the man took off his hat, wig, and tinted glasses. The volunteer *became* Teller. We had *just* seen Teller behind a prop, and yet there he was across the table from Penn. I was as surprised as everyone else and *completely* fooled. Until I saw it a second time.

When I looked where I was supposed to look, the illusion was sound. But when I knew what was coming, I also knew where to look, and the misdirection failed. It wasn't a flaw in the magic effect—very few magic tricks can withstand a second viewing. But from a magician's perspective, the first time you see a trick it's entertainment, and the second time it's education.

The truth is that magic's golden rule of never repeating a trick is more of a guideline, and one that has faded with time. There are numerous tricks—entire acts, even—that are built around the repetition of and variation on a single idea. These illusions are enhanced with every repetition. René Lavand (see page 60), an Argentinian magician, performs a masterpiece routine called "The Three Breadcrumbs," in which three wadded balls of bread keep appearing inside an empty teacup. He displays the balls—each a little bigger than a pea—and despite putting them in his pocket, flicking them off the table, and throwing them over his shoulder, they appear together in a previously empty teacup. At the end of the act, we're no closer to understanding the methods he uses. But we're *amazed* by the recurrence of the same effect despite the repetitions.

As an audience member, if you want to appreciate a magician, you have to break magic's golden rule. Anything worth watching is worth watching again, and that includes magicians. It's the reason I changed my flight to see Penn & Teller's show again. I was fooled, sure, but seeing the performance a second time allowed me to see what had initially been made invisible.

The second time we see a magic performance can be an education, and a distinctly different, experience. We can appreciate nuances like this one, for example: Was the hilarious interplay with the spectator truly organic or somehow instigated by the magician? The first time I saw Las Vegas magician Mac King, he caused a shockwave of laughter in the middle of his act. Onstage in front of a packed showroom, a spectator had chosen a card, then was asked to sign it. However, she signed her name on the *back* of the card instead of the front, so the audience could see it when Mac worked it into the deck. This made it completely obvious which card she took. It was an innocent mistake, but it was three minutes of gut-gripping laughter and genuine interaction. The second, third, even tenth time I saw Mac King, though, the same thing happened. Through nonverbal cuing, he *creates* the funniest moment in his show. He tricks the spectator into signing on the back without saying a word, and then he acts utterly shocked when she does it. Everyone who sees Mac for the first time thinks they are seeing him on the funniest night of his career.

When you watch a great magician a second time, you get to track her show. How do they transition from their opener to the next piece? How do they select her volunteers and minimize that awful minute it takes someone to get from their seat in row W to the stage? How is their technique? Does their misdirection work?

When I watch a magician for the second time, I like to sit in the back, alone if possible. I'm studying the performer, looking for context, for evidence of the magician's personality behind the magic. But I'm often watching the people around me more carefully, too. Are there lulls in the performance where people check their phones for missed texts? Or are they so enthralled, their eyes never stray from the performer? Are they reacting in all the right places or does the magician's script still need editing?

In the early days of television, magicians feared being recorded because they were afraid their acts would become irrelevant immediately after the broadcast. Before the emergence of television, magicians spent decades perfecting their ten-minute acts; they could tour the theater circuit for life without changing a thing. But after a single appearance on *The Ed Sullivan Show*, everybody would have seen it at once—it was used up.

Today things are harder still. The twenty-first century brought YouTube, which makes it easier than ever to watch magicians over and over. Any recorded magic show has to withstand the scrutiny of multiple slow-motion viewings, pauses, zooms, and Google searches.

Magicians cope with this new technology the way we always have, by staying two steps ahead. Television magicians like David Blaine and Justin Willman work with the brightest inventors in magic to devise airtight tricks that amaze both in the moment *and* after a million views. They know their material will be scrutinized more tightly than it would be with a live audience, so they rely less on misdirection and more on perfect technique and ingenuity. The closer you look, the more you enjoy.

✦ ✦ ✦

7

SERIOUSLY, HOW DO YOU SAW SOMEONE IN HALF?

SHARING SECRETS,
REAL SECRETS, IMPORTANT ONES,
WITH EVEN ONE OTHER PERSON,
WILL CHANGE THEM.

—ERIN MORGENSTERN, WRITER, ARTIST

✦ ✦ ✦

P. T. Selbit invented "Sawing Through a Woman," which was loaded with symbolism, mostly of the sexist variety surrounding the treatment of women at the time. Its creator was born Percy Thomas Tibbles in 1881, and he ascended the ranks in magic through clever inventions and whimsical plots for tricks. He reversed the letters of his last name, Tibbles, dropped a *b*, and toured the world as P. T. Selbit.

In January 1921 on a London stage, Selbit sent a seismic shock through the magic world when he made a startling announcement:

Ladies and gentlemen, it gives me great pleasure to demonstrate a modern mystery and a scientific marvel, the inexplicable problem of solid through solid, which I shall now demonstrate this evening by attempting to saw through a woman.

Selbit did just that, binding a woman at the hands, neck, and feet and placing her in a coffin-like box. He penetrated the box with sheets of glass, and then, with a razor-sharp saw, Selbit dramatically sawed through the box—and the woman. After a tense moment of silence, the woman emerged from the coffin unharmed. The audience let out a collective gasp of astonishment.

Context was everything. This was, as noted magic historian Jim Steinmeyer observed, the *exact* right illusion for the time. World War I was over, and the general public was acclimated to death, gore, and violence on a scale previously unthinkable. Before World War I, it would have been considered in poor taste to put a woman in harm's way, even theatrically. But the Roaring Twenties were about excess, and "Sawing Through a Woman" was provocative, fast paced, and, for the first time, acceptable to the public.

One of Selbit's chief "innovations" was the choice to use a woman, which played into the social narrative around women at the time. Magicians had been beheading and dismembering cast members for centuries, but not typically women, who were considered socially off-limits in such shows, so the sight of a beautiful young woman being slowly severed in two onstage, and then made whole again, was shocking, if not still about a man controlling the action. Just months before Selbit debuted the illusion, the Nineteenth Amendment to the Constitution, granting women the right to vote, was passed in the United States. So the plot of the illusion was powerful, particularly to a Jazz Age audience craving social change.

Steinmeyer points out that Selbit may not have been the first to saw through someone. The French magician Jean-Eugène Robert-Houdin wrote about a similar illusion in which a person in a box was sawed in two, but when each half of the box was opened, a full person emerged from each half. The effect is that a person was sawed into twins, which was remarkable, but the audience had no emotional investment in the transformation.

The change in women's fashion likely played a role, too. It was 1921—gone were movement-inhibiting petticoats and restrictive dresses laced up to the neck. Now a woman's stage costume could be more formfitting and flexible, allowing the box to be smaller. In Selbit's illusion the woman was confined to a box not much larger than her body, making the illusion more deceptive. (Not to mention, a woman in a hoopskirt simply wouldn't fit into a rectangular wooden coffin.)

Within six months of the debut of "Sawing Through a Woman," it was already being performed by several magicians across the Atlantic and in the United States. Horace Goldin, a heavyset, mostly silent performer, improved the box. He allowed his subject's head and feet to protrude from the ends, and he and others could separate the box to show two separate compartments—one with the woman's torso, and the other with her legs.

But Goldin's most important innovation was the way he framed the illusion. He didn't play it for laughs, the way it's often done now. ("With my luck," the line goes, "I'll end up with the half that eats.") Instead, Goldin leaned into the inherent danger of the illusion. He would have ambulances outside the theater, and in between shows, stagehands would emerge from the backstage door to empty buckets of "blood" into the sewer grates. These offstage details made the onstage illusion scarier. And the media noticed, which is partly why the illusion became a mainstay of performers and has remained so ever since.

With every great innovation, first there is imitation, and then come the hordes who only want to figure out how it's done. And Goldin had just this problem while touring the United States with his version. Early cinema companies saw the sensation the trick was creating and made films exposing Goldin's illusion, showing his exact methods. He sued the companies but lost because he couldn't prove that his ideas were proprietary.

Then, in an effort to protect his methods from rival magicians, Goldin decided to patent his "Sawing a Woman in Half" illusion. But in patenting the illusion, he made it even easier for the public to access the patent blueprints. Camel cigarettes reproduced the patent drawings in ad campaigns (see page 30), exposing Goldin's trick to millions of would-be ticket buyers before he could reach them with his show.

Meanwhile, P. T. Selbit chased the success of *his* version, "Sawing Through a Woman," for the rest of his career. He later created "Destroying a Girl," "Growing a Girl," "Stretching a Lady," and "The Indestructible Girl." But the timing was never the same as the original.

———◆———

If you really want to know how to saw a person in half, Google it. You might be disappointed. Or you might find that the secret to this century-old mystery is brilliant and creative, and that you might enjoy inventing similar illusions. Every magician starts out like you, with an itch to know how something works. But the act of pursuing the secret is the magician's first step. It isn't my place to force-feed you the secret. "The dignity of the artist," wrote Marc Chagall, "lies in his duty of keeping awake the sense of wonder in the world."

◆ ◆ ◆

8

WHAT HAPPENS IF A MAGICIAN REVEALS A SECRET?

In 1997, a magic special aired on Fox starring the "Masked Magician," a hooded figure who performed some of magic's most iconic illusions and then, after the commercial break, revealed exactly how they were done. The show was called *Breaking the Magician's Code* and came with the sensational subtitle *Magic's Biggest Secrets Finally Revealed*. It was a ratings smash. Four more specials followed.

And many magicians lost their minds. The International Brotherhood of Magicians, one of the two largest magic organizations in the world, filed a lawsuit and petition against Fox, the network that aired the special. The actions were largely symbolic, since magic effects aren't protected under intellectual property laws. But with every rant, complaint, and threat, magicians brought more attention to the show.

The shows were hugely popular, and for a time working magicians couldn't go anywhere without being asked about the Masked Magician. Even old-timers who'd seen it all predicted end times for the craft. In the 1940s, the magician community was similarly angered about an ad campaign for Camel cigarettes in *Life* magazine (see page 27). In comic book form, the ads exposed a couple of illusions alongside the slogan "No Tricks in Camels." But *Breaking the Magician's Code* was different: This was a *lot* of magic—hundreds of years of developments, all exposed to millions of eager viewers. By a guy in a mask.

The Masked Magician was almost immediately revealed to be Val Valentino, a middling Vegas performer who achieved very little success, before or after the specials aired. "The main reason I did the program," he said years later, "was to get magicians talking about the future of the magical arts." He claimed that by exposing certain tricks, he would demonstrate the importance of showmanship for those tricks.

But the truth is Valentino traded secrets that didn't belong to him for a paycheck. Thankfully for the magic community, not much came of Valentino's disloyalty. Mostly the shows revealed only the kinds of secrets that you can expose quickly on television: forklifts and pistons and motors, secret audience plants, and camera tricks. The ratings eventually declined, and the shows were phased out. The problem magicians had with the show was that it dumbed down the craft. When the only things being revealed are simple, rudimentary, and outdated methods, viewers can't help but think that the only things that separate a magician from his audience are a simple secret and some phony props. That's a tragic oversimplification and a consequence of the Masked Magician.

◆

Magic has a strict code of ethics. Revealing a trick is a privilege reserved for each trick's creator. We're rigid about that. Penn & Teller recently asked if I could teach a trick for their pandemic-sensitive magic special *Try This at Home*, and I chose to teach the way I successfully predict a randomly chosen person's height. I can teach this trick without angering the magician's mob because I invented it. But I can't expose how David Copperfield flies because it isn't my trick.

In the last fifty years of magic, there has only been one successfully copyright-protected magic trick, and it occurred just a few years ago. In *Teller v. Gerard Dogge*, Teller identified a magician in

Belgium who copied, almost exactly, his beautiful signature effect "Shadows" and offered it for sale.

In this effect, Teller displays a vase with a rose inside as a spotlight throws a shadow of the rose and vase on a white backdrop. Teller then touches a knife to the shadow, and the rose's leaves and petals fall from the vase. It's a beautiful illusion that he has been performing for decades. When the illusion went on sale without Teller's knowledge or consent, Teller was able to successfully defend his invention in court, winning a settlement of $545,000. Teller had wisely copyrighted the *visible action* of the trick as a pantomime play (rather than the secret method of the trick). This meant he didn't have to quibble about slight variations of the secret; it was clear that Teller's opponent had created an illusion that looked exactly like "Shadows," and that was all that mattered. The case was a landmark of sorts, showing the first positive step magicians can take to protect their secrets.

The Teller case is a notable exception, but magicians don't protect their secrets in courts. Modern patent and IP law makes it nearly impossible for a magician to defend the originality of a piece. Teller had the time, lawyers, and money to beat an unexceptional magician off the grid. More than a legal triumph, it was a PR win for magicians.

But the real story of how magicians protect themselves is more interesting and, dare I say, instructive for other industries. We police ourselves. The reason there isn't more theft and copycat magic is that magicians don't put up with it.

A paper was published at Yale University outlining this unusual, law-free approach to toeing the line in magic. It works like this: If I invent a trick, I have the option to publish that trick, or not. If I publish the secret, I establish it as my own. I get the pride of sharing an idea I'm proud of, and I can profit from the sale of my idea. But that also means others are welcome to use and improve it. If I choose *not* to publish the trick, it's hands off. Other magicians are *not* allowed to do the same trick or anything that roughly approximates it.

So what happens when Michaeldini, the Minnesota Houdini, *does* copy my trick? I call up Michaeldini and I say, "Hey, it's Joshua Jay from New York. I heard you're performing my 'Signed Dollar in Coconut' routine in your show. I've spent years on this thing and it closes my show, so I would kindly ask you to stop performing it."

And then Michaeldini stops. You may not believe this works, but it does (most of the time). Michaeldini takes it out of his show, ideally with an apology, and life goes on.

The magic world is *tiny*. We all know each other. And Michaeldini would know that even though I don't live in Minnesota, I know the other professionals there. And Michaeldini works for the same agency I do. Michaeldini has custom props made by the same craftsperson I use. If I shared with any of these people that Michaeldini is a thief, he would quickly find his business in peril— death by a thousand little problems that would trickle into his life. His referrals would dry up. He would find that fewer people would build material for him. He might be asked not to come to the local magicians' club meetings or find that he wasn't welcome at the seminars he attends to learn new material. Agents with crowded rosters have no place for thieves, so they might drop him or start feeding work to a competitor. Michaeldini is incentivized to do the right thing and find a new closer.

The standard theory of intellectual property is that creators rely on *laws* to protect their innovations. Without these protections, there is no incentive to be creative, since copycats can simply mimic their work. But protecting ideas in court is tough, whether the industry is software or fashion or snack foods or . . . magic. Defending an idea in court is costly, and it *heavily* favors the side that is better capitalized.

And yet, the system is imperfect. Magicians *do* steal from each other, unwritten rules be damned. And there's inevitable infighting about what constitutes "different enough." Michaeldini might ask if he can do a signed dollar in an avocado instead of a coconut. And he and I would have to figure that out amicably. He might even claim independent invention. The solution may involve him performing my trick for a fee. It can and does get messy.

But if you pull back the lens, it works remarkably well. Ours is an industry that values ingenuity and originality. The most original magicians perform signature pieces for decades, with their material safely guarded by an altruistic *omertà*, a code that most of us abide by because we expect the same respect for our own material.

The Masked Magician chose to expose material that wasn't his, and so Val Valentino was entirely and immediately discredited. I have never crossed paths with him on any show, nor have I ever even heard about him being booked for any magic show since the specials aired. The honor code can be quite effective—magicians are a vengeful lot.

The hard part is drawing the line between teaching and exposing, an important distinction for magic insiders. Exposure is when an audience expends no effort to learn how a trick or illusion is done. It's exposure if I go on television and reveal one of David Copperfield's illusions. Valentino in a mask is unambiguous exposure because all the audience had to do was sit there and learn a secret they didn't ask for. But if I sell one of my original tricks, why is that not exposure? Because you likely went online or into a magic shop or a library and sought out a way to learn magic before ending up with my trick. You showed sincere interest. You were looking to be taught in some way.

Take this a step further and let's say you spend an afternoon researching how certain tricks work. You find schematic drawings that are hard to follow and explanations of devices that are surprisingly low-tech. You learn that magicians exploit assumptions and trends when we ask an audience member to name a card or color. You find enough of that stuff to raise an eyebrow. But mostly what you find, as Teller puts it, is that magicians are willing to spend more time on a single trick than you could ever imagine. You discover, for example, that there are magicians who can execute a perfect shuffle, where exactly twenty-six cards are woven into the other twenty-six cards with surgical precision. And those same magicians have learned to do it without looking, while telling a joke. You read about things that human hands can do with enough practice that are hard for an outsider to imagine. Now that you've gotten a deeper glimpse of what it takes to make magic, it all just seems so . . . *complicated.*

Casual observers assume that the secrets to magic are elegant and simple, and those who expose them want you to think that's the case. But the truth is that the secret of any magic trick is just the tip of the iceberg. The sleights, the showmanship, and the framing of the piece are mainly what amaze you—and you won't find those secrets taught online or in a book. You can't learn them by having someone explain them to you. Those things are *earned* through a lifetime of performing magic. So even though you won't find many secrets explained in these pages, you *will* get an unfiltered look at how a magician fools your brain, and even how magicians think.

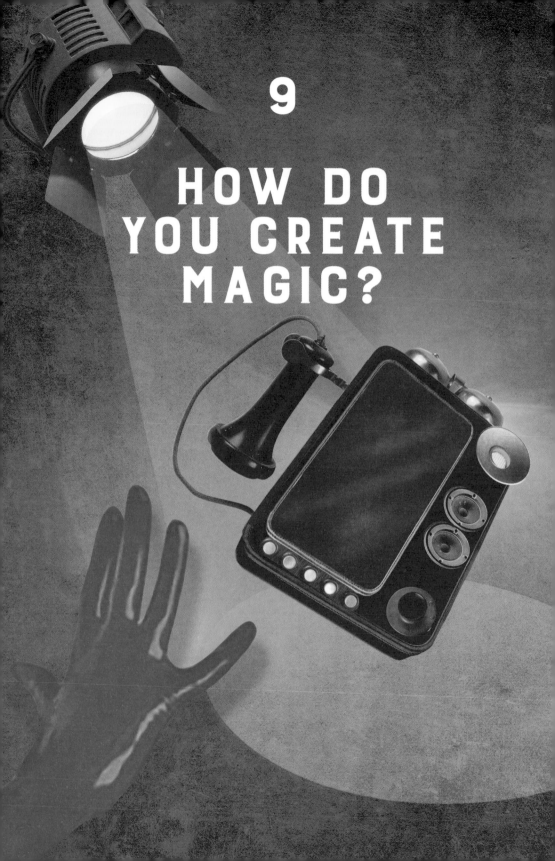

9

HOW DO YOU CREATE MAGIC?

> THE WHAT IS ALWAYS
> MORE IMPORTANT THAN THE HOW,
> IF ONLY BECAUSE THE HOW CANNOT
> BECOME REALLY MAGICAL UNTIL
> SUCH MAGIC IS INDISPENSABLE
> TO THE REVELATION OF
> AN ALL-IMPORTANT WHAT.
>
> —GEORGE BERNARD SHAW, PLAYWRIGHT

Let's invent a magic trick right now. I'm thinking about a levitation, since it's universally amazing regardless of how you present it. What should we levitate? As I write at my desk, my phone is in my periphery, vibrating and dinging and interrupting me. Everyone has a phone, which makes the object relatable. And magicians have yet to fully incorporate phones into their repertoire. So let's float one.

The first thing I do when I create a magic effect is forget about the method. How it works comes later. Instead, I daydream with my hands. In the wonderful children's story *The Magician's Elephant*, Kate DiCamillo writes, "'What if' is a question that belongs to magic." I ask, "What if?" a lot when I'm creating.

Right now, I'm holding the phone on my outstretched left hand and imagining what it would look like if I could really do magic. Would it float upward, like a helicopter taking off? Or do we go the spookier route of suspension, where the phone remains in place as I move my left hand downward, out of the way. I'd love for the phone to just take off, flying around the room like a hummingbird, but I quickly determine there's no practical way to do that. Never mind—how it works comes later.

I start to think *empathically*. If a spectator sees a phone float, what will she think? *It's a fake phone.* (That's what I'd think.) Which means that for the trick to be effective, the phone must be borrowed. I like that a lot because it will add a dimension of drama: At any moment, the borrowed phone could fall and break. And nobody cares if *my* phone breaks. But if a spectator's phone is in peril . . . Yes, I'm liking this so far.

Now, if you float *anything*, a spectator's first suspicion is wires. Whether or not you're using wires, that's what everyone will think, so I rule that out first. Incidentally, this is why magicians roll up their sleeves before making something vanish. No matter how beautiful the disappearance or how absurd it is to conceal, say, a bottle up your sleeve, *everyone* will think afterward, *I saw the bottle go up his sleeve.*

Similarly, we won't use wires in our trick, but *they* don't know that. I need to apply a principle marketers call "pre-suasion." It will be difficult if not impossible to convince someone I didn't use wires *after* I float her phone. So instead, I convince her beforehand.

But the worst thing you can do as a magician is state the obvious. Saying what is implicitly understood only serves to *raise* suspicion. I would never say, "As you can see, there are no wires attached to your iPhone." Why would there be? What an absurd thing to say! Yet novice magicians make this mistake all the time. They begin with statements that arouse suspicion, like, "Ladies and gentlemen, an ordinary pack of cards." When we see cards, we assume they're ordinary until the magician gives us a reason to think otherwise. When the magician *says* the pack is ordinary, our suspicion is immediately piqued. *But is it an ordinary pack? Why? Because he said so? Let me see those.* Now he's in trouble. We want spectators to arrive at the lack of wires on their own.

How about this: I borrow a phone and ask the person to stand a few feet away from me. I hold her phone on my hand and wave my hand above and below the phone. Any wires attached to the phone would either break or cause the phone to jostle—and so I've proved, without my saying so, that there is no wire. Then I float the phone from my hand *onto* her hand. This way, when the phone lands on her hand, she will *know* no wires were involved.

The last part of developing our trick will be the hardest: its raison d'être. *Why* am I borrowing her phone? *Why* am I floating it in the first place? Because I can? No. Too much hack magic falls into this category, and it's tiresome. "I'll cut this rope in two, and I'll put it back together." Who cares? "I'll float this silver ball in front of a cloth." Why?

The best magic has an emotional hook. "I'll show you how to win every single time you play blackjack." I'd like to see that. "My magic mentor taught me his best effect on his deathbed. I'd like to show you that now." Yes please! "This is the hardest trick I do. Sometimes it doesn't work." Whatever is coming, I'm excited.

All magic is metaphor, so to determine the context for our floating phone trick, let's think in terms of metaphor. Houdini escaping from a straitjacket is uninteresting by itself. It's impressive, and if we gazed upward and saw a man writhing in restraints, it might stop us in our tracks or prompt a photo. The same can be said for a nudist walking casually down the street. What separates Houdini's feats from mere diversion is what he stands for: an immigrant who cannot be constrained. Now, *that's* a metaphor that resonated with Houdini's audience at the time, and it resonates still. It's an interesting question to ask yourself when you watch magic: "What's the metaphor?" It helps establish context.

So what's the metaphor with the phone trick we're creating? To me, the phone represents cutting-edge technology. Floating this object is meaningful because we're defying technology with the very *symbol* of technology.

Now to the script. This is very rough, but I'm thinking something like this:

"Can I borrow your phone? Thanks. Phones today are almost like magic: the apps, the video, Siri—in the eighties this phone would have been the greatest magic trick the world had ever seen."

[The magician approaches the spectator and moves her hand into position, extended and flat. He takes a few steps back, places the borrowed phone on his hand. There is silence, and then music softly fades in, something that sounds delicate, like a violin. The phone slowly floats out of the magician's hand.]

"Some believe technology like this will eventually replace magic." [Pause. The phone lands gently on the spectator's outstretched hand.] *"I hope not."*

It's still rough, and maybe a tad preachy, but the potential is there for an extremely powerful piece. We established an effect that has it all: an immediate hook (borrowing a phone from someone), a timeless effect (levitation), and a presentation (technology versus magic). Now all we need is a method. This effect took us minutes to dream up. The method could take years to perfect, which is fine. These things take time.

The longer you've been a magician, the tougher it is to think like a *muggle* (that's magician-speak for layperson). Yet great magic cannot be conjured without empathy. "There is no room for solipsism in magic," writes Jamy Ian Swiss, a revered magic historian and magician. "If the only mind you can imagine is your own, then the only person you will end up constantly fooling is yourself—and many spend lifetimes in magic doing just that." Fortunately, audiences are tough. If the phone trick has a weakness, we can be sure our audiences will point out where. This is what makes performing a new piece so daunting—we're being judged all the time. The only way to find out if a magic trick works is to try it out.

Great magicians don't leave the audience's thought patterns to chance. Every audience brings with them a set of assumptions, a blind spot in the mind's eye. You might assume the coin is real because it appears reflective and shines in the light. You might assume the stage I'm standing on is solid and ungaffed, or not rigged in some way. You might not suspect that I have a pigeon tucked into my right sock. Why would you? If the magician can identify your assumptions, she can use them against you. This is what makes developing magic hard and slow. We might *think* we understand how you'll respond to a trick or idea or line of dialogue, but we won't know until we try. In this sense, magic is always a collaboration between the magician and audience (see page 10).

Dai Vernon famously said, "In the performance of good magic the mind is led on, step by step, to ingeniously defeat its own logic." The magician doesn't fool you. You fool yourself.

In 2010, I was invited to speak about designing magic tricks at Pixar Animation Studios. Their top animators and executives were in attendance, and I delivered a presentation on the use of narrative in magic effects. When I finished, an executive posed a question I didn't expect. "How do you solve problems in your work?"

He explained that much of the work at Pixar is about adaptation. He had found that whenever they encountered a technological or dramatic roadblock, *solving* the problem was less valuable than working around it. He hoped magicians might know something helpful about adaptation. They were working on a short film, he explained, and this film was being designed without dialogue. They asked me about how to convey a series of events *without speaking*. My answer was a trick. I performed a piece from my show—a card trick—that is done without words. I have a card selected, signed, and returned to the pack without speaking. I have a spectator take the deck and throw it in the air, and I pluck the signed selection from the cloud of fluttering cards. I never say a word.

The trick I performed was the solution to an alarming problem I faced on tour in Asia. On the first night, it became apparent that almost no one spoke English. There was no reaction to what I was doing because nobody could understand me. I knew I had to perform a trick that could be understood visually, without verbal cues. Throwing cards into the air and plucking out a chosen card is crystal clear—you could imagine Chaplin or Snoopy doing it in a skit. The choice to pantomime the trick was no choice at all. Nobody could understand my words, so over the course of the tour I evolved the silent routine into something funny. After I came back from Asia, this "adaptation" was my new opener. I still use it today.

Magicians are in a constant state of adaptation—this is how we solve problems. We adjust our material to venues and audiences. Close-up magic—meaning magic that is done in close interaction with an audience, on the street or in a theater—unfolds much like a jazz trio plays standards: with purposeful and unique deviations. In fact, the world-class magician and musician Michael Close dubbed this kind of magic "jazzing," based on its improvisational nature. There are spontaneous twists and turns in jazz magic, but there is always an underlying structure. Author John Irving has to know the *last* line of his book before he starts writing. It's the same with the magic I perform. I know in advance how each effect will end, but what leads up to it is often determined by circumstance.

The most beautiful adaptation I've ever seen was a small moment after a show in Batavia, New York. One of the other magicians performing at the show with me, Rocco Silano, was doing magic for some people at the bar. He has perfected certain magic techniques that allow him to make objects appear, disappear, and transform. They are techniques that all magicians know—difficult techniques that few actually use, but Rocco has mastered them.

He noticed an unattended glass of water on the bar top next to him, and as he moved it, he saw an opportunity. He secretly reached into the glass with his fingers and palmed an ice cube. I caught the move, but that's because I was looking for it—nobody else noticed. Rocco asked a woman to remove the cellophane wrapper from her cigarette box. She struggled with it, and everyone watched as she tore away the clear plastic wrapper. With everyone's focus on the woman, Rocco seamlessly concealed the ice cube. At this point, I had no idea where Rocco was going with his trick. (And as he would later admit, he didn't entirely know, either.)

With his empty hands at chest height and the ice cube safely out of sight, he took back the cellophane and crumpled it between his hands. "What does that sound like to you?" he asked the woman. She shook her head. "Think about it." Still nothing. "To me, it sounds like ice," Rocco said, and then he held the cellophane up to her ear so she could hear how the crinkling plastic sounded remarkably like the slow "sound" of thawing ice.

As Rocco transferred the cellophane into his other hand, he secretly switched it for the ice. He breathed into his fist, pretending to blow "cool air" onto the plastic. He opened his hand to reveal that the cellophane wrapper had been transformed into ice. He gave the cold ice to the woman, and as we walked away, she stood there stunned, cigarettes in one hand and ice in the other. I suspect she'll tell that story for the rest of her life.

The ability to conceal and switch items took Rocco decades to perfect (he is a former world champion of stage magic), but he adapted those skills to a trick that he created *as* he performed. It was a confluence of opportunity and preparation. People often ask me, "What's the strongest trick in magic?" It's the one found in a moment like Rocco had in Batavia with that woman at the bar.

People erroneously describe magic tricks as feats that defy logic. Rather, "magic is the art of making the impossible logical," says Jean-Jacques Sanvert, one of France's great contemporary magicians.

What if the magician introduces the lemon and afterward, unexpectedly, coughs a couple of times? Then, seemingly out of necessity, she changes the lemon into a glass of lemonade. This is equally deceptive, but it also has an internal logic. The best magic contains both wonder and a path to understanding. Teller writes,

"Magic is the connection between a cause and an effect that have no connection in the physical world, but that somehow ought to."

I've come to believe that all the arts are about fulfilling an inborn desire to *make*. Writing is making. Painting is making. Calligraphy is making. But we often think of magic as a performing art, something that takes place on a stage while being watched by others. Yet illusions begin as "What if?" questions that are adapted both before and, sometimes, during the performance. Magic is something magicians *make* long before we share it with the world. Behind the illusion, there is always process.

10

HOW ARE WE FOOLED EXACTLY?

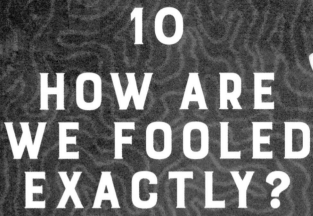

DORSOLATERAL
PREFRONTAL
CORTEX

ANTERIOR
CINGULATE
CORTEX

BRAIN
OBSERVING
MAGIC

FRISSON

SURPRISE!

THERE'S A WORLD OF DIFFERENCE BETWEEN A SPECTATOR'S *NOT* KNOWING HOW SOMETHING IS DONE VERSUS HIS *KNOWING* THAT IT CAN'T BE DONE.

—SIMON ARONSON, MAGICIAN

✦ ✦ ✦

Magic occurs not in the magician's hands but in the minds of the audience. What you see me do onstage is not what I'm actually doing. What you're experiencing—complete, often overwhelming immersion—is what's called "frisson." And although it might be a reach to compare producing a coin to an orgasm, frisson is often referred to as a "skin orgasm." It is one of the few ways our thoughts manifest themselves physically. Like crying, frisson is a physiological reaction to mental stimuli.

In magic, surprise is the key ingredient to evoking frisson in an audience. Music is the easiest trigger for it, though films, magic tricks, or even a stranger's act of kindness can make it happen. It occurs when there is an unexpected change in a pattern, like when a coin is placed in my left hand and then—surprise!—it's not there anymore. That simple trick is a disruption in a pattern that your brain has come to expect through a lifetime of experiences. When the coin is gone, it is a startling, unexpected change. *Zsst.* Goose bumps.

The goose bumps on your arm start as chemicals in the brain. Dopamine is released when a positive surprise occurs. Gambling addicts, for example, experience a rush of dopamine when they are surprised by a favorable turn of the cards. Magic tricks provide a similar surprise and a similar chemical reaction in the brain.

Gustav Kuhn, an expert in cognitive psychology, studies the brain's relationship to magic and deception. He and his colleague Ben Parris were in search of precisely where in the brain magic is processed. "Neither of us seriously believed that magic could be localized to one discrete area," Kuhn admitted. But they did learn that two brain areas were particularly active when people watched magic tricks: the dorsolateral prefrontal cortex and the anterior cingulate cortex.

These two areas are responsible for identifying and resolving problems, and their interplay is key to understanding why we feel astonished. Magic tricks are sorted in the brain as problems to be solved. When they can't be solved, they're transferred to the hippocampus, where dreams are stored. Magician Juan Tamariz (see page 239) intuited this when he described a good magic show as a dream yet undreamed. You input a magic trick into the brain, and when it can't be solved, it's stored as a dreamlike memory. The more shocking the magic, the closer we get to true astonishment, and the more we feel . . . goose bumps.

Physical reactions to the unexpected are an evolutionary by-product. Our hair stands on end when we are alerted to danger in our midst—an unexpected noise or, say, a person floating above the stage. We are jolted into a different frame of mind.

That frame of mind is called "System 2 thinking," according to Nobel Prize–winning psychologist Daniel Kahneman and his research partner, Amos Tversky, who classify the brain as existing in two states. System 1 is our base state, which is what we're in as we begin to enjoy magic, our thinking governed by commonsense, automatic, emotional responses. It's an unconscious state—we aren't thinking about thinking about magic—we're just enjoying the show.

But when there's a glitch, a surprise we can't rationally explain, System 2 overrides our brain, scrutinizing the memory of every stimulus we just saw. *Why isn't the coin in his left hand? Did he really put it there? Did I see the coin in his right hand first? Was I looking away at any point?* System 2 is our rational, calculating side. It's the state you're in when you're 100 percent focused. When System 1 fails, System 2 kicks in to reconcile what you've seen with what you know. And when System 2 fails, you're left with . . . astonishment.

The film director Paul Schrader said, "The best films start when you're walking out of the theater." The same is true of magic. Only *after* your brain has tried and failed to explain the trick does it become impossible.

Impossibility is a process. A magic trick doesn't leave the magician's hands as magic; it *becomes* magical through a sequence in the spectator's mind. It's not a lack of logic that allows us to enjoy magic; it's a healthy dose of logic that *creates* an impossible memory. Jerry Andrus, an inventor and magician, knew this to be true: "Usually when we're fooled, the mind hasn't made a mistake. It's come to the wrong conclusion for the right reason."

Be it science or intuition, these ideas account for the diabolical ways magic is created. Juan Tamariz understands the way audiences think and reverse engineers his effects precisely to evade the brain's thought processes, dubbing his technique the "theory of false solutions."

The idea is to analyze every conceivable solution for a trick—for example, the disappearance of a coin. *It went up your sleeve. You never had a coin to begin with. You kept it in your right hand.* The viewer will choose one of these false solutions that isn't correct but is plausible. As Tamariz places the coin into his left hand, he might choose *not* to show his right hand empty. He could, since the hand is actually empty. But instead he has anticipated that your mind will deduce that if the coin is gone from his left hand, it must be in his right hand. He will then guide you into the logic trap he has laid. And well after the coin is gone from both hands, his right hand might even appear in a slightly suspicious position, all the while strengthening your System 2 thought process to believe the coin *must* be hidden in his right hand. At just the right moment, he can show his right hand empty. And you're *completely* surprised, thanks to his theory of false solutions.

The bigger the surprise, the bigger the astonishment. "The shock of mystery suspends any ability to analyze," says Tamariz, "as well as the desire to do so." Some magic tricks (and movie endings and orchestral crescendos) are so powerful that we give in to the moment and bathe in their intensity. These are the fleeting moments we magicians are forever chasing. But creating them is enormously difficult. One of magic's great paradoxes is that our audiences *expect* surprise. The challenge for us as magicians is to amaze you in ways you didn't expect, to make you think, *I didn't see that coming,* then, *but I should have.*

11

WHO ARE YOUR FAVORITE MAGICIANS?

(PART 1)

✦ ✦ ✦

There are several magicians whose work I admire above all others—Penn & Teller, David Copperfield, and David Blaine, to name a few. One of the most gratifying parts of writing this book is getting to spend time with each of them to learn about their processes. But all of the magicians in this three-part series have one thing in common: You've probably never heard of them.

JERRY ANDRUS
(1918-2007)

Magic is arcane. We magicians keep to ourselves, so much so that some of the best magicians in the world aren't even professionals. They practice their craft between shifts or underneath their desks, away from the prying eyes of their bosses. Perhaps the most prolific magician of all time—with more than two thousand original tricks published—was a machinist in a factory. One of the finest sleight-of-hand performers I've ever seen is a sales associate at FedEx. And then there is Jerry Andrus, a lineman for the Pacific Power Company in Oregon, one of the most creative magicians who ever lived. When I met Jerry, I was just starting to perform on the magic convention circuits. At that time Jerry was already a star, receiving honors and ovations in the convention shows I was opening.

One of the things that made Jerry unique is that from an early age he vowed to *never* tell a lie. Only with Jerry, it wasn't lore—he was serious. When I first heard about Jerry's vow, the playful side of me wanted to test it as soon as I met him.

"What did you think of the guy with the doves?" I asked.

"I don't really care for that kind of magic," he told me.

I tried again. "Did you like the trick I showed you yesterday? The one where the coin appeared on top of the deck?"

"It was over too quick."

Damn, I thought.

It wasn't just that Jerry never lied; it was his delivery that resonated. He leveled blunt, unvarnished truths without an ounce of hesitation or coyness.

Never telling a lie is hard enough in daily life. Try *not* to tell the everyday white lies that get us out of dinner with neighbors or assure our kids what great artists they are. It's not easy, but possible, maybe. What's hard to fathom is how a *magician* can go a lifetime without telling a lie. And yet Jerry Andrus *never* lied, not even onstage. He wouldn't say, "Please choose any card you like," unless you *really* had a free choice. It's a brave, unnecessary, and artistic choice, and it makes performing magic almost impossible. Well, it *would* . . . for anyone but Jerry Andrus.

Jerry's second self-imposed guideline was yet another feat: He performed only original material. If someone else created it, he wouldn't touch it. This is true in a general sense with other magicians I admire, but Jerry was fanatical. He wouldn't even use standard moves in his effects. (It's nearly impossible to explain to non-magicians how impressive this is.) Magic, like everything, is based on certain fundamentals. Everyone—and I mean *everyone*— uses these moves and a hundred others in their own sequences and combinations. They are the building blocks of our craft. But Jerry invented his own sleight-of-hand vocabulary. Every move and moment in his original magic was made up of a dozen or more orig-inal sleights. The sheer creative power required is staggering.

My favorite Jerry Andrus effect was called "Zone Zero." Jerry displayed a large board with a hole in the middle of it. He then presented a bright yellow ball and placed the ball in the hole. When he did, the ball disappeared. He would show both sides of the board, then reach his hand back inside "Zone Zero" to retrieve the ball. The effect is right out of a comic book, with holes that supposedly go into other dimensions. Classic Jerry.

Because he wasn't a professional magician, Jerry cared nothing for practicality. He was free to innovate without the constraints a professional worries about: angles, reset time, durability, or level of difficulty. He published a move in the 1950s called the "Sidewinder Shift," where a chosen card was pushed through the deck and secretly out the other side, concealed between the hand and the wrist. It was so difficult that people didn't believe it could be done. Having seen—or I should say, *not* seen—the "Sidewinder Shift" in action, I can say it was invisible and perfect in Jerry's oversized hands.

Despite his low profile, Jerry is famous among magicians and known also in the skeptic community. He was an outspoken agnostic who opposed pseudo-science in all its forms. His performances could be heavy-handed at times, but he also offered explanations and comfort to his audience as he fooled them. "I can fool you because you're a human," he would say. "You have a wonderful human mind that works no different from my human mind." He wanted people to know that being fooled by something didn't mean you were stupid.

Among his many quirks, Jerry wrote poetry, invented his own button-free dictation machine, and was a pioneer in an alternative layout for the now-standard keyboard.

In 2003, I found myself on tour in the Pacific Northwest and asked Jerry if we could meet up. He invited me to what he affectionately referred to as the Castle of Chaos, the home he had lived in since 1928. (After his death in 2007, a couple bought and restored the house, and it's now a registered historic place open to visitors.)

The house was comically small and in disrepair. It had a distinctive keyhole window in the front, and the whole property, inside and out, was, well, jerry-rigged. He had designed an organ that was integrated into the electricity of the house—as he played, lights flickered on and off. The organ itself was a messy sea of wires that looked more like a homemade bomb than an instrument. He had a treadmill in his kitchen on which he mounted his computer—back when computers were huge and had separate towers attached to monitors. I remember that a pan on his stove was incredibly filthy. "Jerry?" I asked, pointing to it.

Without shame or interest, he replied, "I don't wash my pans." Jerry never lied.

His backyard was what everyone—from neighborhood kids to Jerry Andrus fans around the world—wanted to see. It was an optical illusions laboratory, filled with creations as big as cars, cobbled together with rotting wood and rusted-out nails. There were concentric rings hanging from the trees, which seemed to pass through each other in impossible ways, and a sign with an arrow that always seemed to point toward you, no matter where in his yard you were standing. Whatever fame Jerry had as a magician and skeptic paled in comparison to his notoriety as an illusion designer. Many of the illusion toys you may have played with as a kid were created in Jerry's backyard. He was paid for a few of them, but he wasn't the type to patent his ideas or chase copyright infringements. I was told he died more or less penniless, which is not surprising, because he was clearly unmotivated by money. Even while he was alive, museums featured solo exhibitions of his awe-inspiring optical illusions.

"Box Impossible" is the signature Jerry Andrus illusion everyone wanted a selfie with, decades before selfies were a thing. It was a box with no top and bottom, and when you looked at it from the right angle, your subject was both inside and outside the box at the same time, an Escher drawing come to life. Much like Jerry himself, it begged for a second look.

———◆———

RUNE KLAN
1976-

In 2010, a clip emerged of a shocking, audacious magic trick. Denmark's Rune Klan, a caustic comedy magician, borrowed a woman's shoe and proceeded to bake a bread roll inside it. He poured in flour, then water, then a pinch of salt, lit everything on fire, and—*poof!*—pulled a bread roll from the woman's shoe.

The woman happened to be the queen of Denmark. The clip was a viral sensation, and to this day if you ask any Dane about Rune Klan, they'll respond, "The guy who baked bread in the queen's shoe?"

Magicians have been baking cakes in borrowed hats for more than seventy years, but using a shoe is somehow even more bizarre, particularly when it belongs to a monarch.

Rune and I met as kids—he was twenty-one and I was fifteen. At an age when many of my nonmagician friends were spending their summers at camp, I convinced my parents I was responsible enough to tour the country doing magic shows and lectures. Rune and I toured the country together as "move monkeys," the magic equivalent of skateboarders, our acts filled with unnecessarily difficult moves because, well, we could do them and most people could not. I learned from Rune that to be great, you had to be bold. I knew even then that Rune was a genius destined for great things.

Twenty years later, I believe he has achieved greatness. I'm biased, of course, but Rune is performing the most innovative material in magic today. He's famous now in Scandinavia and has a Warholian Factory near his home, a large studio space in which he spends his days. It has a length of aerial silk chained to the ceiling and a pop-up book the size of a Jeep. The tables are covered with prototypes and inventions, cobbled together with duct tape and sloppy glue jobs. Local magicians pop in and out to work on their own material, and Rune will offer his help if he's not asking for some himself.

Rune found fame early with an edgy comedic style that teenagers loved. But as he and his fans have matured, so has his comedy. In the beginning, he made fun of magic. He was an icon for the teens he played to—giant spliffs appeared from his mouth, a cloth held at crotch level "mysteriously" moved on its own, and when he tried to turn a washing machine into a raccoon, he "inadvertently" revealed a washing machine made of fur with a raccoon tail.

On his first national tour, he wanted to open the show by appearing magically before the audience. His team built a sturdy chamber of Plexiglas that would fill with smoke before he appeared inside. "It just wasn't my style," Rune explained. "It felt more like Copperfield than me." His solution was quintessentially Rune. The lights went down in the theater as *Carmina Burana* blasted. Huge arrows pointed toward the Plexiglas box as it filled with smoke, the production values and garish music conjuring a Cirque du Soleil vibe. Then the music cut off abruptly, and a spotlight shined near the wings of the stage. Rune walked on, sipping a beer. He pointed to the box and said, "That would've been *so* cool if I was in there, right?" It was absurdist, visual comedy, and the audience loved it.

But the shtick got stale. After a handful of tours and television specials, the same old routine wasn't shocking anymore. Rune was older, and making fun of magic felt too easy. That's when Rune blossomed into an artist.

He reinvented himself with a series of penetrating concept shows. In one, Rune partnered with some of the best musicians in Denmark and did beautiful, manipulative magic to live accompaniment, many of the tricks partially improvised each night. No two shows were exactly the same.

In *Childless*, his most recent creation, he explores the ten-year struggle he and his partner faced trying to conceive and, eventually, adopt a child. There are laughs in the show as he parodies his thirty-something friends—the helicopter moms and dads—but it's mostly a heart-wrenching story of wanting a child and not being able to have one. The magic in the show is beautiful, but the story makes you weep.

"If an idea does not scare me, I will not do it," says performance artist Marina Abramović. Rune is the same—restlessly provocative.

My chief complaint about magicians, even great magicians, is that they often lack vision. Magic is boundless in both scope and scale—few magicians master the art of close-up magic, and fewer still can command a stage. They require totally different skill sets, yet Rune has both.

All of Rune's ideas sound like dead ends until I see them performed. "I'm going to do a card trick and talk about my dad's death," he said to me on the phone recently.

"Okay," I replied. What else could I say? It didn't sound like much of an idea to me. But in a couple of years, I'll see it onstage. And it will be wonderful.

———◆———

RICHARD TURNER
1954-

Richard Turner can cut a packet of playing cards and, by feel and weight, tell you exactly how many cards he has cut. He can deal imperceptibly from the bottom and even the center of the deck. Turner, a Texan, has performed on television all over the world as "The Cheat," a riverboat gambler–style character, often wearing rhinestone shirts and a flashy belt buckle. Offstage, he has excelled at *Wadō-ryū* karate and, as a sixth-degree black belt, earned the title of Master Turner. He has even invented a card game called Batty that has a cult following related to the mathematical expertise required to solve it.

Also: Richard Turner is blind.

When Richard performs, his lack of sight is never mentioned until after his show, if at all. When the curtains part, Richard is already seated at a card table flanked by spectators. He is engaging and funny and wildly impressive with his sleight of hand. Most viewers never realize that he can't see the cards or his hands or the audience.

I've never fully understood Richard's artistic choice, but I'm not in Richard's shoes. It seems to me that the poetry—or maybe it's the paradox—of being one of the finest sleight-of-hand artists, who also happens to be blind, would be something to reveal rather than conceal. Surely it would increase the audience's appreciation for his artistry. Stevie Wonder isn't defined by his visual impairment, but it's an essential part of his narrative and is evident in his lyrics and live performances. If the audience was made aware of Richard's disability, the reactions might be stilted or steeped in pity. Richard's choice ensures that the audience defines his show by his exceptional skill set—and nothing else.

I know how Richard accomplishes his sleight of hand—with more hours of practice than anyone I've ever known. I've never seen Richard without a deck of cards, even when we've shared a meal, during which he mostly practices perfect one-handed shuffles. The thing I most admire about Richard is how he achieved his level of skill without the benefit of sight. Repetition practice is not unusual for talented magicians, and practicing without vision isn't an insurmountable obstacle. But the moves Richard has mastered are invisible to the eye, and that requires fine-tuning the angles and the finger positions of each hand. To achieve this, he is uncompromising about his technique. How does he know he's not exposing something from the front angle? How does he know what part of the deck to hide at the right time? Richard is as good at cheating techniques as anyone I've ever seen. All the other cardsharps sit at home all day long, staring into a mirror as they practice. Whereas Richard does it all in the dark.

He's nevertheless uncompromising about his technique. When I see him after a show, he's normally critical of his performance. It always looks flawless to me, but it "feels" off to him, an instinct he surely trusts because he must do everything by feel. The United States Playing Card Company employs Richard as a touch analyst, helping them with quality-control issues on the texture and feel of their cards.

Some years ago, before I ever shared a stage with him, I called up Richard and introduced myself. I told him I would be on tour in San Antonio and asked, sheepishly, if I might spend a few minutes with him to get an autograph. He invited me over to his house, and we spent nine glorious hours together, exchanging secrets.

Sharing magic with Richard Turner is a unique experience. At his kitchen table, he knocked me out over and over, fooling me with sleight of hand I couldn't see, despite staring at his hands from inches away. But how could I show him my tricks?

When I asked Richard for help with my bottom deal, he told me he wanted to "see" it, then placed his hands on top of mine and asked me to do the move.

"Too much tension in your left hand," he began, like a doctor dictating a patient's vitals to a nurse. "You should grip the deck deeper, and you should flatten your fingers to get rid of the finger flash happening as you take each card." We spent several hours at Richard's kitchen table, the master and an apprentice. His hands rested on mine for a great deal of that time, and if an outsider had been looking on, it might have appeared that I was learning by osmosis, soaking up Richard's decades of perfection. If only.

RENÉ LAVAND
(1928-2015)

At first, it would appear that René Lavand had little in common with Richard Turner. He was from Argentina and spoke almost no English, and unlike Turner's "The Cheat" persona, Lavand was suave, weaving stories and poetry into his close-up magic. But Turner and Lavand have more in common than being two elite sleight-of-hand artists. At age nine, they both developed disabilities. Turner lost his vision, Lavand his right hand. While playing at a carnival, René was hit by an errant automobile, and his right hand was crushed. He wore a prosthetic for the rest of his life.

Lavand came to magic later than most. He abandoned a banking career in favor of magic, first as a stage illusionist and eventually as a close-up magician. Lavand pioneered the powerful combination of storytelling and magic. His performances often started and ended with monologues that spanned topics as diverse as Pablo Neruda's poetry, living with war, and Argentinian folklore.

Because seemingly all magic tricks benefit from the use of two hands, Lavand had to invent his own physical "vocabulary" of sleights. He devised ways to shuffle and secretly unshuffle a deck of cards with just his left hand. He learned to false deal from the bottom and second and third from the top. Nearly all vanishes, appearances, and changes are accomplished during a transfer from one hand to another, whether it's with cards or coins or—in the case of Lavand's signature trick—a wadded ball of bread. But without a second hand to transfer *to*, Lavand devised an entire lexicon of new and wonderful sleights that effect these vanishes and changes with five fewer fingers than anyone else.

I first saw René when I was thirteen, at a show in Washington, DC. At the time I loved magic for what it was—something I used to fool my friends at school, a purpose for my restless hands. But René Lavand offered more. As he manipulated the cards, he quoted

Picasso and Borges and talked about the magician's role in our lives: "That's why I've come here—to stimulate *your* sense of wonder," he said. After his show I got to meet him, and I even managed to stumble through my own woefully inadequate trick for him, my thirteen-year-old hands trembling from start to finish.

At certain moments in our development, people come into our lives for just a moment and change the way we think about our craft or ourselves. Richard Turner and Rune Klan were instrumental to me because they weren't over-the-top characters. But René Lavand was larger than life, unlike anyone I had ever met. He opened my eyes to the idea that there was a level *beyond* being a great magician, that it was possible for a magician to be an artist.

12

WHAT DO YOU DO FOR A LIVING?

I CAN'T REALLY DO MAGIC;
I CAN ONLY HELP
YOU TO SEE IT.

—PETER SAMELSON, MAGICIAN

✦ ✦ ✦

"I'm a magician," I say with no small measure of pride, when people ask what I do. This is usually followed by disbelief. "Do you do anything else?" is a common follow-up. People seem unable to wrap their heads around a job that is, at its core, about fantasy. They tend to view it as trifling. Flimsy. A diversion.

This disconnect stems from the difference between what a magician does and what the audience sees. The magician executes a series of rehearsed movements, synchronized with words or music, and what the audience sees is . . . magic. But what the audience sees isn't really there.

It is different from an actor onstage. Lin-Manuel Miranda isn't *really* Alexander Hamilton—we know this as we watch from our seats, no matter how transported we are by his technique, ability, and talent. Wrapped within the performance of magic is an audience *trying* to figure it out—trying *not* to believe, and yet the magic occurs. Call it an unwilling suspension of disbelief.

Because I'm a magician, what you see me do is very different from what I'm actually doing. You see an assistant floating, but I see a network of complex methods and principles interwoven to create an illusion. What connects the magician to the audience? Very little, on the surface.

I can't help feeling that what I'm doing for a living is . . . fake. And what I want, artistically, is to give the audience something real, not something that feels real only for a moment. Fooling people is ultimately unfulfilling. There has to be something more to magic than amusement and distraction.

I'm not the only one to yearn for something deeper than an illusion. "Although I know it can't be done," said M. C. Escher, the fantastical, math-inspired artist, "I want to do it anyway."

Because if all I have to give isn't real, then what is the magician here for? Distraction? Comic relief? I used to be uneasy about the magician's place in the world. Then I went to Canada.

I was in Toronto for my first book tour. There were three of us onstage, each of us authors with new books out. The first author on the panel had just returned from Afghanistan; his book chronicled his struggle with PTSD. He gave a lovely reading. Next up was the guy next to me, who wrote a book about surviving cancer. He took questions from the crowd. It was, as you would expect, a harrowing few minutes. The bookstore's manager introduced me by saying, "And now our magician will judge our pumpkin-carving contest out back."

Real authors do readings and take questions, whereas magicians . . . judge pumpkins. But I wasn't offended. The other two authors wrote about serious, consequential things. I'm a diversion from things like war and cancer. After awarding the winning pumpkin, I performed for a hundred or so people and signed some books. What touched me, though, was talking to people after the show. Nearly everyone I spoke with that night was involved in the Middle East conflicts in some way, or was a cancer survivor. But one person after another came up to see more magic. One kid in particular was unrelenting.

"Why do you want to see so many card tricks?" I asked him.

"Because I'm in and out of a hospital all the time," he explained. "I'm a full-time patient. When we're doing magic, I feel like myself."

I never forgot that kid or what he said. When *we're* doing magic. *We.* He understood that magic isn't something a magician performs at his audience. It's a dance, and he felt part of the experience. And that experience let him step outside himself (and his health issues). Magic made him feel alive.

It makes me feel alive, too. Magic is so much a part of me that it's instinct. I remember a family holiday gathering in my teens where there was a big spread of food, aunts and uncles, and presents. Late in the evening, my mom realized I had been gone for an hour and searched the house to find me, alone, on the floor, practicing. I can't pull myself away from a deck of cards, ever. She asked a fair question: Why couldn't I put magic down for even one evening?

I told her that I do magic because I can't *not* do magic. I don't stop because I don't want to stop.

As magicians, our purpose is to show people something about themselves. Photojournalist Dorothea Lange wrote, "The camera is an instrument that teaches people how to see without a camera." The magician is the instrument to show people how to experience mystery without a magician.

13

HOW OFTEN
DO MAGICIANS
PRACTICE?

YOU CAN'T EVALUATE THE *IDEA* BEHIND A MAGIC TRICK UNTIL YOU SEE IT PERFECTLY EXECUTED.

—TELLER, MAGICIAN

It's a little after 2:00 a.m. right now. When I start to fade, which will be soon, I'll put this laptop down and turn off the lights. But then I'll reach for a well-worn deck of cards on my nightstand. I know exactly where they are, even in the dark. As I do every night before falling asleep, I will lie on my back and stare into the night, practicing card moves in the dark. Some nights it's just a few minutes of shuffling and tinkering. If I'm actively practicing something new, I might work for an hour. Most nights the deck makes it back to the nightstand, but there's a decent chance I will wake up with playing cards all over my bed.

There is also a deck on top of the refrigerator and one in the magazine basket next to the toilet. They're in every coffee table drawer in the house, and I have spare decks in every coat I own. When I fly back to Ohio to visit my parents, I have decks stashed around their house as well. Mom would never touch those decks—she gets it.

When I'm asked how often I practice, I don't know how to answer the question, because I'm practicing nearly all the time. I'm grateful that I'm a magician and not a cellist, because my instrument can be practiced at the movies, on planes, and over a meal. It's not that life gets in the way of practice or practice gets in the way of life; both have, at this point, merged into one activity. It may look like a quick trip to the dry cleaners to you, but for me it's a chance to perfect a new way to steal a card from the deck. Long line at the post office? It's just fifteen extra minutes to work on dealing cards from the bottom of the deck. People are so wrapped up in their own lives that the vast majority don't even notice playing cards disappearing and reappearing at my fingertips. If I'm practicing over a meal, more often than not the server will say, "Card player, huh?" I just nod and keep practicing.

The defining element of magic practice is precision. The pressure of the little finger or a millimeter of motion can be the difference, in a show, between a gasp and shrug. Legendary football coach Vince Lombardi nailed it when he said, "Practice does not make perfect. Only perfect practice makes perfect."

Darwin Ortiz is a magician and cheating expert. During his closing piece, "Ultimate Card Shark," he masterfully deals himself four aces and then a perfect bridge hand. At one point he stops and asks, deadpan, "Do you realize that in the time it took me to learn this, I could have been a doctor?" It's funny. But also true. At the highest level, magic is a lifestyle. You don't practice it between tennis lessons or do it only when you're booked for a show. You live it and breathe it all the time. When it spills over into the rest of your life, you know you're on the right track.

When I encounter new people, I often enlist them to help with a work in progress. "You're a seamstress? How interesting. Let me ask you something: What do you know about secret pockets?" When I watch a film, all I can think about are how the special effects work and whether I can adapt them to my work. I paid attention during Alfred Hitchcock's *Vertigo*, but only because I thought I could use the same plot twist in a card trick. (I did—the trick is called "Hitchcock," and it's a feature in my show.) The French have a term for this type of career immersion, for which there is no English equivalent: *déformation professionelle*, or the notion of seeing the world through the lens of your profession.

I've learned that practicing magic looks alarming to the uninitiated. People have observed me doing the same mundane action—putting playing cards in their case or dropping a coin into a glass—over and over, thousands of times. I also practice in total darkness, so I can learn to perform complex sleights without looking at my hands.

Practice as a magician usually begins with careful analysis of the action we're trying to simulate. If magic is about doing the extraordinary with the ordinary, the first step is learning to recognize what's ordinary. Perhaps you want to learn a "false transfer," the term for pretending to place an object into your left hand while secretly "palming" it in your right hand. You would begin this study *not* by learning the mechanics of the false transfer—that comes later. First, you want to think about something you likely never thought of before. *Exactly what does it look like when I take a coin in my right hand and place it in my left hand?*

No detail is too small in this analysis. What is your left thumb doing during the action? Where are you looking? How is your posture? A key component during a false transfer is the placement of your feet. I am not kidding—this stuff matters.

Once you know what the real action looks like, you begin to understand what the fake, simulated action *should* look like. You alternate between putting a coin in your left hand and doing the false transfer, where you merely pretend to put it in your left hand. You practice in front of a magician's mirror, a three-way panel that shows you three angles in one glance. What you're looking for are "flashes," a magician's term for exposing a move. (If you want to anger a magician, go up to him after a show and tell him he flashed.)

After a hundred times, there is still a clear difference between the take and the fake take. But after five thousand or so times, you're ready for the spouse test. "Which hand?" you ask. If they can tell where the coin is, it's back to the magician's mirror.

There is dire frustration and utter joy in rehearsing sleight of hand, the same duality an athlete feels after an intense workout. Sleights require so many tens of thousands of repetitions that often my hands ache after an intense practice. Learning to *enjoy* this pain separates the very best from the rest. It becomes a matter of pride.

After every action, there is analysis. *Did that look better? What did I do differently? It looks good from the front, but why does it flash from the side?* Roberto Giobbi, one of the great writers in our field, reminds us, "A little better is much better."

Neuroscientists call this kind of self-assessment metacognition, the ability to step outside ourselves and monitor our thinking during practice. Good magicians are masters of this brand of laser-focused practice. It's our safe space. The goal is to hide the mechanics of stealing, clipping, maneuvering, and palming under the innocent action of moving a coin from one hand to the other.

Needless to say, it takes time to get a technique right. The ultimate irony is that the better we are, the less you see. If a juggler practices juggling seven pins, his reward is the audience's appreciation when he performs it. But as a magician, your reward for perfect sleight of hand is that the spectators see *nothing*. "Most arts endeavor to render their technique transparent," writes magician Jamy Ian Swiss. "Only magic strives to reduce it to invisibility."

It is the realization that every magician must confront—that no one will ever see all the hours we put into perfecting a piece. Most of us make peace with it. Others choose a flashier style known as "cardistry," a new movement of stunning and graceful shuffles and cuts. Practiced almost entirely by a young generation, it's our version of skateboarders. They pull gnarly, hypervisual tricks with cards, often using moves that *look* as difficult as they are. Dan and Dave Buck, twins from Southern California, pioneered the genre of cardistry. In their late teens and early twenties, they stunned the magic industry by taking hidden techniques and putting them in plain view, like juggling. The Bucks and their cohorts created moves to boomerang cards out of the pack, to fling cards against their feet, and to spring them from one hand to the other. It's a beautiful style of card handling that is easy to appreciate, and it's a trend that has exploded all over the world.

Me? I'm old-school. My techniques and the sweat that goes into them are personal. Practice is meditation. I know I'll never be able to share with my audience the tiny innovations that I discover through endless experimentation. And that can be unsatisfying when you've poured yourself into your training.

The reason we love magic as children is that we want attention. We want to impress. We want to possess skills that others don't have. Some boys, in particular, want to impress the opposite sex. But those reasons prove hollow after a while, which is why so few stay with magic past adolescence. Reality calls, and magic goes to the back of the drawer. Those of us who stay with it stay because we find other, subtler thrills. We are the ones who are *relaxed* by the riffling sound of a pack of cards before bed. We practice palming in each hand not because it's required, but because it's challenging. When a new trick evades the logic of an audience, it scratches an itch in my head in a way nothing else can. There's an inner beauty to it—a silent, uncelebrated victory that I seek again and again.

HOUDINI

14

WAS HARRY HOUDINI THE GREATEST MAGICIAN EVER?

NO.

15

WHY IS MAGIC STILL SO MALE-DOMINATED?

PATRIARCH

GREAT MEN OF MAGIC

A MAN'S GUIDE TO MAGIC

I'M SORRY,
BUT WE FEEL THAT WOMEN
CAN'T KEEP SECRETS.

—SPOKESMAN FOR THE MAGIC CIRCLE,
BRITAIN'S LARGEST MAGIC ORGANIZATION, 1972

✦ ✦ ✦

Although I have deep respect for the magicians I mentioned earlier as my favorites, it profoundly saddens me that they are *all* oldish white guys. I am continually troubled by, to my knowledge, how few women and people of color practice magic.

The problem is baked into the culture of magic. Since the moment P. T. Selbit created his "Sawing Through a Woman" act, women have been used more as props in magic shows than as equal partners. They have been relegated to objects, first sexualized, then brutalized, forced to "survive" beheadings, have swords stabbed through their midsections, be shot from cannons, and do whatever else magicians require their assistants to endure in pursuit of applause.

This truth is particularly insidious because women were, and often remain, the unsung heroes in many illusions, executing the methods behind the magic in complete darkness, hidden from sight, while the magicians bathe in the glow of the footlights.

The male, magic-loving world hasn't exactly been welcoming to women, either. I've lectured at magic clubs all over the world, and aside from pockets in Japan and China, they are overwhelmingly male, so it's not terribly surprising that sexism and misogyny abound. In Japan, however, I've lectured at clubs where women were the majority in the audience, a refreshing but woefully rare occurrence.

The largest magic organization in the world—the International *Brotherhood* of Magicians—speaks loudly to the limitations of its membership. The Magic Circle, the United Kingdom's largest magic venue and organization, didn't admit women until 1991.

This sexism, deep-rooted and systemic, unfortunately extends to the audience. An experiment led by Pascal Gygax, a German magician and scientist, involved participants watching clips of amazing close-up magic tricks done showing only a magician's hands. Study participants were then asked to rate the difficulty of each trick and also to choose the magician who performed the trick better: "Natalie" or "Nicholas."

Natalie and Nicholas were the same person, of course, but the results were damning. People attributed more skill to Nicholas, even when his material was the same as Natalie's.

Every year, nearly two thousand magicians descend upon Las Vegas for *MAGIC* Live!, the United States' most significant gathering of magicians. With a good showing, careers can be launched there. Everyone brings their A-game, and it's a wonderful gathering of risk-taking magicians vying for the attention of the industry. In 2018, the convention was abuzz about Ding Yang, the woman who "produces a dove with her foot."

When Ding produced a dove with her foot at *MAGIC* Live!, her career was made. An upside-down human with a dove on the top of her foot is an unlikely sight in magic, but a female magician commanding a Las Vegas stage is almost as unusual. It earned an instant standing ovation.

As with most overnight sensations, Ding's story is one of sacrifice and struggle that began with years of acrobatic training in eastern China. Her act involves increasingly difficult stunts on a metal platform, each gymnastic sequence ending with the production of a dove. They appear in balloons and silk handkerchiefs, her performance culminating with Ding suspended upside down, balancing a mask on her right foot. Her inverted left foot shakes a pile of silk handkerchiefs and a dove emerges *on her foot.*

Ding's act is a product of her drive. She already had a standard act, but she wanted to elevate her magic. Juliana Chen, a fellow Chinese magician, saw potential in Ding Yang and helped put together a government-sponsored internship for her to study in Canada with one of the greatest dove-workers in the West: Greg Frewin. Ding left her husband and young son behind to develop the act. She and Frewin, who wanted to put her acrobatic skills to better use in service of the magic, worked on her act for five months, using Frewin's enormous theater in Niagara Falls as a laboratory for testing ideas. By the end, they had honed her act into a sensation.

Where Ding Yang's act showcases physicality and endurance, Tina Lenert's act is centered around love. This iconic act begins with a female janitor—Tina—posed against her cleaning cart, her cheeks smudged with dirt. Magicians recognize the act from the opening pose. When the music kicks in, audiences cheer the way fans cheer a band at the opening riff of their signature song. *Yes,* we think, *we're about to see Mopman.*

Mr. Mopman is the costar of Tina's act, which is an impressive feat for an inanimate object. The upturned mop looks enough like an unkempt head of hair. When Tina wraps her janitor's smock around the stick of the mop, it forms a lanky body. When she adorns Mr. Mopman with a hat, he magically grows arms . . . and comes to life.

Tina Lenert is widely accepted as one of the masters of stage magic, in part because she incorporates so many disparate elements. Her acts combine her background in dance, mime, and music. Born in Venezuela, Tina relocated to Malibu, California, with her parents when she was a teenager, and for a time she was a part of the LA rock scene as part of a band called the Leftovers. She was a founding member of the L.A. Mime Company, but ultimately landed on magic as her means of expression.

"I began thinking about cleaning people and how important yet invisible they are," Tina said of the initial idea for Mopman. "We want our places to be clean, but we don't want to see them being cleaned. I liked the idea of portraying someone who is supposed to be invisible at first, and over the course of eight minutes, is transformed into 'total visibility.'"

All of the theatrical elements from her past—mime, theater, music, puppetry, magic—come together in the eight-minute Mopman act, a sequence that goes straight for the heartstrings. As a janitor, Tina is shy and even unable to make contact even with the enchanting Mr. Mopman. As she stands next to the mop figure (and controls him like a puppet), he produces jewelry and flowers for her, eliciting a coy smile from the overlooked janitor. The choreography of playing two people simultaneously is so seamless that you forget you're watching one person—Tina—carry out complex magic effects spread across *two* characters. Like the very best theater, we not only don't perceive the artifice, but forget it exists. We're wrapped up in a fantasy encounter between a woman and her soul mate. Just before the end of the act, Tina's costume transforms from a shabby janitor's frock into an evening gown. *Blackout.*

◆

Female magicians must overcome the unfair burden of getting audiences and peers to see past their gender and to evaluate their work based on merit. Alexandra Duvivier, a Parisian magician, had it twice as hard. She also had to find a way to distinguish herself from her father, Dominique Duvivier, one of France's most respected magicians.

Dominique is a trailblazing close-up magician with a slew of books and awards and television credits to his name. Alexandra nevertheless found a way to step out from his shadow and earn her own place in the spotlight.

And earn it she did. In the beginning, her father didn't encourage her. "My dad never showed me magic when I was little," she explains. "I had to beg." Only when she proved that she'd work hard did he offer his guidance.

Dominique is the owner of Le Double Fond, a legendary magic venue in the Marais district of Paris. Seven nights a week people cram into the iconic theater-bar for magic shows by the debonair Dominique Duvivier and a small cast of Paris's best magicians. The shows are done exclusively in French, so it's a locals' favorite that sells out months in advance.

In 2001, Alexandra debuted a duet with her father in which they performed a stunning version of the classic Cups and Balls effect, the entire performance done wordlessly to musical accompaniment. The act features a dueling-magician theme in which Dominique pulls off a crazy vanish-and-production sequence, and then Alexandra outdoes her father by doing it twice as fast and with all three balls at the same time. The performance culminates with both of them working together, producing fruit from under the cups and then . . . producing a fourth cup in full view. It's a daring, artistic remix of this classic trick.

In 2006, Alexandra debuted her own one-woman show, *Between You and Me*. She has performed it and other shows thousands of times as the resident magician at Le Double Fond. In 2018, she appeared on Penn & Teller's *Fool Us* and fooled them. For years, too many magicians wrote, inaccurately, that Alexandra was a clone of her father. She's a globe-trotting magician, earning raves for her own material done in her own style. No longer "Duvivier's daughter," she's Alexandra Duvivier.

Ding Yang and Alexandra Duvivier are part of a new wave of female magicians taking primary roles onstage. It's both disappointing and stunning that leading women in magic remain so rare in the modern era. Perhaps even more disappointing is that female trailblazers in magic have been forgotten or uncredited. Consider Adelaide Herrmann. Born in London in 1853, Adelaide started her magic career as an assistant to her husband, Alexander Herrmann. With Adelaide's help, he rose to prominence in Europe and, for a time, became the most popular magician in the world. Of course, Adelaide was much more than her husband's assistant. She was intimately involved—onstage and off—in the show's production, also managing the business affairs for the show and developing her own solo pieces.

When Adelaide's husband died unexpectedly of a heart attack in 1896, she quickly stepped back into the spotlight, touring with Alexander's nephew Leon Herrmann. The two fell out after three seasons together, and in 1899, at a time when there were few female soloists, Adelaide announced that she would tour with a show of her own. Despite the inherent danger of the trick, she even performed the famous "Bullet Catch" illusion in her show, snaring a fired bullet between her teeth.

Adelaide Herrmann is a forgotten treasure from the annals of showbiz, and we would know very little about her role in the history of magic if not for the discovery of her private memoirs. The Herrmann family passed them down for generations, unaware of their significance. In 2010, they were given to Margaret Steele, a magic performer and scholar, who made public Adelaide's fascinating day-to-day accounts as the first well-known female magician.

✦ ✦ ✦

16

WHY ISN'T HOUDINI CONSIDERED THE GREATEST MAGICIAN EVER?

I WANT TO BE FIRST.
I VEHEMENTLY WANT TO BE FIRST.
FIRST IN MY PROFESSION . . .
FOR THAT I GIVE ALL THE THOUGHT,
ALL THE POWER THAT IS IN ME.
TO STAND AT THE HEAD OF MY RANK:
IT IS ALL I ASK.
WHEN I CAN NO LONGER,
GOODBYE TO THE JOY OF LIFE FOR ME.

—HARRY HOUDINI, MAGICIAN

✦ ✦ ✦

Harry Houdini is the most *famous* magician of all time, not the greatest (see page 73). Houdini's most enduring legacy is his fame, in his time and in ours. It's been said that George Bernard Shaw proclaimed the three most famous men in the history of the world to be Jesus Christ, Sherlock Holmes, and Harry Houdini. He then pointed out that two of the three were likely fictitious.

Houdini was a visionary—but of the public relations sort. He achieved numerous "firsts," but they were rarely artistic innovations. More often they were publicity stunts.

Houdini claimed he could hold his breath for ten minutes (he couldn't). He said he was the highest-paid performer on the vaudeville circuit (he wasn't). He claimed to be able to escape from *any* handcuff provided to him (he couldn't).

This is the trouble with Harry. He was talented, but his ambition exceeded his abilities. The right entertainer for the right time, his single greatest insight was positioning himself in a category of one. Houdini wasn't just a magician; he was an escapist.

The History Channel miniseries on Houdini—the one "based on real events"—likely depicts Houdini inaccurately as a pot-smoking secret agent for the US government. The media has a habit of exaggerating the greatest self-exaggerator of all time.

If it sounds like I don't like Houdini, that isn't the case. I own one of his straitjackets and a pair of his handcuffs. I forever regret being outbid when trying to buy the monogrammed "HH" pocket ripped off the pajamas he died in. I collect Houdini because I am fascinated by his ambition. For enthusiasts and magicians alike, there are only two eras in magic: before Houdini and after Houdini.

I won't go down the rabbit hole of recounting Houdini's life. There are numerous biographies of him that mix a nice cocktail of achievement and drama: a rags-to-riches immigrant success story, his mother complex, how he rubbed shoulders with all the great celebrities and statesmen of his era, his feud with Sir Arthur Conan Doyle, his crusade against Spiritualists, and of course, his expertise in escapology. The most crucial piece of his enduring legacy might be that he died suddenly and too young and in a way that historians are still trying to fully understand.

✦ ✦ ✦

17

HOW DO YOU BUILD A MAGIC SHOW?

THE SECRET IS NOT AS IMPORTANT AS THE PATHS THAT LED ME TO IT.

—JORGE LUIS BORGES, WRITER, POET

The secret to putting together a great magic show is . . . there's no real secret. An apt comparison might be how writer Gene Wolfe described the process for fiction: "You never learn to write a novel," he said. "You just learn to write the novel you're writing." My particular approach to putting together a show is about identifying amazing moments in my life that can be spun into magic tricks: running into a friend on the other side of the world, doing magic for a person who is blind, a last-minute change of plans that saved my life. I've turned each of these moments into tricks in my show. At other times, the pursuit of the show itself has nearly ruined my life. Anyone who has devoted themselves completely and fanatically to something knows this dichotomy well.

British magician David Jones once told me a story I'll never forget. He was lost on his way to a show and stopped to ask a farmer for directions.

"How do I get from Birmingham to Newent?" he asked.

"You can't get from Birmingham to Newent," the man replied, Zen-like. Jones was confused.

"You have to go from Birmingham to Worcester to Ledbury, then to Newent."

When you see a magician perform a trick, it usually lasts less than five minutes. But to get to that trick, the magician started with something that had potential but was raw. Through hundreds of tweaks, some trial and error, and the occasional meltdown, she ended up with something that worked.

Intuition is involved. I'm a better judge of what *won't* work now than I was twenty years ago. I know, for example, that magic tricks with rhyming dialogue nearly always fail. Whether it's a satirical rap or a card trick set to the words of Dylan Thomas, it always just seems to come across as trite and heavy-handed. I know now, too, that the more memorization required for a magic effect, the greater the chance of failure. There are some beautiful effects that I won't perform because I know that trying to remember a hundred potential outcomes will eventually result in my failing onstage. But despite my experience, I don't think I'm any better at judging what *will* work than I was when I started. It's easy to remember our mistakes and failed experiments. But the ways to accomplish and present magic tricks are limitless. There are some supposedly unbreakable rules about what will and won't work in a magic show, until someone comes along and rewrites those rules.

I can think of a dozen reasons why David Blaine shouldn't end his show by sitting onstage and taking questions from the audience. Not only has it never been done before, but magic shows—*all* magic shows—end with a closer. A big ending, maybe a personal piece, but definitely some sort of magic firework. Not David's. After his last endurance stunt he comes back onstage wrapped in a towel, and the audience asks him questions. Somehow, it's fascinating theater.

Building a magic show involves a kind of alchemy. There are openers, middle pieces, and closers, and assembling a set list is fairly straightforward. But great magic shows also take advantage of the intangible, irrational *aha!* moments that come when you least expect them. You might be holding your breath underwater or seeing what happens if you try to perform drunk, but some insight is gained, and you find an angle for your show.

Getting the right balance is important. I find magic with spectators onstage to be the most engaging to watch and to perform, but if you do it over and over, it becomes tedious. The goal for any show structure has to be variety. You want to take the audience through a range of material and experiences.

In my thirty years in magic, I've built three acts, but my last show, *Six Impossible Things*, was my white whale. Ambitious in scope and stupidly, recklessly impractical, it occupied my complete focus for three years, and then I performed it off Broadway nightly for a year and a half.

The concept for the show was simple and, I think, uncompromising: an experiential magic show. Each piece was framed in a different environment. Rather than a theater, I chose an escape room with several partitioned environments to create an immersive experience. The audience was on their feet for the majority of the show, often surrounding me. Every magician involved in the planning thought I was crazy to create such unusual conditions.

Each piece in the show began like some of the chapters in this book—with a question I didn't know exactly how to answer. I began with questions like, "How do I do magic without the use of sight?" The answer turned out to be starting the show in total darkness. Each participant was given props and *felt* the magic happen; they couldn't see me, or what they were holding in their hands. The spectators then followed me into a dimly lit basement, where I placed a spectator's first finger inside a cigar cutter and very nearly cut it off (this is a miniature version of the guillotine trick I performed as a child). This sadistic piece came out of the question "Can I create an illusion based entirely around fear?"

During *Six Impossible Things* we did magic seated on the floor, surrounded, and at the end, one on one: just me and you sharing an intimate magic trick. Rather than trying to suit my material to the venue, I wanted to adapt the venue to the material.

By necessity the show was small—limited to twenty guests per night. I created enormous problems by having such a small audience and such an unusual venue (one room was entirely covered in graffiti; another was a 1940s-era kitchen). Early on, twenty Russian lawyers bought out a show and showed up so drunk that half of them couldn't even stand up. When there are five hundred people in a crowd, a few partyers aren't even noticeable from the stage. But when *everyone* is drunk and they're inches away, it's a nightmare. I also discovered that sleight of hand was developed to be seen only head-on. In *Six Impossible Things*, people were watching the magic from all angles, even from behind. The show was the biggest creative challenge of my life. I had never come so close to quitting before.

Based on data I've seen, I'd venture that more than 90 percent of magicians find their material in magic shops, books, or videos. Few dare to create original tricks. The majority of magicians you've seen are likely performing classics in the traditional way. Cups and Balls. Linking Rings. "Borrowed Bill in Lemon." These effects are classics for good reason. Audiences love them.

For better and for worse, the material in *Six Impossible Things* mostly steered clear of the classics. It was original material in bespoke settings. I can't say whether everyone liked *Six Impossible Things*—but it definitely wasn't for the claustrophobic.

The greatest lesson I learned in building that show was the importance of editing. *Six Impossible Things* didn't work when we started, and I couldn't diagnose the problem. The show had strong moments, but it felt unbalanced; there were too many jarring presentations, and the clarity of the magic was often lost in my ambition to present it differently. We tried adding new pieces and rescripting. We bought better lights and brought in another director. But I was stumped.

As a last resort, I tried addition by subtraction. What if we don't add or change anything? Instead, what if we just cut two pieces? What does taking out material do to the rest of the show?

It was an instant improvement. We ditched the opener and the third piece, and then every major problem in the show seemed to unknot itself. We were down, finally, to six pieces—six impossible things. The pacing was fixed, the audience's energy was better, the funny parts were funnier. By including less, the show somehow became more. With the fat trimmed away, the act gained potency.

Whatever mental muscle is involved in creating a show, that muscle is strengthened through experience. This chapter opened with an epigraph from Jorge Luis Borges, and I live my life by his words: "The secret is not as important as the paths that led me to it." Whatever pride I feel about *Six Impossible Things* is sure to fade with time. In five years, I'll cringe at some of my choices in the same way that I cringe now at my older work. At some point, I'll leave all this material behind. But the lessons will follow me to the next show.

18
HOW DO MAGICIANS USE TECHNOLOGY?

SCIENCE IS MAGIC THAT *WORKS.*

—KURT VONNEGUT, WRITER

✦ ✦ ✦

At a recent show, while doing strolling magic, I borrowed a dollar from a man next to me. Right in front of his face, I vanished his dollar and made it appear in his wallet. It's a trick from my repertoire that's both instant and visual and has always served me well. But then this guy I was performing for—he was twenty-five or so—reached for his phone. He Googled "Josh Jay dollar bill trick" and pulled up a spoiler clip explaining how my trick works, then pressed Play while I stood there defenseless as the illusion was shattered for him and the three guests around him.

It used to be simpler: A magician did a trick, and the spectators were left with the sensation of magic. Now thousands of classic tricks are exposed online and others are available for ten bucks (order now and the shipping is free!). Rather than bask in, or wrestle with, mystery, we are conditioned to ask our phones about everything we don't understand.

What are magicians to do?

It's a fascinating magician-specific problem and one that's still unfolding. The conundrum was created by technology and is being solved with the same, mostly in secret, of course. What's happening in the face of wholesale exposure is innovation from magic's top thinkers. Thanks to the intervention of technology, the incentive has never been greater to create new illusions more deceptive than anything that came before.

◆

Magicians are also among the first to adopt new technology and pass it off as magic. Jean-Eugène Robert-Houdin (1805–1871), France's greatest magician, made use of the "ether craze" buzzing around Paris in the mid-nineteenth century in his act. Used as an anesthetic and abused as a recreational drug, ether had a mystical reputation. On his Paris stage, Robert-Houdin opened a bottle of "concentrated" ether and appeared to let his young son inhale the drug and go into a hypnotic-style state. The boy stood on a stool that was placed on top of a bench. Walking sticks were then placed on top of the stools to prop up the boy under each arm. Once the ether had taken its apparent effect, the walking sticks and stools were slowly removed, leaving the boy's limp body suspended in the air. Seemingly "lightened" by the effects of taking the ether, his son remained suspended in air while Robert-Houdin removed the stools one by one. Houdin then lifted the boy's legs to a horizontal position and let go, leaving the boy's body parallel with the stage, but suspended in midair five feet above it, with only one arm leaning against the sole remaining walking stick. Some surely suspected a trick, but others believed it to be a demonstration of a powerful new drug.

Robert-Houdin was also an early adopter of electromagnets, whose powerful pull can be turned on and off by a switch. Robert-Houdin was often credited with stopping a *war* by using an application of this technology, though the story has been somewhat discredited recently. But the legacy of his trick "The Light and Heavy Chest" has endured. The effect began with a small, attractive wooden chest, about the size of a shoebox, placed on a stage. The strongest men from the audience were then invited onstage, where Robert-Houdin cast a spell on them that supposedly robbed them of their strength. The men were then invited to pick up the small chest, but despite their best efforts, they were unable to budge it. Robert-Houdin then invited a little girl to the stage, and she picked up the chest with ease.

At the time, Napoleon III, the first president of France, was getting scared about an uprising in Algeria. Robert-Houdin gave a command performance of "The Light and Heavy Chest" to a group of rebels called the Marabouts. After seeing this "conjurer" take away their strength, they scattered into the desert. Robert-Houdin claimed he had quashed the revolt with magic and science. The truth is he did perform the effect in Algeria, but the rest is open to interpretation.

Georges Méliès (1861–1938) was a magician before he became a cinematic pioneer. Seeing great potential in early film projectors, he bought and modified his own camera, then proceeded to invent or improve upon many of the special effects we still use today: dissolves, appearances, vanishes, splicing, and even hand coloration. His early films, in which he removed his own head, danced with skeletons, and crashed a rocket ship into the eye of the moon, were dazzling technological advances beyond the public's comprehension. But really, they were on-screen magic tricks.

These nineteenth-century methods—simple camera trickery and magnetic chests—are anemic by today's standards, but it's fun to imagine how impressive they would have seemed in context, how advanced and technologically dizzying. To find modern equivalents and also understand how technology is playing a role in modern magic, the best place to look is a dealer's room at a magic convention. Typically, there are dozens of inventors under one roof, each one selling their wares and demonstrating the newest, hottest fad in magic. A dealer's room is like a real-life Diagon Alley.

Recently, heat-sensitive metal was big. For decades magicians have used sleight of hand or switches to "cause" a coin to bend. The disadvantage of a switch is that you never actually *see* the metal bending, only the before and after. But there exists a thing called memory metal, in which the substance can be rubbed at room temperature and it will bend slowly, eerily, in a spectator's hands.

A couple of years ago the hot trick was called "Pyro." It was released by a slick company that caters mostly to young boys interested in magic. Their tricks have fantastic marketing and impressive packaging. "Pyro" is a device worn on the arm that shoots fireballs into the air. You read that right: Imagine a bunch of fifteen-year-olds shooting fireballs from their wrists. What could possibly go wrong?

In 2003, a magician from South America took the magic community by storm when he devised a way to transfer signatures from one item to another. The innovation was incredible, but it raised all sorts of ethical issues. Imagine if you sign a playing card and I cause your signed card to appear on the other side of the room, inside a locked box. Impressive? You bet. But what you don't know is that when you signed the card, I secretly captured an exact duplicate of your signature and was able to apply it, in real time, to another object. The secret isn't mine to divulge, but it's an entirely chemical process. No scanning, resizing, or printing. You sign something, and I have—*in ink*—the exact signature as it rolled off the ballpoint of your pen. That's a trick you don't want to fall into the wrong hands.

The best magicians keep tabs on the latest technology, and it's changing the way we create illusions. "The greater one's science," wrote Vladimir Nabokov, "the deeper the sense of mystery." As the world evolves, so, too, must the material magicians perform. I don't do the trick with the dollar bills the same way I used to. I've developed a better way, one that isn't explained online—at least not until someone figures it out.

19

HOW ARE *YOU* USING TECHNOLOGY?

YOU MUST SURPRISE AN AUDIENCE
IN AN EXPECTED WAY.

—WILLIAM GOLDMAN, SCREENWRITER

As audiences increasingly use technology to instantly find magicians on Google and YouTube—to discover their secrets or watch them over and over again—we're secretly fighting back, weaponizing data and experiments to hone our illusions with new, scientific precision. Yes, even magicians are using analytics on you now.

Although neuroscientists have studied magicians in hopes of finding insights into inattention and misdirection, there was never a scientific examination of magic with the idea of helping magicians. That changed in September 2014 when I received an email from Dr. Lisa Grimm, who asked me to perform magic and speak in her college classroom. Dr. Grimm is a professor of psychology at the College of New Jersey, where she also conducts research on human cognition. She wanted an insider's perspective from a magician. She believed that magicians have a lot to offer the field of psychology, and vice versa. It sounded like an unusual and intriguing gig, so I booked it.

I opened with some magic, then spoke to the group. I tend to use the same general talking points for all speaking engagements, focusing on the basics of misdirection and why magic is important. I shared my thoughts about why people love, and are repeatedly fooled by, magic. I explained that audiences, as Jerry Andrus put it, "come to the wrong conclusion for the right reason."

But as I spoke, I could feel an existential crisis building. I was sharing these thoughts because I believed them, and my beliefs were confirmed by everything I have read or been told by wiser magicians. But where did they get *their* information? Could they be partly or entirely wrong? What if we magicians are the ones making inaccurate assumptions, jumping to conclusions about our audiences? What truly matters in a magic trick? Do we understand magic as well as we think we do? The truth is, we just don't know.

After the show, I shared my doubts with Dr. Grimm about some of the fundamental "truths" in magic I'd begun to reconsider. How much do people really care about the secrets behind effects? What makes for strong magic? Are people as fooled as we think they are? I suddenly had dozens of questions. Dr. Grimm didn't have the answers, but she knew how to find them: through statistics, experimentation, and analysis.

Our collaboration began in January 2015 and continues today. In partnership with the College of New Jersey, we have designed experiments to gather quantitative and qualitative data on the topics of magic, magicians, and deception. Some of our findings revisited what we thought we knew, like whether women like magic more than men (they do) or what the most commonly thought-of cards are (red threes).

One of the most fascinating things we learned is the importance of a magician's introduction. To learn about it, we screened a clip of world-champion magician Shawn Farquhar to a selection of study participants. In it, Farquhar performs the act that won him the grand prize at the *Fédération Internationale des Sociétés Magiques* (FISM), magic's most prestigious competition. Half the participants were shown the clip without any introduction, and the other group was shown the same clip but told that they were watching a world-champion magician doing the act that won him magic's top prize.

Although both groups enjoyed Shawn's act and rated it highly, the group presented with his credentials were *four times more likely* to want to see him perform his full show. Again and again, with different magicians and styles of magic, introductions deepened the audience's appreciation for the magic, and even improved their recall for what they saw performed.

But the most shocking revelation of the survey involved what people liked most and least about magic. Among the most popular things were what you'd expect: 17 percent just wanted to be "amazed," 14 percent liked the mystery of magic, 12 percent liked not knowing how the effects were done, and 10 percent wanted to figure out how the effects were done. (There is a subtle but important distinction between the enjoyment of not knowing and the thrill of "solving" a magic trick, which is a focus of Dr. Grimm's research.) Showmanship was also important, though less so, with 6 percent enjoying it most, equal with those who said "skill" was their favorite aspect.

But none of the aforementioned was the most popular aspect of a magic show. You're going to be . . .

Surprised! Twenty-five percent of people liked the element of surprise best. People of all backgrounds, genders, and ages valued surprise more than they valued being amazed.

This revelation caused me to entirely reevaluate my magic. It made me reflect on the tricks I do and where, how often, and when I offer my audiences genuine surprise. When we developed the study, I predicted people would be drawn to danger or large props or comedy. I thought, to a lesser extent, people loved visual effects and incorporating borrowed objects. But even when presented with these ideas, people gravitated more strongly toward surprise or, as many put it, "not knowing what will happen next."

The idea that audiences expect a surprise gets at one of the core paradoxes of magic, since surprise is the one emotion that must, by definition, be unexpected. And yet just as people go to scary movies expecting to be shocked, we found conclusively that people who watch magic don't just expect the unexpected; they *crave* it.

Conversely, what people don't like about magic shows was also unexpected. More than a third of the respondents in our study said they disliked it when magicians did the same tricks. They used words such as *cliché*, *repetitive*, and *old tricks* in their descriptions. I was convinced that what audiences would potentially dislike about magic shows was the magician. I anticipated most people would find magicians unfunny and unlikeable (and some did), or they would find most magic presentations dorky and outdated, even cheesy (you know who you are, fedora-and-suspenders guys). But given the opportunity, few people expressed these sorts of misgivings. The numbers alone indicate that magicians must forever push themselves creatively.

Unsurprisingly, this "moneyball" approach to magic is controversial. After its initial publication in *MAGIC* magazine, the study was criticized by some who thought the performance of magic was unclassifiable and therefore unquantifiable. Audiences may perceive a trick in one magician's hand a certain way, the thinking went, and perceive it totally differently when it's performed by someone else. Others criticized the way the data was collected (online), believing the only way magic should be studied is live, in person. After the study was published, I spoke on a panel at a magic convention and another panelist took a subtle jab at me onstage. We were talking about opening effects. He explained his opener, then said, "And I didn't need any pie charts to develop [it]." Art isn't science, or so the argument goes.

This systematic approach to studying magic is in its infancy, but it's already changing the way some of us create magic. When asked to think of a number between one and a hundred, which numbers are most common among men or women or children? The results of our study are surprisingly accurate. We have new insights into what age range is most susceptible to a mentalist's suggestion. If I ask you to think of any color, I can make a fairly accurate prediction of what you'll say, based on observable factors in your appearance. And the color you think of tells me something about the playing card you're likely to think of if asked, all based on research.

Thoughts can feel arbitrary, even ethereal. That's what makes it impressive when a magician pretends to read your mind. But what we do isn't random at all. The way you think is a pattern. And your specific thought patterns become more predictable the more data we collect about them. Google uses this data to sell you to advertisers. Magicians use this data to read your mind. I'm not going to share our findings here, but I'll be happy to fool you with them at my show.

The tension between magic and technology has perhaps never been more relevant than in these times of blistering innovation. How, the question goes, can magicians compete with the stupefying special effects in movies? Or the physically immersive new thrill rides at amusement parks?

Magic is certainly not immune to technology. Whole genres of magic were rendered obsolete by the mobile phone likely sitting next to you as you read this sentence. Mentalists were the hardest hit in this sense, as our phones give us access to the kind of information only mentalists knew just a few years ago.

A popular mentalism feat when I was younger involved divining a spectator's chosen song. The mentalist would display a boom box and have a song named aloud from thousands of options. The mentalist would hit Play, and "Wake Me Up Before You Go-Go" would blast from the speakers. (In the eighties, this trick was totally rad.) Now that magic trick is accomplished by anyone with a smartphone and a subscription to Spotify—someone names a song and a few clicks later, it's playing.

A mainstay of mentalism has always been personal information: birthdays, your home address, your sister's husband's name. But now this information is completely accessible on social media. Identifying someone's star sign was once met with utter bewilderment. Now it can be met with a shrug and a near-instant realization that the information is a few clicks away.

But mentalists have evolved, and great mind readers do material that happens now, in *this* moment, with decisions we haven't yet made. The very best mentalists let us in on some of the psychology they might be using—just enough to remind us of the power of our own brains. Derren Brown describes his show this way, with what he terms "soft science." "This program fuses magic, suggestion, psychology, misdirection, and showmanship," he says at the start of his show. "I achieve all the results you'll see through a varied mixture of those techniques."

If you spin the technology argument forward, the question becomes, "Will machines ever create magic?" The answer: They already have. In 2017, researchers at Queen Mary University of London designed computers that create original magic tricks. In fact, artificial intelligence has rendered several simple, mathematical tricks that are among the very worst I've ever seen. They're puzzles, really, and don't have anything resembling an entertaining plot. The news about them made headlines, but the tricks themselves lack a human element I'm not sure computers will ever be able to simulate.

Magic is decidedly low-tech. Cards, coins, rubber bands. It's about proximity, about being within touching distance of the improbable. There's no shortage of tech-powered entertainment, but only magic delivers the unknown. You may not know precisely what's lighting up Darth Vader's lightsaber, but you know it's an effect made on a computer. When you watch great magic, however, there is mystery—something you see and enjoy but don't necessarily comprehend. And as long as the unknown occupies that precious void, there will be magicians to show us the way there.

20

WHAT ROLE DO WORDS PLAY IN MAGIC?

PROPS CREATE INTEREST.
WORDS CREATE SIGNIFICANCE.

—MAX HOWARD, ACTOR, MAGICIAN

✦ ✦ ✦

Magicians use words not just to explain and entertain, but to deceive. Forget sleight of hand for a moment. Words—and *only* words—will make you see things that aren't there, and will encourage you to remember things that never happened.

I failed to appreciate the awesome power of scripting a magic trick until I toured China for the first time. While there, I spoke to audiences through "Rock," my kind but hapless translator. Rock was a teenager assigned by a production company to translate my show each night onstage. Offstage, however, I struggled to understand his rudimentary English.

Rock was a great kid who also felt a deep responsibility to make sure I tried all the spoils China had to offer. He took me to a night food market, where you can eat hooves and horns, and try a bite of fried lizard or a sweet bowl of eyeball soup. "You want snake?" he asked me. I politely declined, pointing out that we had a show the next night in Guangzhou, and I didn't want to risk upsetting my stomach.

The next evening, between shows, Rock again asked, "You want snake?"

"Now?" I asked back. "Of course not! We have a show in twenty minutes."

This became a refrain with Rock, who asked me if I wanted a snake at seemingly every break in our hectic schedule. My patience thinned as the novelty wore off.

"I don't want to eat a snake! No more snakes!" I finally said, losing my patience with Rock.

"But Mr. Josh," he said, confused and a little frustrated, "why don't let me eat snake?"

"Because you'll get sick and then nobody will understand the show. Please, no snake for *you* and no snake for *me*."

Eventually, the production company responsible for my tour called and asked if I disliked Rock, which I found odd. Then they accused me of depriving him of food. I was caught off guard and denied it outright. "Rock tells us that you have stopped his many requests to get you a snack, and that lately you have even forbidden *him* to eat snacks between shows." I then understood that to my ear, when Rock spoke, "snacks" and "snakes" sounded very similar. I apologized profusely for misinterpreting him, we hugged it out, and Rock never again went hungry on tour.

Each night, the language barrier between me and Rock demonstrated the enormous role words can play in a magic show. Magic has the power to transcend this barrier, and some of the most wonderful moments in my life have been performing for people who don't speak English, where the magic simply has to speak for itself. But for me, doing magic without talking feels like performing with one hand tied behind my back.

In any given moment, a person's field of view is enormous, yet our recall for what we see is minimal. What we forget is filled in by our brains, and magicians take full advantage of that. For example, perhaps I borrow a coin from you and make it disappear. It goes into my fist and it's gone. But the words I use during the disappearance can radically change the experience in your mind. Magicians call this "presentational coloration."

"Watch as your coin fades away slowly, dissolving into the air." Suiting actions to words, I might gently knead the coin away between my fingers and toss it into the air like someone might toss a pinch of salt. Although the coin was never in my fist to begin with, your mind compensates, in many cases actually *seeing* the coin fade into a silver powder that disintegrates into the air.

Or, I could spin it differently.

"And just like that . . . *pow*, the coin is gone." This time I might clap my hands together to show the coin is gone. The word *pow* and the audible clap give the impression of immediacy, like the coin vanished at that precise moment in a firecracker-sized explosion.

Words can also misdirect the mind. I might ask you, "Guess: Is your coin heads or tails?" Now I have changed the premise. If I vanish a coin, you will invariably ask yourself where it went, and whether it was ever in my fist to begin with. This is dangerously close to the method I might've used to make the coin disappear. So instead, I might ask you whether the coin is heads or tails. The answer is irrelevant, but the question confirms that there is, in fact, a coin in my hand. I present you with just two options, heads or tails, and you have to ask yourself this question before you can answer it.

Remember: If you can get people asking the wrong questions, they will never arrive at the right answer.

Great magicians are often great writers, too, and they use visceral, descriptive language that will effectively shape your memory of the magic. Earlier I said, "Watch as the coin fades away slowly." I am painting an image of what you will imagine in your mind, and the "slow" pace at which you will imagine it. When I say, "dissolving into the air," I give the disappearance a setting. As the coin melts away, the powdery residue might fall to the floor, but I instead paint a picture of the dust floating upward, lighter than air, like pixie dust in *Peter Pan*.

Think that is a reach? That it wouldn't apply to you? Neuroscientists have shown that most of our experiences are shaped as much by an impression of an event as the event itself.

Words cause us to remember events differently. Early in my set I will often borrow a pair of reading glasses from someone, place them on a table, and animate them. They flip over, suspend, and move, all without being touched. Afterward, I invite the spectator to pick up the glasses. Then I say this: "Did I touch your glasses?" He agrees that I didn't. "And can you examine them in your own hands right now, to make sure everything is as it seems?"

Minutes later, I can recast what happened in a more favorable light. I seem to be summing up the things I have shown to the audience, but if you look more closely, I'm tweaking what I did. "So you lent me your glasses, I caused those glasses to move *in your hands* without touching them, and then you examined everything."

I tell a blatant lie but embed it between obvious truths. It's true that he lent me his glasses, and true that he examined them after the trick. But between those true statements I am embedding an altered memory—that the trick happened in the spectator's hands. Animating glasses is a strong effect on a table, but it's ever so slightly stronger if it could occur in a spectator's hands. Unfortunately, it just can't. But using nothing more than my words, I cause my spectators to remember a trick that's far better than the one I did.

Mentalists use this approach as well. Perhaps I ask someone to write down the name of the first person they kissed but not to show me what they wrote. Later in the show I look them in the eyes and say, "I want you to think of the first person you kissed. Now, be honest and speak loudly so everyone can hear you. Have we ever met before this evening?" She shakes her head. "Did I or anyone else ask you to say a particular name?" She shakes her head again. "Is there any way I could know who this person is?" Another head shake. She and everyone else around us believe there is no way. "Look into my eyes. She thought of her first kiss, and we've never met before. But I'll reach into your mind . . . Now! It's Andrew Gladwin!" The questions I ask are all fair, but the questions also paint an inaccurate timeline. She thought of her first kiss, and I read her mind. I never speak of the inconvenient fact that she needed to write down the name at one point. This is part of the method, but it is rendered invisible by the "recap" I offer.

As Paul Auster proclaims in his spooky *New York Trilogy*, "Remembered things . . . [have] a tendency to subvert the things remembered."

✦ ✦ ✦

21

WHO ARE YOUR FAVORITE MAGICIANS?

(PART 2)

✦ ✦ ✦

RICKY JAY
(1946-2018)

I write this sentence on November 26, 2018, two days after Ricky Jay died. I spent yesterday rereading his books and watching old footage of him performing, trying to figure out how to write about such a talented but complicated figure. Like a dark, twisted magic trick, Ricky's passing was an unwelcome shock. Now everything is different.

What makes Ricky Jay complex is trying to reconcile Ricky the persona with Ricky the person. In my quest to bridge these two very different sides of him, the last forty-eight hours have revealed an aspect of him I never considered before.

To begin, I'm not related to Ricky Jay. I get asked this a lot, and it confuses people. My real last name is Jay; his real last name is Potash.

Ricky was a visionary performer and a singular talent. He is one of my favorite magicians, and his performing style influenced me more than any other magician. From the opening lines of his legendary one-man show, *Ricky Jay and His 52 Assistants*, I was transfixed. He had true power onstage:

*"Ladies and gentlemen, may I introduce my fifty-two
assistants. Notice the contrast of style and character.
They range from ingratiating simplicity to regal splendor.
Some are passive and inert, others brazen and belligerent,
some suicidal, just like you and me."*

Ricky had a reputation for being difficult and cantankerous.
But a person's death affords a perspective not possible when they're
alive, and I've already begun to rethink Ricky.

He didn't associate with many magicians. Instead, he kept to
a cabal of like-minded insiders. He didn't publish the magic he created, nor did he lecture to other magicians. In no way does that
make him less of a performer, less worthy of our praise. But it's
noteworthy.

We're all a product of our teachers, and Ricky learned from
the best. He spent his formative years studying under Dai Vernon,
the most significant close-up magician of the last century. Dai took
Ricky under his wing, shared secrets and techniques, and made
time for him. Dai's legacy is assured not only because he was the
best of his era, but because he was so generous with his work.
Vernon published books and tricks and videos we still study, and he
took on disciples who continue to lecture on his work today.

Generosity is the norm in the magic community. It's ironic
that among the most secretive, closed communities, magicians are
also very generous with each other. The truth is it's the engine of
our craft: the sharing, the mentorship, the tutelage from expert to
novice. It's a theme in these pages because it's one of magic's finest traditions and one that has helped me become the magician I
am, from Jerry Andrus agreeing to meet me over coffee to sitting
across from Richard Turner at his kitchen table. These men are
the giants in our field, and they carved out time for me, a stranger,
not because I had something to offer them, but because they had
something to offer me. This is our way.

For the most part, Ricky wasn't a part of this tradition. I've heard rumblings of him sharing a trick here or there, but he chose largely not to share his work and declined invitations to perform or appear at magician-only gatherings. So be it. He was busy turning into a master.

Ricky gained notoriety early in life for both his sleight-of-hand skills and his world-record ability to scale, or throw, playing cards. He held Guinness World Records in throwing cards, for both distance and accuracy. One of his signature feats was throwing a playing card into the skin of a watermelon.

In the 1970s, Ricky appeared on talk shows with Mike Douglas and Merv Griffin and toured with musical acts like Ike & Tina Turner. But his work reached new heights when he wrote and starred in his own off-Broadway show, *Ricky Jay and His 52 Assistants* (I loved that title, and everything about the show). It was almost entirely card magic, and it caused a sensation in New York and everywhere else it played. Playwright David Mamet, a longtime friend of Ricky's, was the director.

Ricky Jay and His 52 Assistants is, without exaggeration, perfect. From start to finish, it is the pinnacle of card magic—erudite but not stuffy, and pure fun. The premise is rooted in magic's history, and other than the boxy 1990s suits he wears, it still feels current. Throughout the show, Ricky talks about his influences in magic, demonstrating the tricks of his mentors, the whole show exuding his singular personality. He had a dry wit and said cocky things, but his onstage persona was so endearing that you couldn't help but love the guy. He was Brooklyn-born, and there was a harsh bluntness to Ricky onstage and off. When you watch clips of him on YouTube (and you should), your first impression might be that he behaves like a crazy uncle who's having a very bad day. But only Uncle Ricky can manipulate a pack of cards with such elegance.

Offstage, Ricky was an academic and a Luddite. He wrote several fascinating books on the history of performers, most notably

Learned Pigs and Fireproof Women. He was also a gifted character actor, playing a con man in *House of Games* and the Bond villain in *Tomorrow Never Dies.* He hosted a series called *Jay's Journal* on NPR, highlighting weird and wonderful characters from the earliest days of theater. His career was remarkable for the lack of missteps; just about everything he touched professionally turned out well.

What disappointed me about Ricky was that he chose not to pass on his insights. There's no law against this—they were his ideas and he could do with them as he pleased. He didn't owe any lesser magician anything. But that was exactly it, for me, at least—Dai Vernon and all the magicians whose work he studied didn't owe Ricky anything, either. Yet they gave back through their writings and the access they gave him. Had Dai Vernon taken Ricky's approach, there would be no Ricky Jay. Part of what makes Ricky's death such a loss is that so many hard-earned secrets died with him.

How did he approach scripting a magic trick? How did he deal with nerves? How did he achieve the tiny gap above the bottom card of the deck just before he did the Piet Forton pop-out (pulling out a single card while shuffling) without missing even one goddamn time? We'll never know. And that is, apparently, how Ricky wanted it.

That's how I felt until Ricky died. But it wasn't his death that changed my mind. It was Facebook and the rest of social media. As I scrolled through my feeds, they were filled with tributes to the fallen master.

"I'm so sad today. The magic world shares this sentiment. Thanks Ricky Jay. Rest well."

"We lost a giant of magic. Thank you Ricky Jay for years of inspiration."

"Ricky Jay, thank you for everything that you gave to the world."

Outpourings of praise, personal stories, fan art. People were sharing vintage YouTube clips of Ricky. I watched them all. I cried.

I cried because I realized how much he had taught us. It took his passing for me to truly understand that.

◆

SIMON ARONSON
(1943-2019)

My dad died when I was twenty-three. When he passed away, I had just graduated college. It felt, for the first time in my life, like I was in a tailspin. So I called Uncle Simon. He always had the best advice, whether it was about magic, money, or dating. Simon was *always* right.

For the record, Simon Aronson wasn't really my uncle; he was a close friend. He was also one of magic's most revered "amateurs." Before his death in 2019, he had retired from his career as a high-profile Chicago real estate attorney. He also spent twelve years at the University of Chicago, earning degrees in philosophy, economics, and law. Amid it all, he managed to invent some of the most offbeat card effects in the history of magic.

Simon specialized in intricate card effects, many of them relying on complex mathematical principles. Simon's gift for mathematical magic was rivaled by his ability to disguise the math with clever presentations (in an Aronson trick, you would never suspect that any math was involved). In Simon's magic, you may be asked to cut the deck and remember the card you cut to, but in his mind, you've just created a $52 - N = X$ style equation, where N is the number of cards you cut and X is the sound of your jaw hitting the floor when he tells you what card you cut to. Once a decade, he dropped a new three-hundred-page tome on magic, and his many fans would take months to wade through the material, absorbing every detail and footnote like scripture. Simon's magic was deeply deceptive—he was a magician's magician. "There's a world of difference," he wrote, "between a spectator's *not* knowing how something is done versus his *knowing* that it can't be done."

The pages of his books, which read more like math textbooks than magic books, are filled with equations. Although he never appeared on Penn & Teller's *Fool Us*, his tricks did on several occasions. Magicians learn Simon's magic from his books and seek permission to perform them on television. And they have always, so far, fooled Penn & Teller.

A retired lawyer who dreams up a principle that will fool *everyone*: This is the side of magic nobody sees. Not all of our influencers are on the stages of Las Vegas. The real geniuses are often holed away in a room alone, making notations on the world's next great magic effect. We need the next Simon Aronson just as much as we need the next magic superstar.

Simon was a learned, successful magical and mathematical genius, which is why, at twenty-three and unmoored by my father's death, I called him and asked him what I should do with my life.

He observed—correctly, I think—that many of the best magicians in the world used to be perpetually broke, forced to take humiliating shows and work into old age. "Move to Chicago," he told me, "and enroll in law school."

I was in a pretty dark place back then, but even so, I knew enough not to take Uncle Simon's advice. But his suggestion was exactly what I needed to hear at the time. I used to tease him that this was the *only* advice he ever gave me that I didn't take. Still, he was my role model and the smartest creator I've ever met. He died just months after reading the first draft of these pages.

◆

JEFF MCBRIDE
1959-

The closest thing magic has to a university is the McBride Magic & Mystery School in Paradise, Nevada. The school is open to students from around the world, and I count myself as an alum. The reason I went was mostly to spend time with the school's founder and star attraction: Jeff McBride.

You can't miss Jeff in a room. His wardrobe on- and offstage is the same: Japanese kimono robes, elastic-banded workout pants, and, quite often, a fanny pack filled with flashy magic—confetti, streamers, fans, rainbow streamers—that he can and will do at a moment's notice. His hair is a product of another era: shoulder-length frizz with red and blond highlights. *Star Trek: Deep Space Nine* created an alien character based on Jeff McBride, and the industry punch line is that they didn't have to change much. It's meant in the best sense: Though he is defiantly, unapologetically eighties, a tribute to the era that made his career, Jeff possesses otherworldly talent.

Jeff McBride's passion for magic is exhilarating and infectious. I love being around Jeff because, despite having more "flight time," or stage experience, than anyone I know, Jeff still has the same level of enthusiasm as the wide-eyed kids who come to study with him. He absolutely loves to jam on magic, help someone fix an act, and learn the hot new trick. And magicians from around the world pay big money for the opportunity to work with him, both alone and in classes alongside others.

Jeff's act is still iconic, despite how it hails from the eighties. He enters the stage in a white kabuki mask. Every time he removes a mask, another appears. The masks change colors, float, and dance around the stage. The grand finale of his act—timed with an awesome crescendo of eighties synthesizer music—is the removal of the last mask, revealing, for the first time, his face. I've never seen it fail to get a standing ovation.

The act, and all of Jeff's work, incorporates his wide range of interests. He has studied ballet, jujitsu, and mime, and each is featured in his show. Even now, in his sixties, Jeff *still* does the required somersault-flip on cue. His energy for performing never seems to flag.

Jeff holds Mystery School in his home, which is a shrine to all things mystical and alternative. He's a member of the neopagan movement, so along with his exquisite sleight of hand, we students are forced to endure a fair amount of jabber about the alchemical importance of earth, wind, fire, and air. When I attended his school, there was drumming, and at one point, we sat in a circle, passing a crystal wand to whoever wanted to speak.

It's a hippie-like experience, Jeff's well-named Magic & Mystery School, one that's easy to make fun of if you're on the outside looking in. I mean, here's a guy in a kimono, with highlights, teaching card manipulation to a room full of people who—let's be honest—don't fit into a crowd any better than he does. Yet, when I walk through the beaded doorway to Mystery School, I'm home. This is my tribe, and I'm in the presence of one of the best. And whether he's helping a kid find a way to produce a porcelain piggy bank for a stage act or helping me script a piece I just can't crack, we're all there together, trying to figure things out.

———◆———

DERREN BROWN
1971-

Derren Brown ought to be on everyone's list of favorite magicians—even though he's not a magician anymore. Derren is a mentalist, though these distinctions are hazy. Although you might see a mentalist one night and a magician the next and have very different experiences, from the other side of the stage (ours), they have more in common than it might seem.

Magician or mentalist, Derren Brown is special. He's a star of stage and screen in the United Kingdom and has dozens of television specials and West End shows to his credit. Magic celebrities often do material that is unimpressive to other magicians. In their defense, magic on television usually requires the tricks to be broad and overly simple to appeal to the widest possible audience watching at home. There is rarely a distinct point of view or creative storytelling in most of the magic seen on television.

Derren is the exception. His television work is highly innovative. He once persuaded someone without any experience to fly a plane and, in another TV special, staged a scene to persuade a spectator to commit murder. He demonstrated how to predict the winning horse in a horse race. (Reveal: You persuade people individually to bet on different horses, then show only the footage of the person you persuaded to bet on the winning horse.) His material is known to barely toe the line of credibility—to lure you into miracles you can almost believe in.

Derren began as a strolling magician, doing close-up magic in a restaurant. His first television special, *Mind Control*, aired in 2000 and was a hit, making him a household name in the United Kingdom.

As a sort of prologue to a stage show in 2008, Derren revealed that he was gay in a riveting monologue without any "mentalism" content. He'd made his sexuality public in 2007 through a newspaper story, but his onstage reveal unfolded in the larger context of the secrets we do and do not keep as humans—and why that is. It was a beautiful piece of theater, and a quantum leap forward for the credibility of magic. Ours is a craft not widely perceived as self-expression, yet Derren proved to critics and audiences all over the world that a mentalism show could do more than demonstrate what someone is thinking; it could show what the performer is *feeling*. Magic can give its practitioners a voice for self-expression.

Another of Derren's most enduring contributions to our industry was making mentalism cool again. When *Mind Control* aired in

2000, it awakened a new generation to the power of mentalism. David Copperfield's magic specials were wildly popular, but whereas viewers knew David was a showman, they thought Derren was *real*. Derren convinced someone that they should assassinate a celebrity, and he carried out an art heist using only suggestive techniques. The penance we've paid for Derren's trailblazing has been twenty long years of copycat mentalists doing watered-down versions of his material all over the world.

Derren's other insight was *not* claiming to have powers. Instead, he always insists that his feats can be explained by learned, believable skills—a combination of magic, psychology, misdirection, and showmanship. He's like a real-life Sherlock Holmes, able to deduce what country you will think of based on the color of your socks. It's not any truer than claiming he can read someone's mind, but the subtle shift is brilliant. Audiences don't leave his shows asking, "How did he do that?" They leave his show saying, "It's *so* impressive how he does that."

22
DO MAGICIANS
GET FOOLED?

YOU WILL BE FOOLED BY A TRICK IF IT INVOLVES MORE TIME, MONEY, AND PRACTICE THAN YOU (OR ANY OTHER SANE ONLOOKER) WOULD BE WILLING TO INVEST.

—TELLER, MAGICIAN

I love being fooled. *Love it.* But with every show I perform and every invention I create, my doorway to wonder closes a little more. I wish I were fooled more often, if only as a reminder of the sensation I've spent my life attempting to conjure. It's a rare moment of double consciousness when I'm able to see through the eyes of both magician and audience. Lots of old-timers claim they haven't been tricked in decades, but I don't know a single magician who can no longer be stumped.

However, the last time I was *badly* fooled was in Copenhagen. I was eager to see my friend Rune Klan (see page 55). Performing for magicians is an odd sensation. I can't speak for Rune, but when a fellow magician is in my audience, the rest of the audience falls away and I am, in my head, performing for an audience of one—wondering at every stage whether he noticed an original detail or a new wrinkle that might have duped him.

Rune's show began with him walking onstage with only a large cloth—no set, no boxes, no trapdoor. He waved the cloth in the air and covered himself briefly. When the cloth fell, he was leaning against a motorcycle. The engine roared. I was fooled. Badly. I had *no idea.*

After the show, Rune took me backstage and blew my mind again, this time by sharing his method. (I'm sharing the workings of his "Appearing Motorcycle" because he has consented, and he is no longer performing the piece.) "I couldn't come up with a way to make a motorcycle appear on the stage because it's so big and heavy and loud," he explained. "Then I realized, I don't have to make a *real* motorcycle appear." With that, Rune slid a flat cardboard cutout set piece into view. It was a *picture* of a motorcycle, life-sized, utterly unconvincing up close. "With the right lighting and the sound of a roaring engine, *this* looks like a motorcycle. And making it appear is as easy as flipping the board upright, like this." Rune fooled our ears and our eyes with a cardboard motorcycle. Add a little smoke, favorable lighting, and . . . *abracadabra!*

This illusion is so bold that it works. That's because Rune understands how a spectator will experience it. When we hear the sounds of a motorcycle and see what looks like a motorcycle, we accept it. Our senses betray us, and we are utterly, satisfyingly astonished. As spectators our only question is "Where did that come from?" A magician's job, writes Teller, "is to leave you with a beautiful question, not an ugly answer."

I exposed a secret to bring this moment to you. But I suspect you would be indifferent to the story if I merely told you about an appearing motorcycle. This is the magician's dilemma: The full ingenuity of moments like this one deserve to be etched in stone. Instead they're recounted at magic conventions, remembered only as magicians' lore, if they are remembered at all.

There is one trick that has fooled magicians (and audiences) for more than a hundred years: the Robert-Houdin Mystery Clock. Jean-Eugène Robert-Houdin was an extraordinary nineteenth-century French magician whose background was in clock making. He is considered by many to be the father of modern magic, and it was his analytical, horological background that helped him create some of the most storied feats in magic history. But to me his most enduring legacies are the remarkable clocks he built. These impossible timepieces would *completely* mystify you, I'm quite sure, even if you held one in your hands. You'll have to take my word for it, unfortunately, because Robert-Houdin Mystery Clocks are exceedingly rare; fewer than seventy remain, and they fetch more than $100,000 at auction. David Copperfield has a room full of them.

The most outstanding Robert-Houdin Mystery Clock is the Glass Column Clock. It's pretty to look at, but if you aren't paying close attention, you might miss what it is that will fool you. The clock has a decorative base out of which is raised a thick glass tube about ten inches in length. At the top of this clear glass tube is a glass clock face. This, too, you can see through. There are Roman numerals and hands on the clock face, but the hands are suspended on the glass. Despite keeping time, no wires are connected to the hands. No pulleys, no gears, no batteries. Time, itself, becomes a mystery. Yet the hands turn slowly to keep time. Remember that the clock dates from 1839, decades before reliable batteries and power sources and more than a century before wireless technology. It is a breathtaking suspended illusion.

Some of magic's secrets are diminished when you learn how simple (or complex) the solution is. But the Robert-Houdin Mystery Clocks are enhanced by the secrets they hold. Robert-Houdin didn't intend these clocks as magic tricks, but their elegant workings are essential to appreciating his ingenuity.

So with great reverence, I will share the method with you now. The secret of the Mystery Clocks is hidden, audaciously, in plain sight. The clear glass tube you can see through isn't hollow, nor is it solid as you might expect. Rather, there is a tube *within* the tube, and that inner tube rotates secretly, undetectable even to a watchful eye, because it is transparent. The base of the clock holds the usual gears, and the rotating inner tube rotates the hands on the clock face via another glass-on-glass mechanism. What you perceive as a clock face made of solid glass is actually several thin layers, each one rotating, secretly, in sync with the passing of time. Houdin's clocks are perpetual magic tricks, ones that have been astounding onlookers for as long as they have been keeping time.

Imagine you're watching a magician and, inadvertently, you see something you shouldn't. In other words, he flashes. You lent him your credit card, and as he apparently places it in his right pants pocket, you notice that he has secretly and with great speed flicked it behind his back, into his awaiting left hand. Nobody saw it except you. As a magician, I would be impressed by the skill. But I would no longer be astonished.

This is what makes magic so difficult. You can still appreciate a song if a couple of notes are off-key. An errant brushstroke can be found even in the works of masters. But one tiny mistake in a magic routine, and the illusion is shattered. Magic demands precision and perfection. Anything less is hack.

Fooling another magician is something different altogether. The public is fascinated by the romantic notion of a magician's magician. It's part of the reason Penn & Teller's *Fool Us* has been such a hit show. We want to see someone school the masters. *Fool Us* is, as I write, entering its eighth season. I confess that I don't entirely appreciate the allure of the competition element, but it is an undeniable success—not just in the United States, but all over the world. The premise is that magicians perform original pieces, and then Penn & Teller try to figure out how they're done. I can imagine that in a pitch meeting, someone asked, "What about *American Idol* meets magic?"

The format has a lot going for it, however, because we, the audience, get to watch a variety of material and styles, and then we see Penn & Teller try to reason through how they might be accomplished. It is this generation's variety showcase, and the best place to see good magic on television. The competition aspect of it is Hollywood schlock but was added to appease the close-minded execs who green-light these things.

When I got a chance to perform on the show, I didn't know if I would fool Penn & Teller, but I thought I had a chance with "Out of Sight," an original piece I created to perform for people who are blind (see page 164). The effect has an intriguing plot centered on doing magic for people who aren't sighted: I don a blindfold to take away my own ability to see, then perform an entire piece of mind reading without the aid of sight. And even if it didn't fool Penn & Teller, I knew it would be different from anything else that had been performed on *Fool Us*.

Before the show, the producers gave me two unbreakable rules. The first: Do not bait Penn & Teller. They *hate* when a sequence leads them to believe, say, the person is hidden under the tablecloth. But when the tablecloth is whisked away, a flag with "WRONG" written on it is there instead of the person. Which I get. The point is to do great magic that naturally deceives the brain, not to set a trap to fool two knowledgeable magicians.

The second rule: Never argue with Penn & Teller. The producers decide if Penn & Teller have guessed the secret, and then the performer exits gracefully. I've heard talk of magicians who argued a technicality onstage, in front of the audience. Those segments were cut from the show.

When I performed "Out of Sight" on *Fool Us*, first I produced a card chosen in the mind of an audience member, then after correctly guessing his card, I revealed that all the other cards in the deck were blank. And then, because I could, I gave the deck to the spectator as a souvenir. From this, Penn & Teller assumed I *had* to do a deck switch, meaning that I would have needed two decks: one with cards and one with blanks. After locating the chosen card, I would have had to switch the rest of the cards at the edge of the table. Although it didn't make the final edit, Penn even gave me a kind compliment on how deftly I had performed the deck switch. Their confidence level in dissecting my trick was high.

The problem was *I didn't do a deck switch*. But there, onstage in front of the cameras and a packed audience, I remembered rule number two: Never argue with Penn & Teller. What do I do? They solved the trick, so they thought, and the host of the show even ended the sequence, "So, let's give another round of applause for Joshua Jay." Crushed inside, but with a smile plastered across my face, I started the long walk back to the wings (this was entirely edited out of the final cut of my performance).

"Hold it," the host Jonathan Ross called out. "I'm just getting a word in from the producers. Josh, come on back." A moment later Penn & Teller charged the stage, a trophy came down from the ceiling, and confetti fell from the rafters. I had fooled Penn & Teller, and for a few very long, depressing seconds they had fooled me, too.

What fools a magician might surprise you. Many magician-fooler tricks are of the "double duke" variety, where a trick will take place that appears to use a well-known method, and then . . . *ta-da* . . . the solution we expected is a dead end.

Sweden's Lennart Green pulled the ultimate magician-fooler trick in the early 1990s. Green competed at the most prestigious magic competition, the Fédération Internationale des Sociétés Magiques (FISM), in 1988, with an act of card tricks that appeared so impossible the judges assumed he was using trick cards. Green located named cards instantly and sorted shuffled packets into numerical order without any apparent manipulation. He was subsequently given middling scores for taking what was presumed to be shortcuts with his work.

Green entered the next FISM three years later in Lausanne, Switzerland, and did the *same act*. Only this time when he finished, he dropped the cards on the head judge's table. It was a completely normal pack. That year, he *won* the competition.

There's an old adage in magic that if a layperson understands 1 percent of a magician's method, they are not fooled. But if a magician *doesn't* understand 1 percent of a method, she is fooled.

When I was very young, I met an old-timer magician who performed his act in the last days of vaudeville. Near the end of his performance he caused a wineglass to disappear in a way that, to this day, baffles me. I was only nine when I saw him do it, and I was stunned. So I asked him how it worked. His response—an old vaudeville line, I'm sure—taught me something fundamental about asking other magicians to explain their tricks, even to fellow magicians.

"Can you keep a secret?" he asked. I nodded that I could. "Me too," he said.

Those moments of being totally amazed are mostly gone to me now. It's the toll we pay as we improve in magic. Figuring out my first magic trick at nine years old was, in many ways, the defining moment of my life. But it was also the last moment I ever truly experienced magic as a spectator. I can still be fooled, but my role in magic is clear now: I show people the doorway to wonder. The paradox is that this is a doorway I can, myself, never walk through again.

23

WHY DO SOME PEOPLE HATE MAGIC?

THERE'S A LITTLE BIT OF MAGIC
IN EVERYTHING, AND THEN SOME LOSS
TO EVEN THINGS OUT.

—LOU REED, MUSICIAN

✦ ✦ ✦

My favorite episode of *The Twilight Zone* is called "A Nice Place to Visit." Rocky, the main character, dies and wakes up in a seemingly perfect afterlife. He wins every spin of the roulette wheel, gets every single thing he wants, is surrounded by beautiful women. But after a month his perfect world becomes dull, and he tells an angel that he's bored with heaven and wants to go to "the other place." The angel replies, "But this *is* the other place."

At every show I do, I ask how many people in the audience are seeing magic for the first time. Inevitably, more than half the hands in the audience get raised. Magic isn't a universally popular performing art—and that's how it should be. It's more popular than, say, puppetry or miming, but our appetite for music, theater, and television is bigger. If you get tired of Radiohead one day, you simply change the playlist to something else.

I know that the likelihood of magic theaters overtaking comedy clubs is low, and that MTV won't start a magic video countdown anytime soon. But I'm content with magic's position in the entertainment universe. You believe it, you seek it, and you see it when you need it.

When it comes to magic, less is more. The more material a magician shows an audience, the less the audience appreciates it. My friends are forced to watch all my works in progress and then get quizzed on every moment. Did it fool you? If I asked you to describe what you just saw, what would you say? Would you like that better if it was done with credit cards instead of playing cards? My friends are always generous with their time, to a point. They can't wait to help at first, but picking too many cards is like eating too much cake—you can overdose on astonishment as easily as sugar.

TV is the medium best suited to prove this point. It occurs most often when a nonmagician is given creative control of a magic show. A TV or Las Vegas show producer decides that the ratio of magic per minute needs to be amped up. The result is rock-and-roll magic. No setups or premises, just changes and disappearances and surprises. *Boom. Bang. Ta-da!*

You've likely seen it, too. Mat Franco stunned audiences on *America's Got Talent* in 2014. He was young, engaging, and fun, but most importantly he was doing something different. Five of the first six *AGT* seasons were won by singers, which make up more than half the acts on the show. Mat came in and found a selected card by cutting open the judge's table. He was the first magician to win the show. The next season it felt like there was a magician on every week. Some were talented performers, but the audience was desensitized to magic.

Elsewhere, magic remains on the fringes of variety. You might see one of us at a comedy club or on a cruise ship, or you might go a decade without seeing a magician live.

And that's how it's supposed to be.

Magic is scarce onstage because it's scarce in real life, maybe because the emotional range is narrower. There are films about love and loss and destruction and Watergate. There are, as yet, no magic show treatments about the Napoleonic Wars. We tend to watch magicians for more or less one thing, and it's what we can't reliably get anywhere else: astonishment. You can watch all the Marvel movies you want, but movie magic has a simple explanation—it's computer generated. If you want to see magic that makes you think and feel and drop your jaw, you watch a magician. Magic's appeal is in its rarity. It loses its power if it becomes common—just ask my friends.

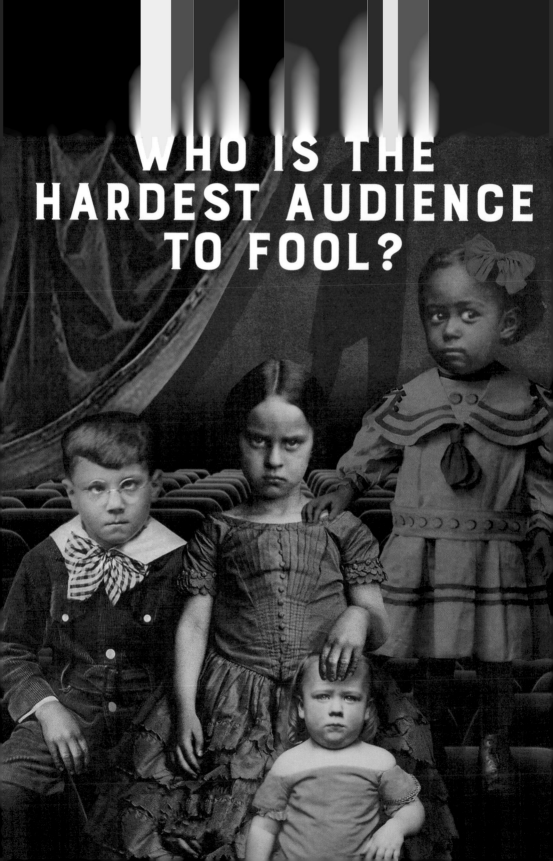

WHO IS THE
HARDEST AUDIENCE
TO FOOL?

THE INTUITIVE MIND IS A SACRED GIFT, AND THE RATIONAL MIND IS A FAITHFUL SERVANT. WE HAVE CREATED A SOCIETY THAT HONORS THE SERVANT AND HAS FORGOTTEN THE GIFT.

—ALBERT EINSTEIN

Recently, I was performing a show at an event called G4G, a gathering of theoretical mathematicians, scientists, logicians, magicians, puzzle freaks, and origami enthusiasts. Five hundred wicked-smart nerds in a Ritz-Carlton ballroom, waiting to watch me do magic. A journalist cornered me backstage and asked if I felt nervous performing for such a distinguished audience. I said I wasn't overly concerned, that the principles of magic deceive even the brightest minds. She seemed deflated. "Well, then," she asked, "who is the hardest audience to fool?"

I replied without hesitation: "Children." (Parents, no doubt, guessed this immediately.)

"I would've thought drunk hecklers or something," she said.

I thought for a moment. When adults drink, they become unpredictable, grab things they're not supposed to, shout out how they think something is done. But kids act that way *all the time*.

When it comes to solving magic tricks, surely an adult with thirty, forty, even fifty years of life experience would have an edge over an eight-year-old. Yet seasoned magicians fear the intellect of children.

Because: A five-year-old's imagination is boundless. And for magicians, that is dangerous. Consider, for example, a child who looks into the sky and sees a bird flying. Next she looks down at her cat. "Can cats fly, too?" she asks. This is the kind of preciously naive question that makes adults swoon. "No," we say. "Cats can't fly." Children experience our world like it's Neverland, until they eventually learn it's not.

Young children are often unimpressed with magicians because their line between reality and magic is blurred. A child's world is overflowing with magic that you and I take entirely for granted. Cell phones, microwaves, airplanes—these are astonishing magic tricks if you have no idea how they work. Competing with these incredible machines is the burden of the children's magician.

Children's magic is often derided as artistically bereft among magicians. But I have the greatest admiration for those who can make effective magic for kids. Silly Billy, the stage name of David Kaye, is a leader and pioneer in the field. He writes about the difference between doing magic for children and magic for adults. He believes magic for children isn't really about magic. It's about *interaction.*

"We want the children to point, scream, yell out, 'Turn it around,' answer a question, wiggle their fingers to make the magic happen, and say magic words," he explains. "In my kids' show, I get four interactions per minute. That's one interaction (laugh, call out, wiggle fingers, etc.) every fifteen seconds."

As adults, we're trained to apply our previous experiences to new situations. We use logic to make assumptions. This is why we're fooled. Kids don't make the same assumptions we do because they lack life experience. Instead, they rely on intuition.

Pulling a coin from someone's ear is classic—your uncle might've reached behind your ear and plucked out a quarter at some point. When this trick is performed well, adults are astonished by it, and most fail to make sense of it. "How did that quarter get there?" As with all good magic effects, the illusion causes the spectator to defeat his own logic.

A child is not so easily dissuaded. She wants me to repeat it, this time showing both hands empty first. She wants to inspect the ear beforehand, and for me to do it slowly next time. Kids are a magician's worst nightmare.

If solving magic tricks is your bag, forget everything you know and try to see the world through a child's eyes. Children say what they think, which can be awkward if you're performing for them. I use this to my advantage, which has resulted in an awkwardness of its own. I have on several occasions knocked on the doors of my neighbors and asked if I can do a magic trick for their kids. Me, a thirty-eight-year-old man, asking Joey's mom if Joey can come to the door for a minute and evaluate my latest trick. Children have the stillness of mind to see through the trappings of many magic principles, and they listen to the inner voice that most adults ignore. If I can fool Joey, I can fool anyone. "The most sophisticated people I know," Jim Henson said, "inside they're all children."

Howard Thurston, one of the great turn-of-the-twentieth-century magicians, developed his own tactic to deal with children. Among Thurston's most famous tricks was human levitation. Each night Thurston would invite a different little boy onstage to be the audience's eyes and ears, walking the boy right under the floating lady to inspect the illusion thoroughly. The boy would be so close to the illusion that he most *certainly* would have seen the secret: a complex network of thin wires imperceptible from a distance. But the kids never talked. How come? The story was passed down to us from an old man who, as a boy, was invited onstage by Thurston during the levitation trick. When the boy looked up, he saw a vast network of wires and pulleys, but before he could say a word, the dapper Mr. Thurston whispered so only the boy could hear, "If you touch those fucking wires, I'll kill you."

This method was darkly brilliant. From the audience's vantage point, the boy looked shocked at the miracle above him. But in reality, the shock was hearing an F-bomb from such a mild-mannered magician. This method also ensured the secret would remain safe after the show. (I mean, what six-year-old is allowed to say *that* word to his parents?)

Wonder declines with age because as we move through life, we are less amazed by the things we experience. Planes in the sky no longer beckon us to look up and admire. We flip light switches without a thought for the marvels of electricity. We think little about the miracle of our very existence because we are too acclimated to the mysteries we don't understand. "If boyhood questions aren't answered before a certain point in time," writes my favorite author, Norman Maclean, "they can't ever be raised again."

Wonder is forever linked to our childhood, which is why magic makes us *feel* like children. When we are astonished by a magician, we revisit a state of mind we may not even consciously remember: our youth. In this sense, magic is designed not for children, but for the child within each of us. Nietzsche wrote, "The struggle of maturity is to recover the seriousness of a child at play." We're all in search of life's reset button, to take us back to a time when cats might fly like birds. For adults, magic is a temporary escape from reality. For kids, magic *is* reality.

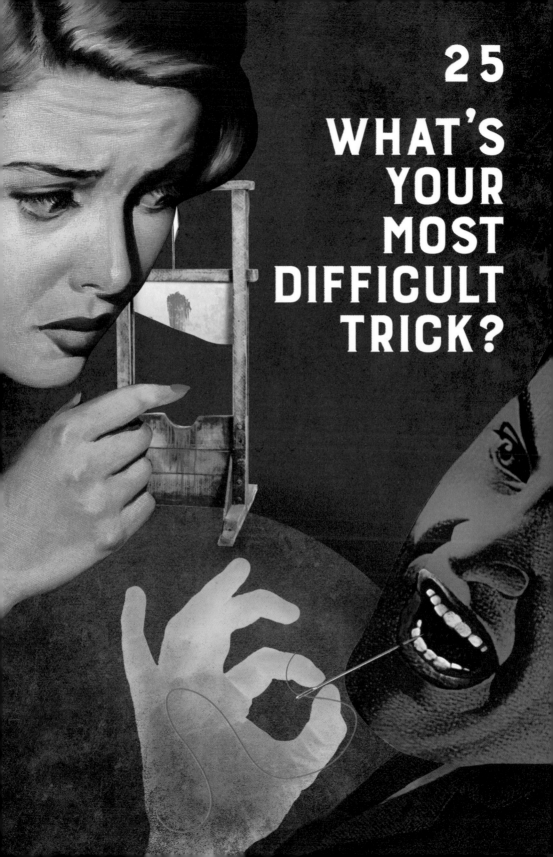

I HAVE FOUND THAT IF ONE WANTS TO CONVEY AN IMPRESSION OF GREAT SKILL, IT IS ADVANTAGEOUS TO ACTUALLY POSSESS GREAT SKILL.

—DARWIN ORTIZ, MAGICIAN, WRITER

An enormous part of a magician's job is to distort the level of difficulty in a trick. We're often doing intense mental gymnastics while thinking on our feet while pulling off crazy sleight of hand while cracking jokes. All so you never realize what's going on right under your nose. On the other hand, there are many effects that look prodigiously difficult—like getting out of gaffed (or trick) handcuffs—that are as easy as slipping off winter gloves.

There are magicians whose material requires a perfect shuffle. That is, a deck that must be split into two *exactly* even piles, twenty-six and twenty-six. Then, by touching the ends together, the cards must weave perfectly, every other card, and "zip" into place. This move requires a year of dedicated practice to master. Many magicians I know simply cannot rely on this special shuffle because their hands are too unsteady, or their eyesight isn't good enough. I have a trick that requires one. My friend Paul Gertner's signature trick is "Unshuffled," in which he is required to do *four* perfect shuffles in a row, without fumbling. He has done it on live television. Guts.

The most difficult thing in my show that recently wrapped in New York is actually the part that looked the most random: selecting volunteers. The difficult moves and misdirection in my show were so rehearsed, so subconscious, that I barely felt them anymore. But the single decision that affected the impact of the magic more than anything else was who I invited to participate. The right spectator will scream and laugh and gasp at all the right moments. The wrong one will feign indifference. Complicating matters, the right one for my Act One, in which I simulate cutting off a spectator's finger, is entirely wrong for Act Four, where I tell a story through a deck of cards.

In Act One, I look for someone with a thin finger because the hole in the cigar cutter won't fit just anyone's pinky. I also look for someone shy, so I scan the audience for someone who is *not* making good eye contact. I may chat with one or two candidates for a moment, then choose the one with the least spark, who I think I can scare most thoroughly.

In Act Four, I ask a spectator to sit on the floor while I spin a tale about how a man and a woman first met. The story is sweet—saccharin, even—but the twist ending is that it's about my parents, which makes it my origin story and so all the more worthwhile. Worthwhile, that is, if the person I selected is into it. I've chosen spectators who keep a running commentary of interruptions, and it's a mess. And younger people, in general, can't handle the inevitable sentimental factor inherent in a piece like this. I'm looking for someone middle-aged, who seems genuinely interested. And because it's a romantic piece, I'm looking for someone who, based on who they are sitting with in the audience, seems already coupled so I don't come off like a sleaze trying to use a love story to pick up someone during my show.

You might think my selection process overwrought, but I can say without exaggeration that it is the defining variable in the show. I might be off my game on a given night (or I might be particularly strong). The difference in my performance is almost indistinguishable to the crowd. But the participants—they make the show what it is.

Harry Lorayne, now in his mid-nineties, is a magician and memory expert. He was a mainstay on *The Ed Sullivan Show* and talk shows hosted by Merv Griffin and Mike Douglas in the 1960s and '70s, always demonstrating extraordinary feats of memory. Some had a trick to them, but one in particular was entirely real. Harry would meet every audience member, one by one, as they entered the theater or ballroom, often introduced by the host of the event: "Harry, I'd like you to meet Alfred and Elaine Jolovitz. This is Joe and Pam Martuccio, and this is little Eli Bosnick." Harry would meet as many as three hundred people or more on their way into the theater.

Later in the evening Harry would perform a show onstage, and at the end, he would ask everyone to stand up. He would then go down every row and recite every person's name back to them: "That's Elaine Jolovitz! Alfred Jolovitz! Joe and Pam Martuccio! Eli Bosnick!" In a time way before earpieces and hidden cameras, this was a legitimate demonstration of a superpower memory, and it's *stunningly* difficult. As a performer, I have even more respect for Harry's closer, because he would often do it several nights per week. This means the mnemonic system he used to remember the names had to be mentally "cleared" in his head after each performance, so he could do it again the next night.

I love this genre of performance, and it's the rarest kind. The method to the trick is *exactly* what you say it is. Magicians spend so much time lying to an audience about what they're doing that it's refreshing when they do exactly what they propose. When everyone is expecting a lie, the most shocking surprise is the truth.

Todd Robbins, an eccentric and world-renowned sideshow performer and historian, believes that people see magic tricks that are fake and think they're real, whereas they view sideshow stunts that are real and think they're fake.

In 2016, David Blaine bridged these gaps with a unique blend of magic and sideshow feats. We'll cover David's complex career and personality later (page 254), but Blaine is, in my estimation, doing the most difficult material in our industry. I'm not talking about card sleights or mnemonic feats. His touring stage show is a mixture of magic and stunts, and most (if not all) of those stunts are *real*. He pushes an ice pick through his hand. And would you like to know how he does it? *He pushes an ice pick through his hand!*

Later in the show he sews his lips closed with a real sewing needle and thread. The method? *He sews his lips closed with a needle and thread!*

The show closes with him holding his breath for more than ten minutes in a tank of water. How? There's only one way, and it took David years to learn, but it's a trick without a secret.

My favorite scene in my favorite film, *Catch Me If You Can*, pivots on master con man Frank Abagnale and how he passed the Louisiana bar exam. He impersonated an airline pilot, a doctor, and a teacher, but nobody could figure out how he cheated to pass the exams. "How did you do it, Frank?" asks Tom Hanks, playing the investigator.

"I didn't cheat," he replied. "I studied for two weeks and I passed."

26

COULD YOU CHEAT AT CARDS?

TRUST EVERYONE,
BUT ALWAYS
CUT THE CARDS.

—FINLEY PETER DUNNE, HUMORIST

✦ ✦ ✦

Yes. But I never have, except for maybe a night or two in college, and only then to make a point. Cheating is wrong, cheating is illegal, and cheating is sleazy. It wouldn't be difficult for a skilled magician to take money from his friends, but that magician wouldn't end up with many friends. When people ask if I cheat at cards, what they're *really* asking is whether the clandestine skills magicians have worked hard to achieve can be used to clear out a high-stakes poker game. People like to romanticize clever heists and casino takedowns, but it's an unanswerable question. Although I haven't been caught up in any cheating scandals, there are magicians who have been seduced by the dark side of the force.

As a practical matter, the best magicians possess more than enough talent and skill to cheat at cards. It is certainly feasible in a private game under the right conditions that a magician could tilt the odds in their favor. But a magician with world-class skill is unlikely to get mixed up in a cheating scheme, because there is far more money and far less risk to performing in the best venues around the world.

And shaking down casinos is tougher than it used to be. Most major casinos forbid players to hold the cards, with poker as the notable exception. That doesn't mean cheating is impossible, but in the twenty-first century, it is often done more with technology than sleight of hand. Most of the cheats caught today are busted for having "computers," electronic devices taped to their legs or chest that signal, with vibrations, what cards other players have. They're often operated by someone who has a good view of the dealer's cards. The most commonly caught cheat is the dealer himself, someone who has worked their way into the casino system and is now cheating their employer with a secret team of accomplices. (But this is mostly the stuff of ridiculous film plots like *Now You See Me* or *Ocean's Eleven*.)

A magician's only reliable shot at cheating at cards would be in private games. I befriended a cheat when I was younger and living in Ohio. This guy worked a Midwest circuit of country-club poker games usually made up of groups of doctors or lawyers. He'd socialize with these people and get himself a seat at a local high-stakes game, usually composed of older men. I remember he told me the biggest haul he ever scammed was from a group of judges.

This man—I'll call him Alfred—knew how to do only two things with cards. That was all he needed to scrape together a living cheating at them. His first skill was that he could give a deck a false shuffle, meaning he could mix a deck convincingly, in a variety of styles, but secretly maintain the order of the cards. What Alfred would do was collect people's hands after a round was played—a flush, a pair, a full house, maybe—then appear to mix them back into the deck. But actually he would retain them on top of the pack, ready to be dealt out.

Alfred's other skill was secretly glimpsing the bottom card of the deck and dealing it whenever he wanted. If it helped his hand, he could deal it to himself. If it didn't, he would deal it away to another player, and then repeat. These two skills gave him an insurmountable edge at the poker table.

The rest of his job was restraint, believe it or not. With the ability to fleece high-rolling midwestern professionals, he could take every hand dealt. But Alfred knew that would only get him strange looks, so he mostly played honest, or so he told me during one of our late-night diner sessions. "I would have to cheat *not* to take too much money," he explained. "But at some point in the evening, the pot would get big enough that I would take it, and I always did."

I went with Alfred to a game only once. I was in my teens and blinded by the romantic idea of the lone card cheat—a secret artist who possessed skills undetected by discerning card players. Alfred was a modern-day Robin Hood—cheating the rich and giving to . . . himself. I wanted to see him in his element. I didn't give any thought to what men do to other men who steal from them in such games.

On the night in question, Alfred and I entered a McMansion outside Toledo, Ohio. There were beers and drinks while a college football game blasted from the big-screen TV. Finally, it was time for poker. I wasn't playing, we told them. I was just Alfred's friend. I sat a few feet away from the table and watched as the game began. Almost immediately, I noticed a poorly executed glimpse on the bottom of the deck, followed by a shuffle that screamed crooked to my knowing eyes. But it wasn't Alfred dealing. We had, against all odds, come across *another* cheat at the same table!

This person was known to the other players, so we guessed he had probably learned a couple of techniques to give himself an edge. But here was Alfred, who would momentarily be cheating a cheater. Alfred saw what I saw, and we wanted no part of it. We made an excuse and bolted.

The odds of sitting at a card table with two cheats is something so strange, so *completely* unbelievable that it's more fitting as a plot twist in a novel. And eventually my story *did* become a novel. I first shared it in an essay while I was in college, and years later I received an email from my professor asking if I would mind if he wrote a story around the notion of two cheats in the same game. *Bluff* is the book, and Michael Kardos is the author (and my former professor). It's a great read. My role was replaced by a female magician named Natalie.

Cheating and magic are similar. As an outsider, you'll never really know just how clever Houdini's mysteries are precisely because you don't know how they're done. And we'll likely never know if anyone has ever pulled off a cinema-worthy heist, because the success of such a crime is directly tied to us *not* knowing it happened. That's the difference between a great magician and a great cheater: The very best magicians are celebrated for their work; the very best cheats are invisible, unappreciated, and unsung.

27

WHAT MAKES DAVID COPPERFIELD SO ICONIC?

MAGIC TO ME IS ABOUT
MAKING DREAMS REAL.
MAKING THEM LOOK REAL.
MAKING THEM FEEL REAL.

—DAVID COPPERFIELD, MAGICIAN

It's three in the morning, and I'm in a room with David Copperfield, two of his assistants, and a seamstress at his private airplane hangar just outside Las Vegas. For the last thirty minutes, David has been pulling a curtain off a window. It's a theatrical curtain made to resemble a real one, fixed into place with magnets. First he pulls it from a corner, then shakes his head. "That's not right," he says softly. "Again." Two of his assistants retrieve the curtain and reaffix it over a windowpane so he can try again, this time pulling from the middle of the cloth. "That's better, but still not fast enough," he says, his voice hoarse from just having finished his third ninety-minute show of the day at the MGM Casino. Back on the wall it goes.

The lobby of the airplane hangar is lavishly appointed in leather furniture that faces this window, which looks out on a painted white tarmac dotted with aircraft. Next to his private jet is the original spacecraft from *My Favorite Martian*. There's a helicopter tricked out with missiles and machine guns, and a full-scale model of one of da Vinci's flying machines. David explains that he is working on a new idea where he can invite guests to look through the window into an empty hangar, then cover the window with a curtain, and when he whisks it away, *whoosh*, the spacecraft will be in view. Tonight, he's working on the *whoosh*.

I sit back and take in David's world. Over and over and over he pulls the curtain off the wall. I struggle to discern the difference between a slight upward motion and a downward yank, but David knows what he wants—and he's not getting it. It becomes apparent that the curtain itself is the problem. David doesn't like the hem, and the group decides the magnets that attach the cloth to the windowpane are too close together. Then there's the problem of how to cover the window in the first place. David tries to articulate to his team a contraption that will allow the window to be shown, cover it for a few seconds, and then be whisked away with a theatrical flourish. I don't follow David's idea exactly, but the seamstress notes his suggestions and disappears into another room. It won't be the last we see of her this evening.

David Copperfield tends to evoke thoughts of big things. This is the man who vanished the Statue of Liberty and walked *through* the Great Wall of China. But he's working on the smallest of moments with a piece of fabric. These moments matter, but I hadn't considered the effort they require. David sweats details like this. "I hate it," he says. "The process of getting it right is hard. Now let's get you your hat."

There's a huge, two-hundred-year-old bank vault safe in the lobby, and David unlocks the device and removes a captain's hat with the initials *DC* on the brim. I put on my new hat, and David begins the tour. "This is like Disneyland," I tell him, wearing my souvenir hat, surrounded by flying gadgets both real and fictional. He laughs and points up to an enormous neon *D* that for years served as the original *D* at the Disneyland Hotel, where he once stayed as a boy.

David explains that his vision is to make the hangar a place where he can give tours to children and teach them about flying. David isn't a pilot, but his latest fascination is anything related to flight. There are stations in the hangar with pictures of the Wright brothers and small experiments to demonstrate the basics of aeronautics. Later in the evening, sitting in the living room of his jet,

I wonder aloud how a guy who gives fifteen shows a week for 750 people per show wants to make time to teach a dozen school-children about the fundamentals of flight. But David doesn't see this place in terms of time, bandwidth, expense, or audience size. Like everything else in his life, his hangar isn't a hangar; it's an experiential theater—and the project consumes him.

When we're finished chatting in the G4, we go back to the lobby. The time is now 4:30 a.m. The assistants are still there, and they've modified the curtain with a new cord hanging down the right side. David pulls the cord, and the cloth drops in front of the window. He pauses a beat and then whisks it away. "Yep," he says.

I turn to the seamstress, but she is expressionless. "Are you hard to work for?" I ask David.

"I don't know. Ask them."

Saying David Copperfield is the greatest living magician is like saying Steven Spielberg is the greatest director or the Yankees are the greatest baseball team. You might disagree, but the burden of proof is on you. He is an icon who has starred in twenty ground-breaking television specials and won twenty-one Emmys. He holds eleven Guinness World Records and has sold 33 million tickets.

My parents took me to see his show when I was young. Toward the end of the show, David spoke of aviation and his general fascina-tion with flying machines. Then, David flew. Through hoops, inside a box, and while holding a falcon, he *flew*. Even as a small child I knew it wasn't real, but it felt so real. "David Copperfield can *fly*," I remember telling my friends at school. When David's feet left the ground in that show—that was the moment when I knew how I wanted to spend my life.

David Copperfield was born David Kotkin, the son of Jewish parents from New Jersey. By age ten, David was performing as "Davino, the Boy Magician." At eighteen he was cast in the Chicago musical *The Magic Man*, and he's been lighting up the stage and small screen ever since. For forty years, David has held the top spot in the world of magic, but the last decade has been a transitionary period. He has chosen to walk away from television. Gone are the dance numbers, the daring escapes, the industrial fans gently blowing his coiffed hair. David is in his sixties and searching for new ways to bring magic to his big audiences.

"The Alien" is what's torturing David lately. It's his most ambitious segment in years, spanning the entire second half of his show, a segment he continues to refine, long after its debut. The premise is madness—I struggle to understand it completely. David explains to the audience, in earnest, that his father was once stationed near Roswell, New Mexico, the alleged site of an alien spacecraft crash in 1947. Then he spins a tale about an alien who knew and befriended his father. The same alien comes back to visit David, to deliver a note his father wrote thirty years earlier (apparently aliens are unreliable postmen). It gets weirder from there. The alien talks with a Brooklyn accent, cracks jokes, farts, and hugs David as they carry on a lengthy conversation. David is charged with returning his alien friend to his home, and the routine culminates with the production of an enormous spaceship that floats over the heads of the audience. The routine is part *E.T.* with a strong Pixar sensibility, and is, even by David's admission, a work in progress. "People hated it," he said. "But we try to make it suck less over time."

I grew up on David Copperfield—everything he touched was polished and precise. His material never showed any fault lines, so it was humanizing to listen to David wrestle with "The Alien." Virtually every other magician I spoke with while researching this book—Penn & Teller, David Blaine, Juan Tamariz—echoed the same point about giving up on material that didn't test well or work out. Cutting material is, to me and my contemporaries, part of the process. But not for David. "I really can't think of [a trick I've cut]. I know things have sucked for a long time, but when I believe in them, I finally make them good." "The Alien" isn't as spectacular as David's well-known stage classics, like "Flying" or "The Fan," but it's getting there. "The Alien" would have been cut from most shows long ago, but after hundreds of performances, it has morphed into something better, something new.

I marvel at Copperfield's brave gamble. He doesn't have to take risks, yet he's choosing the most artistically challenging piece of his career, and he's on the cusp of breaking into an entirely new genre: fiction through magic. "The Alien" isn't about the creature's powers or the spaceship that appears over the audience's head—it's about a story. David is, in a sense, making a movie onstage with magic, and the sensation of watching the piece is akin to watching a film. The audience *knows* the alien is an animatronic machine, and that David's father never befriended an eighteen-inch alien. But what engages us with "The Alien" isn't what engages us with his other illusions. This is a suite of magic with a through line. David is our tour guide, and while watching "The Alien" I feel just like I felt at his hangar—part of a larger, indescribable experience.

It took an alien to coax out the human side of David, but his most personal performance is one that most are unlikely to see. When he's not onstage or on his plane (or at his private island, Musha Cay, in the Bahamas), he's at his private museum just outside Las Vegas. The museum is invitation-only. David allows five people to visit at a time and gives each tour personally. They begin after his last show of the night. Magicians dream of being invited on the tour, since invitations come only from David himself. Seeing Copperfield's museum is like seeing Graceland if Elvis were giving the tour.

The tour I was on started just after 1:00 a.m. The building is biographical, its contents a history of David's interests and aesthetics housed in a resplendent monument to all the greats in magic, including, sometimes awkwardly, David himself. The outside is cleverly disguised—it looks like an old-fashioned tailor's shop, a loving tribute to his late father, who worked as a tailor in New Jersey. To the right of the entrance is a re-creation of David's star on Hollywood Boulevard.

For decades, David has been buying up magic's most precious treasures at auction. He is a completist, and he has a feverish desire to own the best items in the best condition, whatever the cost. He has managed to acquire nearly every notable collection and piece that has come to market in the last two decades. Even I—who can't hope to compete with David—have been locked in hopeless bidding wars against him at industry auctions.

I would estimate that perhaps a third of magic history's treasures are within the walls of David's museum, so the collection must be concealed from the public out of necessity, for both safety and secrecy. The museum used to be disguised on the outside as Butchie's Bra & Girdles, a lingerie storefront that mysteriously never opened. It was considered a provocative conceit at the time, but David has matured and so has his museum. The collection is now a tribute to his late father, Hyman Kotkin, who died in 2006. When David speaks of his dad, here and at his show during "The Alien," he does so with genuine affection.

When David arrives, the lights on the storefront change. I meet the other guests on the tour: Patrick Culliton, a Houdini expert; and Eddie Dawes, one of the foremost scholars on magic history, now ninety-one years old. There's also another magician with Patrick, who I will soon learn is blind.

A false door in the changing room of the tailor shop leads us into the lobby of the museum. David disappears for a bit, and Chris Kenner, his consigliere, head of operations, and a seminal magic creator in his own right, explains the rules of the museum before playing a video hyping David. In the four-minute clip, we're reminded that David has won more Emmys than any living performer, that he has vanished the Statue of Liberty, and that Rick Ross rapped a song all about him.

David reemerges and, with five of us huddled around, asks to borrow a ring, which he clearly places into a box and leaves in my care. Also, he has someone think of *any* celebrity, write it down, and keep hold of the paper as a record. The ring? The thought-of celebrity? To what end we don't know.

David then resumes the tour, escorting us through a labyrinth of magic illusions and ephemera. We are treated to unspeakable wonders. Every notable magician in history is represented with their own shrine: Howard Thurston, Harry Kellar, Harry Blackstone, and even Doug Henning, whom David succeeded as America's most popular illusionist. Adelaide Herrmann (see page 79), America's most popular female illusionist, is represented with props and posters, as well as the stunning dress she wore on tour. The artifacts are the centerpiece of the museum, of course, but the displays rival even the most opulent museum exhibitions. There is lighting and music in every room, and as David speaks about Houdini's straitjacket, for example, the item is illuminated from above and accompanied by gaudy orchestral music playing softly as David narrates.

Since there are no crowds, there are virtually no barriers. Everything is within touching distance, and as long as you ask first, David is pretty chill about letting you hold the items. At one point, sensing my excitement, he pulls me aside and motions me up a steep flight of stairs, where a secret vault is located. Inside are all the private writings, diaries, and notes of Robert-Houdin (see page 92), the most influential magician of his age. And handing me the folios, one after the other, is the most influential magician of *our* age.

Next on the tour, David presents us with a secret harness fashioned by Robert-Houdin, used to make his son float in Paris salons in the early nineteenth century. Robert-Houdin artifacts are, perhaps, the rarest from that era; I had never even seen one. The man who is blind quietly asks his friend Patrick to describe the item to him, not realizing that Patrick is still in a different gallery. Without hesitation David lifts the harness from its case and says, "Here," placing the fragile object in the blind magician's hands. His fingers pore over every contour in the rusted metal and leather gadget. He wants to touch something Robert-Houdin touched—magic by osmosis.

Next we walk into a complete re-creation of Martinka's, America's oldest magic shop. Panel for panel, prop for prop, David had experts and historians reconstruct the entire magic shop showroom, just as it would have appeared at the turn of the twentieth century in New York City. Many of the artifacts are original to Martinka's. At this point, David takes the stage and asks me for the ring box he gave me earlier. But when I look in the box, the ring is gone. He proceeds to perform a century-old illusion, much like it would have been demonstrated on the counters at Martinka's. An empty, examined flowerpot is filled with dirt and placed on a table. Without anyone touching it, a plant sprouts and grows before our eyes, and on the highest branch, the ring reappears. This is a museum tour, but also clearly a show.

When we walk into the next room, only a small kiosk is visible, lit from above in an otherwise endless expanse of black. It is the Macy's counter where David first encountered magic. At great expense and research, he obtained the *exact* kiosk that he happened upon as a boy. It's filled with the original tricks (all in original packaging). David offers a brief demo of beginner tricks, including the one that hooked him on magic, the Coin Board. Afterward he gifts me his first business card—these are a rite of passage for young performers: "Davino Boy Magician" it reads, with a conspicuous misspelling of his specialty: "Chirdren's Parties." I choke up for a moment, standing inches from the man who first kindled my interest in magic, listening to him explain his own origin story.

"Then, I discovered Tannen's," he says. Music fills the room, and slowly, warm lights flood the walls of the space. We are now surrounded by Tannen's Magic Shop, circa 1969. Tannen's is a New York magic institution and still one of the finest shops in the country, one of the few that survived the internet age. Every counter, sign, and feather flower bouquet feels like they're in the right place. He even has the famous floor emblem of the shop's logo.

Vintage photos of the shop taken in 1969 confirm that the shop is an *exact* replica from that year. I had only heard of Tannen's glory years. Now I am standing in the shop where my heroes hung out and swapped tricks—when David Copperfield calls me over to see something.

I would have loved an extra hour in any of the rooms I visited that early morning, to take it all in or snap a secret photo as proof that I was there. But when I stray too far from David, he corrals me back to the group. His enthusiasm to share the history of magic as carefully assembled in his collection is awe inspiring. You can't help but care about every poster and prop and Houdini letter—because *he* cares.

David is relaxed onstage during his show, but there's never any doubt you're watching theater when you watch David Copperfield. Chatting with him in his airplane hangar gives you the measure of him only as someone who has decided to buy himself some very expensive toys. But at his museum I got to spend time with the real David Copperfield. I'd met him many times before, but I had never seen him as he was that night.

The next stop is up a steep flight of stairs to the poster gallery. Eddie Dawes hesitates. At ninety-one, he has rarely gotten up from his wheelchair to this point. But David is determined to get him up the stairs at any cost so that he can continue the tour with everyone else. The moment is yet another reminder of magic's great equalizing power. I am in a room with the world's most famous magician, a man who is blind, and a ninety-one-year-old historian, and we are equals, each of us taking turns sharing stories about our heroes, asking each other questions about the legends immortalized on the museum walls. "Do you recognize that one, Eddie?" David asks, pointing to a large Chung Ling Soo lithograph on the wall, the only one like it known to exist. The central figure—a man in a robe—is dancing, almost jumping out of the picture's frame.

Eddie nods, knowingly. "I first saw that poster when I performed in Liverpool and came to your house afterward," David says, "when we took it from under your bed and spread it out on the floor." David had purchased several choice items from Eddie a decade earlier.

Mike Caveney emerges, barefoot, from some unknown corner of the museum. "Josh? What are *you* doing here?" he asks. Mike is one of the most esteemed historians and authors in magic, and also a sought-after performer. He authored one of my favorite books on magic and also performed at my wedding. "David has me come out a few times a month to help with research," he says. "I'm reorganizing his library tonight." David not only fills his museum with the finest objects, but hires the brightest minds in magic to research and catalogue it.

The library, which David tells me will be the biggest magic library in the world when completed, will be where David hopes magicians can come to do research. I ask how that will be possible when the only way to get in is by personal invitation from David himself. "I'm going to endow it," he says, and then he lays out a vision in which the museum itself remains private for magic scholars, but its contents travel around the world on loan in temporary exhibitions.

There's an entire room dedicated to Robert-Houdin's Mystery Clocks (see page 122). There are perhaps seventy known to exist in the world, and almost half of them reside in this room, most of them shiny and in working order. These clocks sell for more than $100,000 each. With the clocks are automaton machines built by Robert-Houdin himself—figures that come to life and perform magic tricks, bake cakes, and play music. All of them were built in the nineteenth century. They aren't just magic treasures—they are unique human achievements, each one of a kind.

Every show needs a closing act, and David has fittingly designed his museum experience to end with Houdini. A room showcasing everything from Houdini's Water Torture Cell to his baby shoe and bathtub is the last stop of the tour. In 2017, Houdini's Harlem town house went on the market (for just over $4 million and sold for around $3.6 million). David didn't buy the house, but he bought the bookshelves from the new owners, and had them cut out of the walls and transported to Las Vegas. The entire library as Houdini displayed it is preserved in a photograph. David has—you guessed it—reconstructed the library *exactly*.

Suddenly, on a chair just to the left of the shelves, a bodiless head begins speaking. I was the one David asked to think of a celebrity earlier in the tour. The disembodied head ponders for a moment, then calls out, "Win-ston Church-ill." It's four in the morning, in Vegas, and the dead are reading our minds. It's time to go back to the hotel.

28

IS MAGIC ART?

THAT IS THE MISSION OF TRUE ART—
TO MAKE US PAUSE AND LOOK
AT A THING A SECOND TIME.

—OSCAR WILDE,
POET, PLAYWRIGHT

I have vivid memories of the first magician I saw as a child. The year was 1988, and the location was my basement. Mike Bishop, a popular local magician, performed at my seventh birthday party. I've forgotten the tricks he did that day, but I remember vividly how I felt. Details might fade from the mind, but magic embeds emotion in memory.

Yet when people see most magicians, their experience falls well short of profound. "The great tragedy of twentieth-century magic," says Max Maven, one of the industry's most prolific creators, "is that magicians have taken an art form that is inherently profound and rendered it trivial." Most magicians present their tricks as puzzles designed to confuse. And if you're even a little confused, you can't be amazed.

YouTube is filled with clips of people performing simple tricks for their dog or toddler. There's a YouTube clip with more than thirty million views where an orangutan is stumped by a zoo handler who vanishes a large nut. The orangutan stares blankly for a moment, then falls backward laughing. The reaction is indistinguishable from a human's reaction to being fooled. It will melt your heart.

But it is not art.

At least not in my eyes. For magic to be magic, it has to deceive. For magic to be *art*, a magician has to make you feel an intense emotion. There's usually a point of view or evidence of a narrative. And there must be a feeling that this magician is the only one who could have presented her material in this way. Producing a dove onstage is just a trick, but the narrative is the creation of life. When Penn & Teller burn and restore an American flag, we experience a range of emotions. We're fooled—sure—that's what makes it a magic trick. But we're intrigued and engaged, and then reflective about what we've just watched.

And the narrative need not be trick specific. I have teared up watching Mahdi Gilbert, a friend and fellow magician, perform flawless but straightforward card magic. Mahdi was born without hands and feet and has learned to use the webbing of his appendages to shuffle, deal, and do exceptional sleight of hand. For me, the experience of watching a magician excel without fingers is a spiritual experience. I'm humbled and grateful to be in his presence. The narrative of his show is the self-evident story of his life.

The very best magic asks us to look at something we know and see something new. But the meaning has to sneak up on the viewer, and a delicate touch is essential. Most magic shows start with a bang. You have to impress before you can suggest. The right to tell an audience a story—to transport them—has to be earned. Author Philip Pullman suggests that stories must begin in delight and end in truth: "If you start with what you think is truth, you'll seldom end up with delight—it doesn't work that way round."

As magicians, we can't slap meaning onto a magic effect— that has to occur in the spectator's mind, what art critics call "the beholder's share." During a magic trick, I call it the "spectator's burden." I used to end a trick by producing a small porcelain rabbit. After the trick one night, a woman in the audience stared through me like I was a ghost, tears welling in her eyes. Later she explained, "I had that exact rabbit toy when I was a little girl. And when you made that rabbit appear, it took me right back to my childhood." Sentimentality be damned, these are the moments that define my life. I gave her the rabbit and haven't done the trick since.

✦ ✦ ✦

29

WHAT'S THE WEIRDEST SHOW YOU'VE EVER DONE?

A LITTLE MAGIC

CAN TAKE YOU A LONG WAY.

—ROALD DAHL, AUTHOR

✦ ✦ ✦

I did a show at Pablo Escobar's estate where I performed at a wedding for a prominent New York banker. But that's not the weirdest show I've ever done.

I did a show at a hospital in Brazil for a little boy named Benjy with an autoimmune disease—an actual boy in a bubble. To choose a card, Benjy put on a rubber glove and stuck his hand through a small hole, where I placed a fan of cards within reach. But that's not the weirdest show I've ever done.

I did a show in which a politician—a famous guy we all know by name—was in attendance with an escort on his arm throughout the evening. At one point I removed my phone to take a picture of an obscene ice sculpture I found funny. I was almost tackled to the ground by the Secret Service, who looked over my shoulder as I deleted all photos of the event. Still not the weirdest show I've ever done.

I did a show for Steve Paul, the iconic music impresario who was an early champion of Jimi Hendrix, the Doors, and Pink Floyd. He invited me to his apartment and asked everyone in attendance to sit cross-legged on the floor—the same floor, he made sure I knew, on which John Lennon and Andy Warhol had sat. He served chocolate chip cookies and water and insisted on complete silence during my show. He shushed anyone who laughed or applauded during my set. "Just internalize it," he told his guests, ticked off at the noise. Still not the weirdest show I've ever done.

I donated a show to a center outside New York City for people who are blind, where my entire audience had to "feel" the tricks since they couldn't see. Not the weirdest show I've ever done.

The weirdest show I've ever done was when I was eighteen and a man named Jerry hired me to perform at his seventy-fifth birthday party. At a strip club in Raleigh, North Carolina. A mere three months *after* I was legally allowed in strip clubs. Now I was the headliner.

When I walked in, the floor manager pointed to a small platform where a woman was suspended, topless, upside down, on a pole. Flanked by two other topless performers, she was surrounded by a pack of ravenous men—my future audience—fighting each other to slip dollar bills into her thong. "You'll do your show up there," he said.

I replied, half joking, "And I assume the women will be up there dancing during my show."

He removed the cigar from his mouth and ashed it on the ground. "You bet your ass they will."

Minutes later I found myself onstage, with an audience of zombies. Their heads faced my direction, but every pair of eyes was fixated on the women to my left or right. I went through my act trick for trick, line for line, but was barely heard over announcements like, "Another round of applause for Shari . . . and now welcome to the stage our *naughtiest* girl, Nasty Natalie!" I was onstage in front of a hundred people, performing only for myself.

The low point was when Jerry, whose colossally bad idea it was to hire a magician for his strip club birthday bash, walked up to the front of the stage, egged on by his friends. At first I didn't understand what he was doing, but as he made his way toward me, holding up a hundred-dollar bill, I understood. All I could do was play along, kneel down, and allow Jerry to tuck his money into the waistband of my pants.

That was the weirdest show I've ever done.

The performance venue is arguably more important for magicians than for any other performing artist. You can stage *Les Misérables* on Broadway or at GlenOak High School, and it works in more or less the same way. The quality of the show and the set may vary, but words are spoken and sung on a stage, with an audience watching below.

But for magicians, venue dictates material. When I was presented with the challenge of performing for Benjy, the boy encased in a protective bubble, I knew the moment I was escorted into the room that my material wouldn't work. Stealing his watch was out of the question. So although a setting can destroy a magic performance, even the most challenging venues are opportunities in disguise. That day, Benjy and his family were witness to a show that nobody will ever see again.

I invited Benjy to select a card through the hole in his bubble. His gloved hand maneuvered a card from the spread. Without fanfare, I stepped back, displayed Benjy's card, and shuffled it into the deck. I threw the deck at the bubble and the cards fluttered across the room. But then Benjy noticed one card was stuck to the bubble's wall . . . on the *inside*. (The method didn't put Benjy in any actual danger—and I have to give a nod to Benjy's caregiver for her secret help in pulling off this unusual illusion.) Benjy peeled it from the wall to verify it was his card and, with a look of silent bewilderment, tacked it to the bulletin board next to his small desk among the well wishes and photographs. That card wasn't just a playing card anymore. It was, I hope, a memory of something impossible.

When I received an invitation to perform for a group of students who were blind, I took the show both out of curiosity and altruism. How the *hell* was I going to pull this off? It's an interesting challenge to perform for people without sight because magic is an almost entirely visual medium. I can't think of many magic effects that work if you aren't able to see them. There's Richard Turner, the virtuoso blind card cheat from Texas (see page 57), but he's the one who can't see—we, the sighted audience, marvel at what his hands produce. Yet even his material would be lost on an audience that shared his condition.

So how do you amaze an audience that can't see? You fool their minds. I spent the two months leading up to the show developing material tailored precisely to an audience that sees with their fingers.

Here's what they experienced: I passed out metal forks to each guest and invited them to inspect the forks carefully with their fingers. I asked everyone to lay the forks on their outstretched palms and concentrate their energy on bending the metal. I then asked each guest to rub the fork gently along the handle with their free hand.

As they rubbed, laughter built from the crowd. Each fork was bending, some forks faster than others. For some spectators, the forks bent at ninety-degree angles. For others, the tines splayed out in a fan of their own accord. Throughout, the audience could *feel* the metal as it bent.

I can't say for certain what those students experienced with the forks, but I was fighting back tears, witness to a moment outside myself where I pushed my craft into a crevice it had yet to fill. Until that moment, magic was to those students like the sunset or cubism or a touchdown—things they could experience only through the words of others. But that day, fifty students who were blind held a moment of magic in their hands. They had experienced wonder *firsthand*, wonder they could touch and feel, and they had a now-useless fork to keep as a reminder.

That performance also led to the development of my original piece, "Out of Sight," in which a spectator holds a deck of cards and merely thinks of one. Without questions or manipulating the deck, I announce the name of the thought-of card and reveal that, actually, all the cards in the deck are blank, except for the selection.

I realized after my first performance of "Out of Sight" that the best possible presentation was telling the story I just told here—about the experience of doing magic for people who were blind. I performed "Out of Sight" for Penn & Teller on their show *Fool Us*, sharing the overwhelming experience as I performed this feat of mind reading (see page 124). As a prize for fooling Penn & Teller, I got to return to their Las Vegas stage six months later and close their show with an encore performance.

The experience of performing for the students who were blind was so meaningful to me that my most recent show, *Six Impossible Things*, re-created the entire scenario. Guests were escorted into a New York City basement, then seated in a circle of chairs. An usher distributed forks. Then, without warning, the lights faded to black. My voice emanated from the middle of the room, and in total darkness I guided people through the same fork-bending experience I had created for the audience of people who were blind.

The first ten minutes of my show took place in total darkness, where the audience was forced to experience magic with their other senses. (Ten minutes is just about the limit sighted people are willing to sit in complete darkness, by the way.) After tricks, there was no applause, and stunts were often met with tense silence. This was a difficult adjustment for me. Openers are usually pacesetters—they establish the mood and vibe of a show. It was definitely a risk to turn off all the lights and force people to feel around for magic in the dark. But it was also the thing people talked about months after the show was over. None of it would've been possible in a five-hundred-seat theater, and certainly not at a strip club.

30

WHAT DO YOU THINK ABOUT WHEN YOU PERFORM?

THE AUDIENCE ROARED WHEN THE QUARTET TOOK THE STAGE, AND I LEANED BACK AND SHUT MY EYES, PRETENDING THE APPLAUSE WAS FOR ME.

—DAVID SEDARIS, AUTHOR, HUMORIST

✦ ✦ ✦

When you watch a magic show, we're watching you, too.

Hello, Hawaiian shirt.
The braid in that woman's hair.
A Mickey Mouse watch.
Who's laughing?
Who's not laughing?

Everything means something.

The Hawaiian shirt is a bold fashion statement. The guy wearing it is likely someone with confidence, not easily embarrassed. I might involve him later in my show.

The woman with the meticulous braid in her hair has flawless hygiene—she clearly pays attention to detail. Therefore, she is likely to notice details others might not. I'll be careful about how, or if, to involve her.

The Mickey Mouse watch doesn't tell me much, but the man is wearing it on his *right* hand, which means he is most likely left-handed. Anything he does with his right hand will be easier to influence. I'll make sure he chooses his card with his nondominant right hand.

Everything you do at my show tells me something about you. And what you *don't* do tells me just as much, if not more. Sir Arthur Conan Doyle's most brilliant plot device takes place in "The Adventure of Silver Blaze" when Sherlock Holmes solves a crime by identifying the dog that *didn't* bark. I look for the person who isn't laughing. When you laugh, you're at ease, and that's often when we execute the sleight or the switch. Those who don't laugh are problematic. They require extra attention.

Magic can be threatening, particularly the kind of close-up magic I do at times. For some, magic is just a problem to solve. If someone can't figure it out, they can become frustrated, even hostile. I've found that men are often threatened if their wives or girlfriends are enjoying the show a little too much.

For this reason, I will often pay extra attention to the man or make him the hero of a trick early in the set: "Jon, I can't find Susan's card. Would you touch any card in the deck? That one? Wait! Did *you* just find her card? Amazing!" Once he is on my side, he isn't threatened, and everyone enjoys the show.

It's important to identify alpha males and females. There is always one or more in a group. It might be the CEO at the company party, but it's more likely to just be the loud guy, the ringleader. You know the type: He has to have the last word, he has to say something funnier than everyone else, and in many cases, he is the one paying my fee. A guy like this could become a problem, even a heckler, if he feels threatened. A joke at his expense could be the last laugh in the show. But make a fan out of him, and everyone follows along. I have found that this is the key to celebrity performances. I was once hired to perform magic at an event for Ben Affleck's charity. An hour into the gig, I felt a tap on my shoulder: "Ben would like to see some magic now." Okay then.

I was escorted into a room with thirty people, a mixture of friends, hangers-on, and publicists. But the dynamic was odd. People weren't watching me. They were watching Ben Affleck watching me.

I borrowed a dollar from him, folded it up, and caused the name George Washington to disappear from the bill. Ben showed no reaction, so nobody else did, either. I folded the bill again, and this time when I unfolded it, the name Ben Affleck appeared *printed* on his bill. He freaked out. And about three seconds later, so did everyone else.

A magician takes every advantage. When I walk into a room before a show, I talk to myself, often out loud. "Are there tricks that won't work in this space? What's behind me when I perform? That window might be a distraction. Then again, maybe I can use it for my 'Card Through Window' effect. A couple is getting engaged after the show? Perhaps I can produce the ring for them."

My set list can change within seconds of being introduced, all in the service of giving the best show. The best magicians often take advantage of (and credit for) unusual circumstances.

31

AND WHAT ABOUT RIGHT BEFORE YOU GO ONSTAGE?

TO ACHIEVE THE MARVELOUS, IT IS PRECISELY THE UNTHINKABLE THAT MUST BE THOUGHT.

—TOM ROBBINS, AUTHOR

✦ ✦ ✦

I'm backstage right now in New York. Alone in my dressing room, I can hear the rustle of the audience filing in and finding their seats. In just a moment I'll close this laptop and put on my jacket. Then I'll pop a breath mint and reach into my pocket for the crumpled, aged scrap of paper I read to myself before every performance. I know by heart what's written on that paper, but reading the words is comforting to me.

Perform like it's the first time and the last time.

It's an old musician's parable I keep close at hand. An orchestra is about to begin a performance of Beethoven's Fifth Symphony. Backstage the conductor says, "I know all of you have played this piece innumerable times, and the audience has heard it many times. But tonight, I want you to play for two distinguished guests. One member of your audience is a little girl who is hearing Beethoven's Fifth for the first time. The second member of your audience is an old man, who will be hearing it for his last time."

Every show, just before I walk onstage, this is what I think about. Someone out there is seeing magic for the first time, and I'm their ambassador for the craft. Someone in this theater will watch my show and make a determination about all magicians based solely on what I do.

When I was a kid, I had crushing stage fright. Even though I was performing at all the neighborhood kids' birthday parties, I would shake through my entire first trick before slowly gaining enough composure to be present. My dad used to comfort me by asking, "Are you nervous?" I would always nod. "Good. That means you care."

Thousands of performances later, I don't shake anymore. I have the opposite problem. I've become so comfortable that I'm at risk of giving a careless performance. This note—*Perform like it's the first time and the last time*—is a reminder to care as much now as I did at those birthday party shows. This is the single best piece of advice I have for anyone else in entertainment. It's my mantra. It was passed to me at the right time in my career and has given me my strength backstage, where I need it most.

One of my goals is to pass this mantra on to the young magicians who come to my show. Here's how it works: I have the venue staff alert me when they observe any wide-eyed kids there who look to be aspiring magicians. We get a lot of kids who see magic on television but want to see it live.

After my show, when I get the signal from our host, I'll pull the young magician aside and explain my preshow ritual. Then I give them a handwritten note with these same words. I wish them luck on their first show, and then I make them promise that they will read these words before *their* next performance.

32

HOW DID HOUDINI DIE?

I KNEW, AS EVERYONE KNOWS,
THAT THE EASIEST WAY
TO ATTRACT A CROWD
IS TO LET IT BE KNOWN
THAT AT A GIVEN TIME AND
A GIVEN PLACE SOMEONE IS
GOING TO ATTEMPT SOMETHING
THAT IN THE EVENT OF FAILURE
WILL MEAN SUDDEN DEATH.

—HARRY HOUDINI, MAGICIAN

✦ ✦ ✦

I am in the midst of a lifelong research project on what I call "tragic magic." I collect and uncover stories of all the magicians, assistants, and spectators who have died in the performance of magic. This includes actual decapitations, staged murders, drunken escapes, and careless mishaps. In my years of research, I've discovered more misinformation about Houdini's death than anyone in magic history. However, by assembling the totality of research and scholarship around the incident in 1926, we can unpack what likely caused Houdini's premature and tragic death.

First: He was exhausted. At fifty-two years old, he had spent much of his life touring the world. He was no longer the perfect, muscular specimen advertised on his posters, and was unable to match the physically demanding stunts of his youth. He had fractured his ankle in a recent show and was hobbling around, icing his ankle between shows to dull the pain.

On the afternoon of October 22, 1926, Houdini was backstage at the Montreal Princess Theater, lying in a recliner and reading his mail. He had invited two students backstage from nearby McGill University to sketch his likeness. Under circumstances that have never been entirely clear, a *third* student, J. Gordon Whitehead, later found his way backstage.

Whitehead was thirty-one at the time, older than the average student. And probably larger, too, at six feet, three inches, by eyewitness accounts. As Houdini reclined backstage, he chatted with the three students, recounting the importance of a balanced diet and insisting they feel his forearm muscles.

Whitehead changed the subject and asked Houdini if it was true that he could absorb any blow to the abdomen. It was reported that Houdini would sometimes invite audience members onto the stage to punch him in a test of his strength. Interestingly, historians have been unable to substantiate any claims that Houdini boasted of being able to weather punches. It's also important to remember that this stunt would've been performed when Houdini was prepared for the blows: hunched forward, stomach muscles tensed and condensed to absorb the shock of a punch. Although you wouldn't choose to be punched, even you could withstand a fairly rigorous gut punch if you knew it was coming.

J. Gordon Whitehead gave Houdini no such notice. He delivered what eyewitness accounts reported to be four strong blows to the stomach, causing Houdini to partially fall over, recoiling. Whitehead then delivered several successive blows, until Houdini, the wind knocked out of him, whispered that it was "enough."

What neither Whitehead nor Houdini knew that afternoon was that the famous magician was suffering from appendicitis. Less than a week later and very ill, he registered a fever of 104 degrees. Still, he declined medical treatment and continued his tour to Detroit. Eventually, he was unable to perform and was taken to the hospital, where he immediately underwent surgery. It was discovered that his appendix had ruptured. In 1926, two years before penicillin was discovered, a ruptured appendix was a death sentence—with modern antibiotics, Houdini likely would have lived.

The historic debate is what role, if any, J. Gordon Whitehead played in Houdini's death. Does trauma to the abdomen exacerbate an ailing appendix? There are conflicting reports from medical experts then and now, as well as long documents that consider the minutiae of this inconclusively. I asked a general surgeon after one of my shows, "Would being punched repeatedly in the abdomen *cause* an appendix to rupture?"

"Well," he said, "it certainly wouldn't have helped."

The unsolved mysteries don't end there. J. Gordon Whitehead's behavior was too strange to ignore. He was fascinated by the occult, and several Houdini scholars believe he was a stooge sent by angered Spiritualists to harm Houdini. There is absolutely no direct evidence to support this claim, but the fascination is understandable. The motive is clear enough: Houdini blazed a trail of exposure wherever he went, outing fraudulent mediums for what they were: charlatans. In the Roaring Twenties, Spiritualism was big business, and Houdini was the face of the revolution that eventually snuffed it out. Whitehead died in seclusion and squalor in 1954.

Another issue some consider a factor was money. Houdini carried life insurance that eventually paid Bess, his wife, double indemnity. To get double the promised amount, authorities had to conclude that Houdini's death was an accident and not just a case of a ruptured appendix. There was certainly a motive from Houdini's camp in general, and from Bess in particular, to find fault with J. Gordon Whitehead's suspicious behavior. And in the end, Bess *did* receive a double indemnity payment from the insurance company.

All of these details are fascinating but not germane to Houdini's legacy. He didn't die in a failed escape in the Hudson River, as some fantasized accounts have claimed, or during the Water Torture Cell, as depicted in the film *Houdini* starring Tony Curtis. He died in a hospital after four agonizing days, eventually passing on Halloween. The part of Houdini's death that sounds the corniest—and the most fabricated—is actually true. He promised his wife that if anyone could come back from the dead, it would be him. And their agreed-upon code word that he would send from the world beyond was . . . *believe*.

33

WHAT'S WORSE— SCREWING UP A TRICK OR DEALING WITH HECKLERS?

✦ ✦ ✦

Eventually, every magician screws up a trick. For me the screw-up came on live television, December 17, 2008. It was my first appearance on the *TODAY* show—the hosts were Kathie Lee Gifford and Hoda Kotb. Those four minutes were the worst of my professional life and are forever preserved thanks to the magic of YouTube. If you dig deep enough, you can still find the clip online and see for yourself what went wrong. But if we ever meet, I'd prefer that you not bring it up. Okay?

By its very nature, close-up magic is interactive. But it shouldn't be delivered *at* spectators, like lines of a play. Magic tricks are conversations with real people in real time. A good magician *strives* for an authentic experience, not a recitation of scripts and sleights. This is what makes close-up magic the fullest artistic expression of our craft. It is also what makes close-up magic dangerous.

The danger is that if you seek an authentic, unplanned interaction, you might just get one. The trick I chose to perform is my interpretation of an effect that dates back to the 1970s. The idea is for two signed cards (in this case, signed by the two hosts) to *fuse* together to create an impossible object: a single card with both cards' faces merged. The problem arises at the 3:27 mark, when I had to secretly palm a card in my right hand and deposit it on a tabled packet of cards. This is, by any measurement, a difficult task. It was poor judgment on my part to even attempt a move like this on television. Though I had thousands of performances under my belt by then, I had absolutely no experience on television. Rookie mistake.

Kathie Lee detected the move, I'm ashamed to say, and she called it out. "Hey, I saw that," she said. In the moment, I adapted by executing another sleight to "prove" she didn't actually catch anything. That was it. I finished the trick, they reacted in all the right places, and it was done.

The number of times I've been busted in front of an audience is small; I'd say fewer than two dozen times. Most of them occurred with fewer than five people watching. On one regrettable night a prop broke midtrick, and there was no way to recover. Every mistake cuts deep, but the professional embarrassment I felt after this *TODAY* show appearance was a low point. I've never encountered a spectator who noticed something was wrong in that clip—but I know I made a mistake, and it weighs on me still.

◆

Less-experienced magicians are forever asking me about hecklers. At my seminars, I've heard heartbreaking stories about audience members who insulted a magician, or broke his props midtrick, or shouted an obscenity at the critical moment. "How do you deal with hecklers?" is the question they ask. But what they *want* to ask is, "What do you say to people to shut them up?"

Magicians call them "heckler stoppers"—lines that blast someone into silence, cauterizing the wound in one deft insult. I have a collection of them in the recesses of my brain, but they're the nuclear option, to be used *only* as a last resort when war is the sole path that remains.

But I'm quick to tell magic students that if they're seeking advice on handling hecklers, they're asking the wrong question. It ought to be "Why am I getting heckled?" Most people who interrupt a magic show aren't doing it to throw off the magician—they want attention. More often than not, the magician is ignoring his audience, and someone has decided to *force* an interaction by shouting out something. I have found that giving a heckler the attention he seeks takes almost no time and allows you to continue with the show.

"I'll bet you use this trick to pick up girls at the bar!" is a common one. Quickly dispelled by pointing at my wedding ring with the reply, "I only use my powers for good." Done. Over. On with the show.

However, magicians can also invite heckling when they act like fools. It's human nature to knock someone down who is knocking down someone else. "Say 'stop,'" the unrefined magician asks, riffling too quickly through his cards. Before she has a chance to respond, he blurts, "I like a woman who doesn't know when to say 'stop.'" Gross.

I treat my audiences respectfully. Most of the humor in my show is about my own failings, not theirs. As a result, I have very few encounters with hecklers. Occasionally, though, it's a problem. And the problem is usually from alcohol.

In the end, it's worse to screw up a trick than to be heckled for the simple reason that the former is a failure of *my* job, whereas the latter is a failure of the audience's job. But both make for a bad day at work.

◆

The rudest person I ever performed for was a guy who interrupted me constantly with theories about my tricks. At one point he thrust his hand into my pocket, trying to find where a coin was hidden after I made it disappear. The guy just *couldn't* live with mystery. I told him he was insatiably curious, which is magician-speak for "asshole."

Then I realized a haunting truth. That guy was just like me. I became a magician for precisely the same reason he couldn't contain himself—because I can't bear *not* knowing how a trick works. I simply have to know how it's done. I am insatiably, obnoxiously curious about anything I don't understand. This makes me a terrible spectator, unable to let go and live in mystery.

But it's also what makes me a good magician.

✦ ✦ ✦

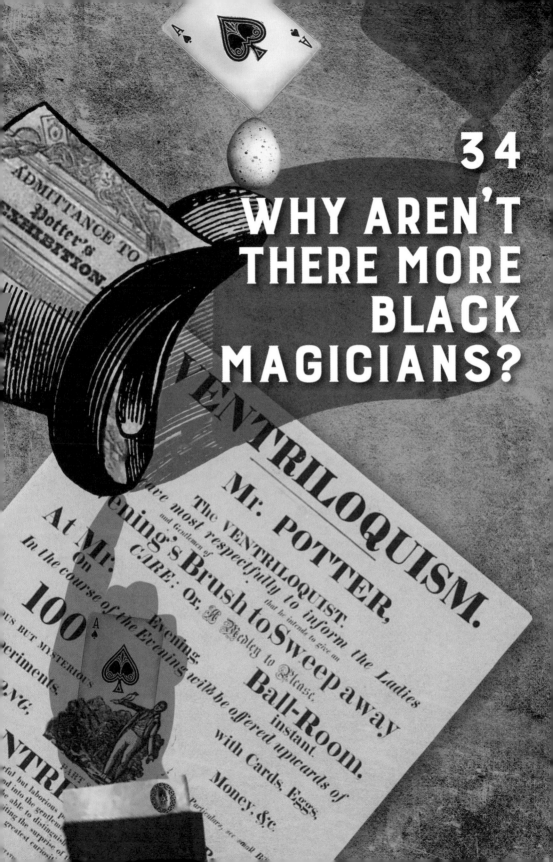

34
WHY AREN'T THERE MORE BLACK MAGICIANS?

I'VE MISSED OUT ON SOME OPPORTUNITIES BECAUSE OF UNDERLYING RACIAL ISSUES FROM UNSCRUPULOUS MAGIC AGENTS. BUT PERFORMING MAGIC HAS ALWAYS BEEN THE EQUALIZER FOR BLACK MAGICIANS.

—KENRICK "ICE" MCDONALD, MAGICIAN

It isn't just women who have been excluded from magic: Black magicians are vastly underrepresented in the current scene and nearly forgotten from magic's history. Magic has always been a visual medium, and its history is often told through the colorful lithographs and advertisements magicians used to promote their shows. Many of the great figures in magic told their own stories through popular memoirs or by passing their shows on to a successor.

But Black magicians were mostly excluded from these traditions, and there is scant visual material on any of the Black performers of magic's golden age, from the 1870s to the 1930s. Black magicians were not welcome at most venues, except for those that catered exclusively to Black communities. Despite these barriers, Black magicians have left a rich legacy, and it's undeniable that there are more Black and other magicians of color now appearing on regular magic circuits.

The first famous magician on record in the United States was a Black man: Richard Potter (1783–1835). America was in its infancy, and so, too, was its magic scene. Potter, whose mother was likely enslaved, flourished in Colonial America with a combination of magic and ventriloquism. He toured for a time as the assistant to a white, Scottish magician. Then, in 1811, Potter continued as a solo artist, becoming one of the most popular magicians in the country and a figure some historians refer to as America's first Black celebrity. So successful was Potter that he purchased 175 acres in Andover, Massachusetts; the area still bears the name Pottersville.

A century later, Benjamin Rucker (1889–1934) gained notoriety, touring the States under the pseudonym of Black Herman, in honor of Prince Herman, Rucker's onetime teacher and performing partner. Black Herman was a distinctive character. The few photos of Rucker that survive depict a debonair performer, dressed in tails and a top hat. His repertoire consisted of powerful classics of the time, including escaping from audience-tied restraints, making rabbits appear, and causing a bird to emerge from a flash of fire. He did bigger tricks, too, performing a suspension effect called "The Asrah Levitation" in which an assistant floated and then vanished in midair (see page 205).

But Black Herman's showpiece was his rendition of "Buried Alive." He would perform the feat outdoors, where he would cause his pulse to slow and then stop entirely. It wasn't legitimate, of course; there's an age-old secret to make it impossible for someone to find your pulse for a brief period of time. Herman would then place himself in a funeral casket that was lowered into the ground. He would apparently remain there, sealed inside, for three dramatic days. Black Herman's casket would then be lifted out of the ground, where he emerged and escorted the audience back inside the theater to finish his show.

The secret to the trick was Black Herman slipping out of the casket before it was lowered into the ground. He was then free to go to the next town on his tour and secure the land and contracts needed to mount his show. He would return to the previous town days later to slip *back* inside the casket and complete his signature trick. And so Rucker went, from town to town, year after year.

Black Herman's show would have been a fascinating glimpse into his era and community. In the North, he enjoyed audiences composed of both white and Black members, but in the southern states, Jim Crow laws mostly forbade him from performing for mixed audiences. He instead played to entirely Black houses in those regions. And his show was no mere imitation of those performed by other magicians. He incorporated elements of his life and culture onstage, like calling out the sounds of birds found in his ancestral African homeland. During his rope escape, he referred to the techniques he used as the same as those used by his ancestors to escape from the bonds of slave traders. It would appear he was quite convincing: A 1924 newspaper clipping revealed that Black Herman was arrested for "Black Magic," specifically citing the fact that he fired a gun at a card deck and caused it to inexplicably disappear. After his shows, Black Herman offered special talismans for sale, whose powers, he claimed, could ward off racism. Details of more specific obstacles he faced in his career as a Black performer are, sadly, lost to time.

Henry Box Brown's (1816–1897) greatest trick occurred before he even began his career in magic. Born into enslavement at the Hermitage Plantation in Virginia, Brown devised an escape so daring that it would presage a successful career in entertainment: He mailed himself to freedom.

Carrying out a plan hatched with a group of abolitionists in Philadelphia, Brown conspired to "accidentally" burn his hand with sulfuric acid on the day of his escape. This gave him the required time and privacy to enclose himself in a box lined with cloth and marked "Dry Goods." The box had just one air hole and was transported for twenty-seven hours by train, wagon, and steamboat before arriving in Philadelphia, where his abolitionist cohorts received the box—and the man—safely in the North.

Brown would go on to be an acclaimed showman, author, and eventually, magician. He performed feats to mesmerize animals and conjuring tricks onstage, though reports of his magic career are rare. He died in Canada in 1897.

Today, Kenrick "Ice" McDonald is the world's foremost authority on Black magicians. McDonald, himself a magician of color, faced a different sort of adversity than Richard Potter or Henry Box Brown. Ice was born into a religious family, and his father didn't immediately approve of his foray into "the dark arts." He had to practice in secret and teach himself his craft. "I personally knew it was not a dark art," Ice says. "I just liked the way it made people feel." Ice's signature performance is a bird act in which he makes doves appear and vanish from silky and sequined foulards. In 2014, Ice was sworn in as the first-ever Black president of the Society of American Magicians.

The magic landscape has become more inclusive in the last decade, but its biggest obstacle might be its unrecoverable past. Adelaide Herrmann and Henry Box Brown are fascinating figures, but their stories aren't the only ones. We'll likely never know about the specific magic tricks or significant struggles of the nameless women (see page 75) and performers of color (see page 184) whose stories have been censored by history. The challenge, then, is to help the next generation of women and underrepresented performers blaze a new path.

35

DOES MAGIC LOOK DIFFERENT IN OTHER COUNTRIES?

THE ESSENCE OF THE BEAUTIFUL
IS UNITY IN VARIETY.

—MOSES MENDELSSOHN, PHILOSOPHER

✦ ✦ ✦

When I was seventeen, I did a nine-month lecture tour around the world. I saw twenty-three countries on that tour, but it was the magic that I saw *in* those countries that I'll never forget. I understand how this might sound, but here goes: In Japan, the magic *looked* totally different from magic in Argentina. The way people shuffled cards in China, for example, was different from how they shuffled cards in Australia. Audiences in the United Kingdom responded to my work in a totally different way than in Morocco.

In Japan, magic was topical in nature. It was much less about the magician and more about a fascinating prop, or the impossible way a paper could be folded. Japanese magicians were often introverted, doing astounding tricks without theatrics or bravado. It was spare and lovely. In France, the magic fed into popular impressions of French culture: fancy shuffles and ornate, multiphased effects. In Argentina, the magicians were suave, fooling you in slow motion.

In the analog age, countries were more isolated. The magic shops in a given country carried mostly products *from* that country. So if you lived in Italy, you looked up to Silvan, a famous Italian illusionist, and learned from other Italian magicians. If you lived in Japan, Dr. Sawa, a dentist and one of Japan's most prolific magicians, was your guru.

The internet has changed all of that. Now every magic shop carries everything, so *all* magicians learn from the Card College series of books, written by author and performer Roberto Giobbi. My DVD *Unreal* sold as well in Asia as it did here in the States.

I remember the surreal feeling of going all the way to China and seeing a local magician perform one of my tricks for me.

Now so many of magic's secrets are a click away. If you're willing to pay for the downloadable video, you can study vintage tutorials with Dai Vernon, the greatest close-up magician of the last century. For years, the only way to meet Dai Vernon was to go on a pilgrimage to his home in Canada. Now you can study with him through your phone, in bed, in pajamas. My friend in Ecuador had to fashion his own props when I visited him in 2001. There was no alternative—he was forced to invent things as he worked. Now he orders props online from America on a Monday, and by Thursday they're sitting on his doorstep. On my last tour of Japan, I noticed the magic was more advanced than I'd seen previously, and completely Westernized. The tricks, the plots—even the style of movement—resembled the Western magic on which I was raised. The magicians were learning magic from the same places I was.

Although the internet has dulled much of the vibrant culture of magic, individuality persists in places. What these places seem to have in common is that they're less influenced by North American culture. In countries where English is not prevalent, the magic culture feels better preserved. Quite simply, if magicians can't fully understand the American teachers online, they seek out local help, which reinforces local traditions and also encourages budding magicians to come up with their own unique styles.

In Paris, near the St. Germain metro stop, you can often come across a magician called Bebel. Just "Bebel"—nobody knows his last name. Bebel has long dreadlocks and a club foot, uses an ornamental walking staff, and sits when he performs. The things Bebel does with playing cards are incomprehensible. Illuminated by the soft yellow glow of the Paris streetlamps, he does street magic, French-style. This translates as tricks often improvised, a tad confusing, but flashy and amazing: Four aces are here, and then, *boom*, they're over there. The red deck is now blue, back to red, then vanishes entirely. Everyone loves Bebel's magic, but magicians are particularly impressed because it's rare to see such technical material used in the real world. Usually a magician reserves a particularly risky or flashy trick for other magicians. Professionals usually conform to safer material—especially in the streets—that can withstand extra scrutiny or inclement weather or a child's grabby hands.

You won't see Yann Frisch, another French magician, on the streets of Paris. Yann performs in the city's avant-garde theater spaces and, occasionally, even circus tents. Classically trained as a mime, Yann won magic's world championship, the Fédération Internationale des Sociétés Magiques (FISM) (see page 97), in 2012 with the most unusual act unveiled at the competition in decades.

Yann's act, which I described earlier (see page vii), is performed silently. So-called "silent acts" *usually* mean there is musical accompaniment instead of talking, but Yann's entire act is done in silence. It begins with him onstage sitting at a table, looking confused. The character he plays is troubled and increasingly frustrated as the magic seems to happen to *him*. The simple, beautiful premise of the act is built around a cup of water that changes into a red ball. And, for nearly eight minutes, red balls disappear and reappear everywhere they shouldn't be. Yann is hapless against these menacing balls, growing ever more frustrated because he simply wants a drink of water. The built-in humor, the visual magic, and the *extreme* difficulty of the moves he's doing make this act not only championship quality, but among the best renditions of ball-and-cup manipulation ever devised. The routine is based loosely on the classic Cups and Balls effect in magic, one that is basically a rite of passage for all magicians. But there is much more at play: There's a narrative and an unusual character, and there's inherent drama stemming from the performer's inability to stop the magic. The act is avant-garde and new wave and bold, which is to say, so very French.

Magicians often comment that my magic has an element of the French style in it, and this makes sense. To learn from French masters like Bebel, I studied in France in 2003. At the time, I considered France the magic epicenter of the world. The reasons were many: Le Double Fond, a close-up magic theater in the Marais neighborhood (see page 79), opened its doors and featured magicians doing some of the most interesting material developed in France at the time—and it clearly rubbed off. The French style differs from American magic in that it's fluid, rhythmic, but not always overtly fancy. I adhere to strict, self-imposed limitations on the amount of skill that I show when I shuffle or spread cards, but like the best French magicians, I do try to make it aesthetically attractive. The French keep cards and coins in motion, as if the objects are lighter than they really are, and moving of their own volition. It's ballet meets tango, only executed with fingers.

The culture of magic innovation in France is a credit to the French government, which recognizes the importance of supporting professional artists. In France, magicians who perform more than forty-three shows a year are entitled to unemployment benefits for *all* the other days they are not performing. As long as they can prove they will not receive income from other work, the French government's staggering, wonderful position is this: We will pay you to keep improving your craft so you don't have to wait tables. It is called *L'exception Culturelle*.

But even France's magic scene has been eclipsed in the last decade by Spain, and without the help of the Spanish government. I asked one of Spain's most talented magicians, Woody Aragon, if the Spanish government supported its artists like France does. "In Spain," he said, "if you don't work, you go hungry."

Most magicians would agree that Spain is now the epicenter of the magic world. Boasting perhaps the most distinguished magician alive in Juan Tamariz, Spain is sprinkled with magic dinner theaters and bars, and, largely thanks to Juan's influence and openness with his disciples, there is a national understanding of card magic. Spanish audiences *get* the subtle differences between one card magician and another because they have grown up watching close-up magic on television. In the United States, a vast majority of the public has existed on a limited diet of fantastical, stunt-based magicians like David Blaine, and we are unused to any other flavor. In Spain, magic is as much a part of life as concerts or comedy.

Beyond Spain, the future of magic seems to be brewing in a most unexpected place: South Korea. Sensational acts—most of them built for large stages—have emerged from there recently and taken top prizes at magic competitions. Theme acts are popular in South Korea: Yumi Chen sitting in front of a vanity mirror preparing to go out leads to a series of unexpected magic moments: Her hair changes, she vanishes a blow-dryer, and her entire costume changes without cover. Ted Kim created an act where his clothing, props, and set all change with a combination of magic and image-mapping technology: Highly accurate light projectors cause patterns and pictures and even videos to appear on his body. So while Kim is wearing a simple white frock, it fills with fish and animated polka dots, all in the blink of an eye. His act is surreal, like watching a video game come to life. Yu Ho-Jin won FISM, the world championship, less for what he did and more because of his pacing. He stood almost entirely still throughout his act, every movement slow and graceful, and despite no rapid motions, he changed a silk scarf into playing cards and back again. He showed his hands unmistakably empty and then caused cards to appear and even float, barely moving his fingers between sequences.

In a fitting twist of irony, if you want to see performers like Yann Frisch and Bebel and Ted Kim—some of the last paragons of magic originating from and honoring their culture—you'll have to look them up . . . on the internet.

36

WHAT MAKES
PENN & TELLER
SO DYNAMIC?

CAUGHT UP IN THE DIFFICULTY OF MYSTIFYING, MAGICIANS OFTEN FORGET THAT THE FIRST JOB OF ANY ARTIST IS TO COMMUNICATE A BEAUTIFUL IDEA. WITHOUT THAT, ANY TRICK, EVEN A REAL FOOLER, IS AN EMPTY EXERCISE.

—TELLER, MAGICIAN

✦ ✦ ✦

Many of Penn & Teller's tricks were conceived over food. On their early tours, the world's most famous magician duo would discuss new ideas in diners and rest stops over burgers and fries. At a Minnesota diner one night in the early 1980s, Teller finished his food before Penn and decided to practice sleights for the classic Cups and Balls. The trick is foundational for magicians. Nearly every great magician has a version, and the trick dates back at least two thousand years, when it was first performed either in Egypt or by Roman conjurers.

Teller rolled two paper napkins into balls and emptied his water glass—and then his fingers started dancing. From where Penn sat, across the table, the sight was absurd. Teller was doing Cups and Balls moves with a clear cup. Even though Teller's sleights were clearly visible, the effect was still amazing. Penn was struck by the realization that the misdirection was so strong, he was missing the moves, even when they were exposed. On a purely aesthetic level it was beautiful.

Then came the idea: Could one do Cups and Balls with clear cups and get away with it? No, it turned out, one could not. But *two* might.

"Cups & Balls and Cups & Balls" is the title of their routine, and it has been a mainstay of their shows for more than thirty years. The routine evolved into a quintessentially Penn & Teller trick, with all the hallmarks of their brand. It is performed at first with opaque cups, a lovely choreography of their four hands alternating actions, lifting cups and revealing small balls. It fools us as each ball appears where it can't be, and then, finally, the cups are lifted to show three giant foil balls and a leather-covered baseball. But that's just the beginning.

"We did that for a while," Penn says at this point in their script, "but we want to zoom in and show you a Penn & Teller Cups and Balls." In other words, they're about to expose the trick. Each of them places the balls, large and small, back into their pockets, letting us see the secret starting point for the props. Then clear plastic cups are laid in a row, and the same sequence is repeated, verbatim. This time Penn names the sleights as they're executed. "We take the first ball and pretend to place it in our hand, having already snuck it under the first cup." The explanation is real. It sounds like nonsensical magic jargon to most people, but it's accurate and timed perfectly.

What's fascinating, however, is that the explanation doesn't diminish the magic. Despite Penn's narration, the choreography is so complex, the misdirection so compelling, that you *still* look in the wrong places. You see an inverted empty cup, and a moment later it's filled with a giant, tinfoil ball. You hear what's going on, but by the time you look, it's already finished. Like swimming in a cold pool on a hot day, you experience two opposing sensations that work in concert to deliver pleasure—in this case, wonder. Watch "Cups & Balls and Cups & Balls" on YouTube; it's one of Penn & Teller's most impressive three minutes. Like so many of their best bits, you get the distinct sense they're talking directly to you, performing only for you.

Penn & Teller first performed "Cups & Balls and Cups & Balls" in an early run of shows in Hollywood, two blocks from the famed Magic Castle. Around that time, Teller tells me, they decided to call themselves "the bad boys of magic," to appeal to people tired of smug magicians performing corny illusions to last year's hit songs. "And it became a self-fulfilling prophecy," he explains. Ricki Dunn, a noted (and now deceased) pickpocket, walked over from the Magic Castle to see their show at the nearby Las Palmas Theater. He was so appalled by the apparent exposure of a classic that he took a swing at Penn in the theater lobby. As expected, they leaned into the controversy. For years Penn & Teller were banned from the Magic Castle and censured from the Magic Circle in London. Eventually, they were given memberships and special honors from the Magic Castle, but the Magic Circle still refuses them membership (on the grounds of exposure).

——◆——

Magic's most famous duo actually started out as a trio. Formed in 1975, they called themselves the Asparagus Valley Cultural Society, so named because they met in Amherst, Massachusetts, once the asparagus-growing capital of the United States. Wier Chrisemer, the onetime third partner with Penn & Teller, went to college with Teller, and met Penn Jillette in a hi-fi store. The threesome performed avant-garde variety entertainment—juggling, music, and magic. "We started off as two guys who knew a third guy," Teller says of their beginnings. "We came in with a mutual liking for Wier and a mutual skepticism for each other."

"I dig some people the instant I see 'em," says Penn. "I just want to be near them. I want to make them laugh. I want to listen to them . . . Teller was never one of those friends to me."

As a trio, Penn, Teller, and Wier toured fairs and small theaters for six years as a troupe, and were a long-running cult hit in San Francisco in the late seventies and early eighties. But as a trio they ran out of creative steam and disbanded. Penn & Teller aficionado John Lovick recalls Penn's side of the breakup from an onstage interview in 2004. "Penn said that people think they kicked Wier out of the group, but [Penn] claimed that isn't true. The trio broke up, and later on, the two of them re-formed as a duo. That didn't sound quite right to me. So, after the interview, I asked Penn if it was true that they re-formed as a duo later. He said, 'Yeah. It was about an hour later.'"

Penn and Teller soon found there was plenty of onstage chemistry between a tall, brash raconteur and his small, animated foil. They just had to evolve their points of view.

"Sixty to seventy percent of the time the one who starts the conversation is Penn," says Teller, backstage at the Rio Casino in Las Vegas, where they have performed five shows a week since 2001. It often starts with a provocative opening line or concept.

"I just want to revisit that idea we talked about years ago," Penn said to Teller, "'The Age-Appropriate Escape.' I'm in my sixties and you're in your seventies. What if we did an escape that was age appropriate? Like escaping from a La-Z-Boy recliner?" Teller thought a La-Z-Boy was too mechanical and suggested a bentwood rocking chair instead.

This is how ideas are developed between the partners: Penn might provide a premise, perhaps a topical idea. Teller's immediate interest is in the structure of the idea and its dramatic potential. "The key is that it's a collaboration of two people of dramatically different personalities," Teller says. "Penn is interested in the present. He's connected to the world. He's fascinated by what's happening here and now. I'm a little more unstuck in time and love form and plot. I was brought up on Hitchcock films and *The Twilight Zone.*"

One of their openers, "CellFish," is a trick where a borrowed cell phone appears inside a dead fish. Teller cuts the fish open and sifts through the guts to retrieve a participant's borrowed phone (safely encased in plastic). Teller recalls, "That started when Penn said, 'I'd like to come out at the beginning of the show and ask, "Would you all take out your phones and turn them on?"'" "CellFish" turns the standard preshow cell phone announcement on its head.

They quickly figured out where they wanted to put the borrowed phone—in the belly of a dead fish, naturally. But vanishing the phone was a subtler problem. Teller, who started out as a high-school Latin teacher, found the answer by channeling Shakespeare, for which he has a particular affinity (he has directed critically acclaimed, magic-laced iterations of Shakespeare plays).

"Shakespeare knew what to keep onstage and what to put offstage," Teller says. "You don't want to see Macbeth kill King Duncan in his sleep." Similarly, he explains, they didn't want to vanish the cell phone visually. So they vanished it in a more interactive, humorous fashion: The phone disappeared onstage, but the entire audience saw how it was done—everyone except the phone's owner.

Every trick Penn & Teller create features their point of view. The current iteration of their show has tricks that deal with religion and privacy. In the past, they've patriotically burned and restored an American flag, and outhealed faith healers. But not everything in their show is heavy or controversial. Take "The Red Ball," for example. This piece is based on David P. Abbott's floating ball. Abbott was an ingenious inventor of magic and close friend of Harry Houdini. His floating ball illusion was once popular, but nobody had attempted it in decades. In the P&T version, *the ball never floats.* An audience-examined red, vinyl ball—about the size of a beach ball—takes on a life of its own. Teller tried other ball colors:

"Green and yellow were awful," he wrote to me. "Only red had that quality of being the essence of a kid's toy." This innocent kid's toy rolls, hops, balances impossibly, and finally jumps through a hoop, stopping and changing directions according to Teller's subtle nods and gestures.

The trick was technically original and charming, but Penn felt it lacked their point of view. Why animate a ball in *their* show? "I told Penn that the ending of that trick is that the ball [should] chase me offstage, but it doesn't fulfill the promise that we made to the audience." That promise is the implicit trust that *everything* P&T perform will have a point of view. Mike Close, a friend and collaborator, suggested they point out the obvious. Though the audience can't see any threads, most people know on some level that thread is involved. Why not point it out to the audience? Now, at the end of "The Red Ball," Penn walks onstage with a giant pair of scissors and cuts a string above the red ball. The ball falls from its suspended animation, once again subject to the laws of gravity. After a few minutes of silent fantasy, that snip is a jarring dose of reality. "That brings them over to our side," Teller says of their intentional spoiler moment.

Both men are unafraid to take risks. "We will pursue an idea *way* too far," Teller says. "Go watch our special *Penn and Teller: Off the Deep End*." This 2005 critical and artistic flop was a two-hour magic special, underwater. Half the material had to be scrapped because of weather and ocean currents. Six years later, they tried a different television format: a magic competition. *Fool Us* has been on for seven seasons so far, and has been a ratings smash both in the United States and overseas. Magicians perform their best feats for Penn & Teller and a studio audience. Penn & Teller attempt to work out the methods of the tricks. I was honored, in season two, to fool them on their show (see page 124).

The format makes explicit what many of us do when we watch magic: try to figure out how it works. And paradoxically, by making that explicit, the audience is set free to enjoy the art of magicians. *Fool Us* is a variety show in competition-show clothing. "The viewers are seeing the magic through our eyes," Teller adds, "so there's a level of trust with what they're seeing on the screen."

Penn & Teller perform at the end of each episode of *Fool Us*, which has been both a blessing and a curse. *Fool Us* is responsible for Penn & Teller's late-career resurgence and has resulted in some extraordinary, original pieces. But turning out thirteen new segments each season is also an enormous workload.

And all the work is paying off. Most performers in their sixth and seventh decades are entering the elder-statesman phase—a little less dancing, a little more plastic surgery. But not Penn & Teller. They are unquestionably in their prime and doing the best work of their forty-year career. Their show is an evolving laboratory of signature pieces and new ideas. I've never seen the same set list twice.

◆

"We spent a lot of time in the first six years, really seriously storm-off-the-stage fighting," Teller remembers. "We spent [those early years] of our career disagreeing more vehemently, and having hurt feelings, and then you grow to work with someone for a long time. Now, as time passes and we work more together, what we find is this: We share certain very important things. We are both sober, we are both atheists, we arrive on time and do our job. No show is ever canceled because of hangovers or tantrums."

If you read about Penn & Teller in the media, one recurring sound bite is that they aren't friends. Both have said, separately, that they aren't close outside of work—that they don't hang out socially and didn't start out as friends. I found this disheartening. I didn't want to believe that Penn & Teller are the Fleetwood Mac of magic—great onstage chemistry that masks offstage drama.

"It's rare that we even see each other when we're not working," Penn wrote, "but it's pretty rare that we're not working."

Teller is often credited among magicians as the magic engine of the partnership, since his background is in magic (Penn started out as a juggler). Penn affirms this. "He's probably the best magic mind in the world. He's certainly one of the three best magic minds alive."

But as I spent time with Teller, what became clear is that the two have a special, enduring—if odd—friendship. "Teller and I only fight over art," Penn says about their relationship now. "Respect of skill and creativity is so much stronger in show business than love."

For years, they were duty bound to stay together; now it's something sweeter. Teller speaks admiringly of Penn's singular brilliance and his wellspring of new ideas. "There's a little bit of competition all the time," Teller admits. "Who can solve this? Who has the better idea on this?"

At the end of an afternoon together, when it was time for Teller to prepare for his show that evening, I asked him the uncomfortable, direct question about his friendship with Penn.

Teller describes their partnership like an arranged marriage. They're compatible in many ways, so they work it out. "Eventually, there's a friendship there that's much deeper than the sort of bromance that fuels rock bands. I'm not working with Penn because he's the person I'd pick out of a crowd. I'm working with him because he's a very, very good person to work with."

Then Teller cried quietly for a moment, and we sat in silence. He recalled the moment Penn's first child was born. And then, nearly verbatim, Teller recited a passage from *Fiddler on the Roof*.

It's the scene where Tevye asks his wife, Golde, if she loves him after enduring a lifetime together. Golde ponders the complexity of their relationship and then replies. "Do I love him? For years I've lived with him. Fought with him. Starved with him . . . If that's not love, what is?"

After the pickpocket Ricki Dunn tried to punch Penn in the Las Palmas Theater lobby, both he and Teller persuaded Ricki to join them at Musso & Frank Grill on Hollywood Boulevard. Ricki was still upset that the duo was exposing the classic trick Cups and Balls. He expressed genuine confusion about the motivation for the piece. "Whose side are you on?" he asked them.

It was a defining moment for the twosome. But their answer crystallized their entire worldview on magic. "The audience's best interest is most often served by not knowing how something is done," Teller admits to me now. "But here and there, part of the delight is being taken on a backstage visit that is enchanting and beautiful." He paused for effect. "We're on the audience's side."

37

WHAT'S YOUR FAVORITE MAGIC TRICK?

MAGIC IS HARD WORK. WE USE THE WORD MAGIC TO DESCRIBE SOMETHING DIFFICULT DONE WITHOUT EFFORT, BUT THAT'S AN UNFAIR DESCRIPTION. MAGIC WAS AND IS THE ALL-DEVOURING WORK OF DECADES.

—WARREN ELLIS, COMIC-BOOK WRITER,
NOVELIST, SCREENWRITER

✦ ✦ ✦

I was once asked to name the four greatest magic tricks in history. The question, by Mark Reiter and Richard Sandomir, authors of *The Final Four of Everything*, was easy for me: "Sawing Through a Woman," "Human Levitation," "The Bullet Catch," and "Vanishing the Statue of Liberty." Each is an amazing feat, each comes with an unforgettable story, and each touched the nerve of an entire generation.

In 1921, sawing *through* a woman was as provocative as it was topical (see page 25). The trick emerged at the beginning of a new push for women's rights and played for or against the cause, depending on the viewer's interpretation.

We've all dreamed of flying, which made the "Human Levitation" such a sensation when it debuted. Servais Le Roy wasn't the first magician to levitate a person, but his original version, "The Asrah Levitation," is my favorite. In the illusion, Le Roy's assistant is covered in a sheer cloth and then rises several feet into the air, the body floating up and down at Le Roy's command. What set Le Roy's version apart was the ending. When the assistant's body was just above his head, Le Roy whisked the cloth away and his assistant vanished in midair. "The Asrah Levitation" is still in use today, and that moment—*poof, they're gone*—remains one of the most breathtaking moments in all of magic. It first debuted in 1902, which means Le Roy found a *fake* way to make someone fly just months before the Wright brothers did it for real.

In "The Bullet Catch," the performer catches a bullet in his teeth. At least twelve people (and likely more!) have died attempting this crazy effect. One of the earliest, Madame DeLinsky, was the wife and assistant of a Polish magician. In their version of the trick, Madame DeLinsky would survive a firing squad of six soldiers. However, in 1820 one of the soldiers failed to prepare his gaffed gun correctly and accidentally shot DeLinsky in the abdomen. It is believed she was pregnant at the time.

The most famous version of the trick was called "Condemned to Death by the Boxers," a nod to the Boxer Rebellion, an uprising in China aimed at driving out foreigners near the turn of the twentieth century. This was the version created by Chung Ling Soo, the world's most famous "Chinese" conjurer. Soo was a marvelous magician, but his biggest secret was that he wasn't really Chinese. Born William Ellsworth Robinson, he invented the persona of Chung Ling Soo because he thought, correctly, that a foreign act would be in greater demand on the vaudeville circuit. Dismayingly, he appropriated this persona from a legitimate Chinese magician named Ching Ling Foo, who was a sensation not only in his native China, but also in the United States. Robinson chose a name that sounded similar to Ching Ling Foo and called himself Chung Ling Soo. To complete the transformation, Robinson donned a wig and grease makeup onstage to darken his complexion. Robinson-as-Soo never spoke onstage, and created a fake backstory in an attempt to legitimize his appropriated onstage persona. However unethical and unfair this was to Ching Ling Foo, Robinson's act was a crowd pleaser, and it led to a successful career as a "Chinese" conjurer.

As Soo, Robinson performed his version of "The Bullet Catch" for years—it was the standout piece of his show. But on March 23, 1918, on a London stage, an assistant fired a gun at Robinson and a real bullet entered his chest and exited his back. "My God," he said. "Something's happened. Lower the curtain." As shocked as the spectators were to see a man shot onstage, they were equally shocked to hear him speaking . . . *English.* Until that moment, Robinson's real identity was an industry secret. His death four hours later made headlines around the world, and rumors swirled that he had been murdered by his disgruntled wife or his staff, or that he had planned an onstage suicide. In the end, a coroner's examination of the gaffed gun revealed a flaw that caused it to fire. The event was ruled "death by misadventure." You can still see versions of "The Bullet Catch" on TV and in some live shows, and the trick remains deadly. The magician Kofi Brugah died performing it in 2007, in Ghana. It endures because it scares us. The narrative? *Invincibility.*

"Vanishing the Statue of Liberty" was performed just once, in 1983, by David Copperfield. People have vanished their assistants, helicopters, even elephants, but the reason people still talk about *this* effect is the carefully chosen narrative. Copperfield *vanished* a landmark that symbolizes the United States and our belief in freedom. Copperfield's momentary vanish of the Statue of Liberty is woven into that history of the eighties in the same way as Michael Jackson's moonwalk or Ronald Reagan telling Mr. Gorbachev to "Tear down this wall." Even today, more than thirty years after it aired, people *still* ask me about it.

What's remarkable about the trick is that, though people still talk about it, you couldn't find it on YouTube until recently. And for good reason. This illusion, like all the best illusions, is a product of its time—it's hard to appreciate it in the context of now. There's an annoying voice-over, a ludicrous "sonar" device to track the statue, and an old-school miniature model of the statue to explain how the illusion will happen. When the statue itself vanishes, we see a milky black haze where it was in the sky, and . . . *that's it.* A moment later she's back and the illusion is complete. Like Mom's cooking or a first kiss, our imagination fills in the gaps and distorts our memories, turning moments into myths.

I love all four of those tricks, but none of them are my *favorite*.

My favorite piece is by Penn & Teller, one they periodically mix into their show, though I think it should be a permanent addition. The piece is called "Honor System." It goes like this.

Before the show, audience members are invited onto the stage in single file to examine a wooden crate and a large, clear Lucite box. The walls of both boxes are solid. So I already appreciate the unusual interaction in which the audience gets to walk on the stage and *touch* the props. Every other illusion in magic you watch from afar, skeptical of the silly contraptions. This one is stripped down, hands on.

Penn & Teller then come onstage and Teller is placed into the Lucite box, which is then placed into the wooden crate, which is locked. Penn explains that Teller will escape from the boxes and offers a fascinating choice: mystery or knowledge. "Keep your eyes open if you want to know the secret," Penn says. "Keep your eyes closed if you want to be amazed." He invites those who wish to be amazed—to remain in mystery—to close their eyes until they hear music play. When they open their eyes, Teller will have escaped from the boxes. *Abracadabra.* Those who simply want to *know* how it works are welcome to watch. Penn delivers a very Penn & Teller line at this point, as he urges those who keep their eyes open *not* to talk about it after the show, lest they spoil it for those who choose mystery. "In other words," he says, ending the piece, "if you can't shut your goddamn mouth, then shut your goddamn eyes."

Those who close their eyes hear laughter just before the music starts. And then, when they open their eyes, Teller is somehow, impossibly, *there*. And now that he is out of the box, the show begins.

If you keep your eyes open, you're in on a secret. The first thing you do is look around to see whose eyes are open and whose eyes are closed. Then you witness the simple, entertaining method. The crate isn't simple after all, but an amazing mechanical device. It telescopes open like a crazy puzzle box, and Teller climbs out with a quizzical look on his face, after which the crate closes up behind him. It's unexpected.

Penn & Teller have always flirted with the issue of exposure, and this piece is their most artful approach to it, leaving the reveal up to the beholder. "'Honor System' started as a conversation Penn and I had driving back from the Minnesota Renaissance Festival in 1976," Teller told me after a recent performance. "To me, the idea is asking, 'Did you come to this show for a question or an answer? Would you like to go home with a question that you can turn over and over, or do you want to go home with an answer you can feel smug about?'" It took them twenty years to find a suitable trick for the presentation. The piece is *so* Penn & Teller, finely attuned to their characters— Penn, the philosopher monologist, and Teller, a Chaplin figure, silently, comically contorting into the box. Nobody else would do a piece like "Honor System." And nobody who sees it ever forgets it.

The framing of the illusion is also what makes it brilliant. Penn & Teller have found a way to take an otherwise mundane illusion and turn it into a completely interactive piece. "The challenge," says Teller, "is that it can't just be a trick. It has to be an intellectual conundrum. You have to have something that is fascinating with your eyes open and impossible with your eyes closed. And then we had this delicious idea of doing an escape. If you keep your eyes open, it's very satisfying. But if you close your eyes, it's impossible." On the surface the piece is playful, but at its core it's a deeply personal, existential decision.

"Honor System" doesn't take place on a Las Vegas stage—not really, anyway. The most interesting facet takes place in *your* head, when you are rushed into a decision of mystery or knowledge. I've played it both ways, on different nights. How would you play it? It says a lot about the kind of person you are.

✦ ✦ ✦

38

WHAT DO MAGICIANS DO IN SECRET?

WHAT IS INTERESTING AND IMPORTANT HAPPENS MOSTLY IN SECRET.

—MICHAEL ONDAATJE, AUTHOR, POET

✦ ✦ ✦

Children are widely considered the toughest audience, but for me magicians are the toughest crowd. Let me explain: You can misdirect kids, act silly to knock them off their guard, and play on their willingness to believe just about anything. Now imagine performing for a theater full of magicians. Every person sitting there is not only evaluating your presentation, but also anticipating every secret move you do and the quality of the execution. It's a trial by fire with a jury full of pyromaniacs.

Magic conventions are both the scariest and most joyful places for magicians to perform. They are closed to the public and populated only by us, so I feel I'm among my tribe. But what works at a magic convention isn't always what works for the public. A prominent magician might go on TV and do a standard trick in a standard way. Ellen DeGeneres can't tell the difference. But it would be unthinkable to perform an off-the-shelf magic trick at a convention. To succeed at a gathering of magicians, you need to do original material.

When I was seven, my dad took me to the Columbus Magifest in Ohio, one of the oldest magic conventions in the world. Each year we gather just under a thousand magicians for a weekend of shows, interviews, lectures, and clinics. In 2019, Juan Tamariz headlined the show. Magic shops from around the world set up booths Comic-Con style, demonstrators attract crowds with balls of fire, electronic shops pop off the latest confetti cannons over the crowd, and mentalists bark at passersby, offering to read their minds. Yes, they're selling stuff, including themselves as performers. This is what these people do for a *living.*

But the real reason people come to the Magifest and conventions like it isn't just for the talent or the shows. It's for the hang time. Like jazz musicians looking for a good session, magicians at every level want a chance to sit at a table at 4:00 a.m. and watch the newest underground miracle. And if the deck is passed in their direction, they want a chance to shine. Reputations are made and lost in these chain-hotel lobbies. At magic conventions, it's not uncommon to hear gasps and applause at moments that, to you, would seem totally inappropriate. Until you realize the magicians are applauding *the moves*, not the finales. It is my favorite weekend of the year, and one that I now help run, thanks to taking over ownership of the Magifest ten years ago with my business partner.

Until recently, a vast network of magic meetings happened all over the world. But things are changing. The International Brotherhood of Magicians and the Society of American Magicians, the two largest industry organizations, were once beacons of the art. Both are now woefully out of step with modern magic. I grew up a member in good standing with the Canton Magicrafters Club. My dad served as treasurer one year, and I won the club competition when I was a teenager. I'll never forget the first meeting I attended at seven years old. "I didn't feel like a kid," I told my dad. "They just treated me like a magician." He liked that. So did I.

The Magicrafters met in the basement of a local bank, and the wonders I saw down there changed the trajectory of my life. I had to do an initiation show to become a member, which was until that point the scariest part of my seven-year life.

The local magic scene is no longer. Bureaucracy has eroded the influence of these organizations on a national level, and the internet took care of the rest. Now young magicians share clips online and try to fool each other with YouTube videos. It isn't all bad, I suppose, but there's no substitute for real-life instruction. Membership in all fraternal organizations is down: the Freemasons, the Elks club, and countless others. The decline of magic clubs meant the loss of a magic lecture "circuit" that once allowed me to crisscross the country many times, performing and then lecturing on my own material. Nobody gets rich on lecture tours, but traveling the world and sharing original material is a rewarding rite of passage for many magicians.

And magic clubs around the world are all a bit different. When I toured Japan, it was refreshing to see that nearly half the members were women (see page 75). In Paris, there are several clubs, and each one despises the other. If you perform at one meeting in Paris, don't expect to be welcomed at another. I recently lectured at the Magic Club of Iceland—there were four of us, including me.

The only magic club I'm still active in is called The Magnets. Founded in 2003, this radical club was formed in direct opposition to every other magic club. There are no dues, no officers, and no annual conventions. It's a loose collection of youngish professional and semiprofessional magicians who meet every Wednesday at a midtown Manhattan bar with the sole purpose of helping one another. A few times a year we pool our money to rent a cabin in the woods and invent tricks together, or take a road trip to a magic show or festival. Our membership includes two rabbis and an atheist speaker. Another member is fourteen years old and working with the other Magnets to put together a Rubik's Cube routine. Rachel Wax works in the fashion industry by day but performs at, and hosts, the club's weekly weekend show. Eli Bosnick, one of the club's founders, is the benevolent "dictator" of the group, loosely organizing meet-ups and guest speakers for the rest of the group. When someone violates an ethical rule in magic (stealing material, mistreating another Magnet), they're out. When someone can't afford a prop or a trip, we put on a fundraiser. It works, and it's the best magic hang in New York.

Magic clubs aren't the only endangered species in our industry—magic shops have gone the way of independent bookstores and local record shops. The internet was, unsurprisingly, the grim reaper, of course. But there is an upside: Magicians in every corner of the world now have equal access to resources because many of the great magic teachers now offer their materials online. Magic downloads are their most popular products—you watch a trailer of the trick, and if you're interested or fooled, you pay to download the tutorial. For a price—anywhere from five to fifty bucks—you can follow along with the trick's creator.

But the decline of magic shops led to the loss of much more. There are still a few good ones left: Tannen's in New York City, the Magic Apple in Los Angeles, Midwest Magic in Chicago. These are places where magicians congregate to talk shop or take classes, to see and feel and try props before investing in them. Sadly, most shops can't survive when magic is available cheaper and faster online. Some of the best magic teachers have adapted and offer virtual private lessons. But what students lose in this twenty-first-century approach is interaction—it's pretty hard to pick a card over Skype.

Perhaps the most sacred and beautiful tradition in the magic community is how we commemorate our dead. I don't vibe to any kind of religious ritual, but there's something poetic about "The Broken Wand Ceremony." When a magician dies, their local magic club sends a representative upon request (you can select a theistic or nontheistic presentation). The idea behind the ritual is that when a magician dies, their wand is broken and can never be used again. When my dad passed, I requested a local magician who knew him, Robert Rees. On short notice, Robert fashioned a wand out of fine wood, painted the tips, and (this is the secret part) weakened the center of the wand so it would easily snap in half against the knee. At the funeral, he spoke:

Jeffrey Jay, you once carried a wand, an ancient emblem of mystery. It symbolized the magic power that was yours. Now its power is gone. It is a mere stick, devoid of all meaning and authority, useless without your hand to wield it.

The wand was broken in half and passed to me. It sits on my desk as I type this sentence.

✦ ✦ ✦

39
DO YOU HAVE MAGIC STUDENTS?

RAFIEL

Josh Jay
410 Silk Court
New Franklin, Ohio 44319

I'VE GONE TO THE END
OF THE WORLD
ON THE WINGS OF WORDS.

—DR. WILLIAM CHESTER MINOR,
IN *THE PROFESSOR AND THE MADMAN*
(PLAYED BY SEAN PENN)

✦ ✦ ✦

I've been asked to give private lessons, mostly by affluent dads in New York asking on behalf of their kids. This is a polite, but easy, no. I'm never in one place long enough to teach and have always believed in the "journey" approach to learning, be it magic or writing or origami. You learn by doing. I grew up in a small town in Ohio—I had no teacher. My formative years were spent cross-legged on the floor of my room, feeling my way around the fundamentals, failing, then failing a little less.

If a great magic teacher had been available to me, I would have jumped at the chance. A handful of masters have retired from touring and shifted their focus to teaching magic. But it's my observation that the most creative magicians develop their skills in isolation, rather than being heavily influenced by a magic curriculum.

In 2013, I received a letter in the mail postmarked from a prison in California. "Dear Josh," the letter began, "I'm the prison magician." His name is Rafiel Torre and he is serving a life sentence for murder with no chance for parole in a maximum-security penitentiary in California. His first letter described not only his difficulty learning magic in prison but also the way he constructed his own decks while in "the hole."

I needed cards. We weren't allowed "regular" cards, so we made them. I realized milk cartons could be torn along the creases to make cards: four cards to a milk carton. If you had a cellie, you could make eight cards a day until you had fifty-two. So it took about a week to make a deck of cards. You used pen fillers to write with. Once my cards were done, I started to practice overhand and riffle shuffles with them. In about another week's time, I could do the basic sleights and basic card manipulations I would need to practice some tricks.

Anyone who would go to these lengths to practice magic clearly had the drive to be a good magician. But in prison, he had no way to learn. I agreed to teach him, on the condition that he explain to me why he was there. This is my rule when people write me from prison, as several do. I just feel the need to understand as much as I can about who I'm corresponding with. My first incarcerated pen pal was David Garza, who was serving a prison sentence in Michigan's Upper Peninsula. David was halfway through a twenty-year term when we began writing. We've now corresponded for nine years.

David sent me handcrafted magic tools he built with the meager supplies afforded him in prison: false fingertips made of tinted toilet paper, casino chips made of cereal boxes, and playing cards fashioned from construction paper that look *identical* to factory-printed cards. These objects are proudly on display on my coffee table, symbols of how magic persists in even the darkest places. I've corresponded with David through his release from prison, through a violation of his parole that sent him *back* to prison for a year, and his subsequent rerelease. When I started writing to him, he did very little magic and couldn't even shuffle a pack of cards. Today he's a free man again and a professional magician.

Rafiel wrote to me for the same reason David and all of my other incarcerated pen pals wrote—because they're permitted to read magic books in prison. Prison libraries are filled with books on permissible hobbies for inmates: origami, sketching, and magic. In 2008, I wrote a how-to guide called *MAGIC: The Complete Course*. This book served as an entry point for all of my imprisoned pen pals. Rafiel devoured the book and mastered all the card tricks in it. Then he wrote asking what to do next.

Rafiel will never get out of prison. He explained to me that he was charged with murdering his lover's husband. Before he was incarcerated, Rafiel was a well-known mixed-martial-arts fighter. He traveled the world and competed at the highest levels. There's a documentary about him (and his subsequent murder conviction) online. I've never met Rafiel, but through our years of corresponding, it's clear he's smart, articulate, and wildly curious about magic. He is my only student.

For four years we corresponded through letters, but as Rafiel entered middle age, he was moved to a medium-security facility with limited internet access. Our correspondence spans a range of topics. I thought I had it rough with some of the drunk hecklers I've had to work around. But Rafiel's stories of being beaten for not explaining his tricks bring new meaning to the idea of a "tough crowd." He's had to learn the hard way how to perform magic for gangs, carefully negotiating the line of entertaining powerful, violent men without making them feel tricked. Once, when he wouldn't explain one of his secrets to a guard, the guard ransacked his cell, beat him, and filed a report that Rafiel had attacked the guard. He had to spend three months in "the hole," twenty-three hours a day alone in a cell, all because he refused to tip the secret to a card trick.

Magic, however, has supposed advantages on the inside. "Magic opened a lot of doors for me," he wrote. "It got me into better buildings, jobs, and even got me food when I've been locked in the hole."

The best way to learn magic is face-to-face, where you can impart to students the nuances of timing and misdirection. With Rafiel, I'm forced to describe sleight of hand in minute detail, an exercise where I have to learn how to explain a sleight that takes less than a second to perform in two or three pages of description. It's a close reading of a magic effect, and in the act of teaching Rafiel I'm often learning something new. It's usually a small detail— perhaps the motivation for moving an object from one hand to another. But sometimes it's something more fundamental. To teach Rafiel about misdirection through a *letter* requires me to distill the concept down to its essence. I encourage him to think about his audience and his environment when he performs. In response, he has developed fanciful presentations that transport his specific audience, typically with talk of gambling and recounting stories of life on the outside.

We spend a great deal of each year developing Rafiel's holiday show. Every December, the warden at the prison where Rafiel is held allows him to put on a show for the guards and inmates. It is the most important forty-five minutes of Rafiel's year, and we spend dozens of letters working on every aspect of it. We talk material, transitions, and scripting, and even brainstorm ways for Rafiel to rehearse the material away from his cellmates and guards.

I send Rafiel magic books when I can, but I have to parse them out, since he's allowed to own only ten books at a time. When they arrive, the books are carefully searched, and then a mailroom guard uses a box cutter to slice off the hardback covers, which can be fashioned into weapons. When Rafiel works through one classic magic text, I send him another. His brother is a doctor on the West Coast and sometimes sends funds to me with the request that I pick out something useful for Rafiel. Rafiel has a grown-up son who supports him as well, learning magic on YouTube to show his father.

Mostly I feel helpless as Rafiel's teacher, unable to mitigate the reality of his situation. Instead, I encouraged him to write up his story, describing his lowest moments but also times he's bested his hostile audience and brought joy to what must be one of the most joy-starved audiences in the world. I published his book, *Diary of a Prison Magician*, in a limited printing for fellow magicians. We published it without Rafiel's name attached, for fear of violent retribution by prison guards.

A friend asked how I would feel about mentoring Rafiel if I knew, definitively, that he was guilty of murder. I have no special insight into whether to believe Rafiel. But when I write to him or David or other people in prison, I'm not writing to a murderer or someone necessarily violent; I'm writing to a magician. I don't believe it's my place to judge—my kinship with them is about magic, which for some of them works as a kind of redemption. I can help with the magic; the rest is up to them.

I could claim altruistic reasons to mentor Rafiel and others like him. You could say I'm helping him as a way to spread the craft. And teaching to a gracious student like Rafiel is its own reward, I suppose. But these aren't the reasons I respond to Rafiel's letters and emails.

I help him because he's a magician, and he asked for my help.

40
WHAT IS THE MAGIC CASTLE?

IT IS ACCEPTABLE TO REMOVE
ONE'S JACKET WHILE SITTING IN A
SHOWROOM WATCHING A PERFORMANCE,
SITTING DOWN IN THE DINING ROOM,
OR TO TEMPORARILY WRAP
ANOTHER GUEST WHO IS COLD.
HOWEVER, WALKING THROUGH THE
CLUB SANS JACKET IS NOT PERMITTED.

—FROM THE MAGIC CASTLE WEBSITE

✦ ✦ ✦

Young musicians grow up dreaming of playing Carnegie Hall. Aspiring painters imagine their work on display at the Guggenheim. If you're a magician, your goal is to someday perform at the Magic Castle.

Located in Hollywood and built in 1908, the building had fallen into disuse by the early 1960s, when the Larsen family rented the property with an unusual idea: They wanted to open a private club to watch magic. Brothers Bill and Milt Larsen, along with Bill's wife, Irene, founded the Magic Castle in 1962. Milt, now eighty-nine, can still be seen at the Magic Castle most nights.

The Castle, as it's known, has a haunted mansion quality to it, moody lighting over dark wood and earth tones. The lamps are dim, and there are beautiful stained-glass walls and windows throughout (some of them original Louis Comfort Tiffany designs). It smells like a steakhouse, and *everyone* gets lost on their first visit, wandering the winding corridors that connect one side of the club to the other.

There are a few other venues around the world that cater specifically to magic, but the Castle is the center of the magic universe. Its stages have launched numerous careers. The Magic Castle is to magic what CBGB was to punk and new wave music in the 1970s, a place where brave artists can try anything onstage and see what works.

The most enduring legacy of the Magic Castle is the perfection of the conditions—it is, without question, the best place in the world to watch and perform magic. Many have heard of the place, but comparatively few have actually been inside. It's a private club with steep membership dues. I describe it to my midwestern friends as a country club, but instead of golfing, you watch magic (no question which club I'd rather be at). There are around five thousand members, and there's a waiting list to get in. Dues are a $5,000 initiation fee plus $1,375 per year for nonmagicians, but the Academy of Magical Arts, the acting body that governs the Magic Castle, allows magicians to join for a more reasonable rate.

The only way to get into the building itself is to be a member or know one. Performers get six "comps" per night for the week they're headlining, and these comp passes become so coveted that people seek out the headlining magicians who are announced on the Castle's website with pleas for access. The last time I performed at the Castle, I received three emails from men I didn't know explaining that they wanted to propose to their spouses inside the Castle. People will do almost anything to get inside. As a result, the Castle stopped advance announcements of performers on their stages—people were simply getting too creepy over the passes.

When you walk into the Magic Castle, the first thing that confronts you is the check-in desk. There, a host checks your name off the list and asks for identification. The club serves alcohol across five bars, so it's an establishment for those twenty-one and over. I went on a pilgrimage to the Magic Castle when I was seventeen. At the time, I was doing a lecture tour for magicians. At every stop, I asked if anyone in the crowd could help me get a fake ID so I could get into the Castle. I bought one in Tulsa, Oklahoma, and spent every second of my week in Los Angeles at the Magic Castle, performing at every opportunity. A member friend allowed me to come as his guest, and the ID was passable enough not to attract attention.

Upon entry, the host does a visual inspection to make sure you meet the strict dress code. Men are required to wear full suits, and until the late seventies, women were required to wear dresses. Now various formalwear is acceptable, but nobody is exempt from the stricter confines of the dress code. Last year one of my guests was turned away because his trousers had external pockets. "That's a jean cut," the host explained.

"But these are four-hundred-dollar Versace pants," he replied. The host was unmoved. He had to go home and change.

Even celebrities are turned away if they don't dress appropriately. Johnny Depp was allowed in, but he had to exchange his ever-present neckerchief for a loaner tie. The dress code is a legendary hassle, but it serves an important purpose: There's nothing like the Magic Castle, so there's no model for how to act at a private magic club. The natural inclination is to behave like you would at a comedy club, but that wouldn't work. The Castle doesn't want people to come drunk or play host to bachelor parties. When couples or individuals are exploring the club's many hidden corridors and spaces, there's an air of reverence and sophistication. People in full suits and gowns approach the magic shows as they would an opera or classical music concert. When you're at the Magic Castle, it's a fully immersive experience—the idea is that you should be paying attention.

Assuming you're dressed appropriately and are of age, the host requests that you walk up to a dusty bookshelf, look at a copper owl bookend, and say, "Open sesame." When you do, the bookshelf recedes into the wall and a secret passage is revealed. Into the club you go.

The Magic Castle has five distinct performance areas, ranging from the Close-up Gallery (thirty guests in a horseshoe, practically touching the iconic, green felt table) to the Palace, which is a proper theater that seats 130 people. The five showrooms each have headliners who perform one-week contracts. And when we headline, we are on a continuous pattern throughout the night. The shows are short, mostly, ranging from twenty minutes to forty-five minutes. When I work the Close-up Gallery, I do twenty-eight shows in a week, Monday to Sunday. The best-kept secret to visiting the Castle is to come twice, on a Sunday and Monday night. This is when the talent changes over. So you get to enjoy two completely different rosters across two action-packed evenings.

The Magic Castle is cofounder Milt Larsen's lifelong passion. He imported one of the bars from Ireland and reassembled it in the basement space. One of the original external turrets of the building is now incorporated into the dining room. The Castle has been expanded dozens of times over the years, making the layout labyrinthine and a distinct part of its charm. There are secret doors and staircases, and after years of appearing there, I'm still discovering hidden spaces. The eyes on the old portraits follow you as you pass them. When you close the door on the vintage phone booth, a skeleton appears next to you. As men relieve themselves in the urinal, a laugh track is activated. From what I'm told, those who visit the women's room aren't subjected to the same gentle mocking.

One of the Castle's most iconic current performers is long dead. At a piano just off the main lobby, Irma the invisible ghost pianist holds court. You ask her to play *anything*—from ragtime to rap—and the piano appears to play itself. You can ask her questions, too. "Irma, what's your favorite song?" She plays "We're in the Money." A friend asked her who was going to win the last presidential election and she played "Jimmy Crack Corn and I Don't Care." Irma's lost some of her deceptiveness in the last decade, but none of her charm. In the age of Shazam and Spotify, computers easily recognize songs by their names or refrains. But Irma's been playing nightly since 1963 . . . and computers have nothing to do with it.

Most people come to see the performances, but I think the best way to experience the Magic Castle is to just get lost. It's easy to do. There are three floors open to the public, and the venues are scattered across the sprawling mansion. Explore a little and you'll find rooms with museum-quality magic memorabilia. Or stumble on an impromptu performance. Magician members often invite their own guests and do informal shows, but anyone is welcome to pull up a chair. When you're mingling between performances, it's likely the guy next to you will turn around and ask you to pick a card. The place is crawling with magicians.

The reason the Magic Castle is so revered by the public is easy to explain: It's the Magic *Castle*, a rickety old mansion where the world's best magicians dazzle on repeat. But for us magicians, the Castle is the place to both hone our trade and show off our skills. When you do twenty-eight shows in a week, you can't help but improve. Because the shows are one right after another, it gives magicians the unique opportunity to subtly test different lines or moves. I might open with a particular trick in the first show, but slot it third in the second show. The Castle provides closed-circuit video, so later that evening I can compare one show to another, see how a move looks, or gauge whether a joke needs to be replaced immediately. Comedians "do the rounds" in New York for the same reason, but it isn't quite the same. Every venue has its own quirks and vibe, so there's a benefit to repeating material over and over in the same place, every forty-five minutes. Hidden deep within the venue is the Castle's library, which is open only to magicians. It's one of the largest magic book collections in the world. If a magician needs to research an arcane trick or subject, the Castle library is where they go.

To work the Castle, you have to audition and get booked. If an act is poorly received or a magician mistreats a spectator, they aren't asked back. The Castle also has a history of embracing new ideas. Two-man shows and avant-garde theater pieces are work-shopped in some of the smaller showrooms. In 2019 I was invited to be a lecturer in residence and held a two-day seminar on my work for the magician members. It was like a college course, eight hours per day. Attendees sat at desks and took notes, and each brought a work in progress to perform for the group.

The Castle has its own juniors program, a swap meet, and even an awards show—the Oscars for magicians. Like any long-running establishment, it's had its ups and downs. For years the food was rightly criticized as underwhelming and overpriced. In a recent reorganization, the food and beverage side of the business was overhauled, and now it's excellent (although still overpriced).

In the sixties Johnny Carson and Cary Grant were members, and Hollywood's biggest names were spotted there, enjoying a rare moment out of the public gaze. Photography has always been pro-hibited in the club, which makes it a haven for celebrities (and extramarital trysts). The sixties was also the era when the titans of magic held court at the Magic Castle. Dai Vernon, perhaps the greatest close-up magician of the twentieth century, spent the last two decades of his life there, and nearly every night he could be found on the same couch smoking a cigar. Any magician passing through the club could pull up a chair and see what Vernon was working on. Known as The Professor, Dai Vernon is still at the Castle in spirit—an urn with his ashes was on display for years at a favorite "jamming" spot in the club (they've since been moved to a private area of the Castle). I once had a spiritual moment doing card tricks below the box that houses the mortal remains of The Professor.

In October 2011, the club caught fire and the Castle very nar-rowly avoided catastrophe. Ironically, the fire brought national attention back to the Castle, and the club entered a new phase of cool. Neil Patrick Harris had become club president shortly before the incident. Harris is a magician and one of magic's most public cheerleaders. He oversaw an unprecedented rise in attendance and brought fresh attention to the venue. Under his tenure, the Castle reached capacity many nights each week, and reservations—for those who can get them—are required months in advance.

There's a momentum to the Castle now, one that serves to enhance the experience for both the magician and her audience. The place has an otherness to it—magic works better there than anywhere else on the planet for reasons that are both tangible and not. Some performers say it's the booze—there's always a bar nearby in the Magic Castle. As a result, the audiences are loose, more so as the night goes on. Some performers say it's the difficulty of getting in, proof of the old adage that says the scarcer the ticket, the better the crowd. Maybe it's the perfect acoustics and lighting conditions, or that they don't allow kids. Likely it's a mix of all of that, with a dash of legend added for good measure. Whatever its charm, the Magic Castle is the embodiment of everything integral to the experience of magic. I hope that someday you'll find a way inside.

41

WHO ARE YOUR FAVORITE MAGICIANS?

(PART 3)

> ## ALL GREAT MAGICIANS
> ## SEE THROUGH REALITY AND
> ## INTO THE IMAGINATION.
> ## THEN THEY BRING THAT INTO REALITY.
>
> —BENJAMIN PEARCE

✦ ✦ ✦

ROB ZABRECKY
1968-

If I could hire any magician in the world to perform for my friends and family, it would be Rob Zabrecky. And that's what I did for a recent family gathering.

Rob brought down the house.

That he is so acclaimed in the industry is not surprising. What might be surprising, however, is that he's alive at all. In the 1990s, he was on his way to being a rock star. Possum Dixon was an acclaimed band on the cusp of breaking out, and Rob was the lead singer. But along with their record deal came the rock star lifestyle, and Rob got addicted to heroin.

He kicked it after some years, but when he got sober, he lost his zeal for music. Magic filled the hole, with Rob funneling his creative energy into a brilliantly morose onstage persona. Unexcitable and oblivious to his own humor, Rob uses magic as his vehicle to be weird onstage. In truth, his magic isn't particularly memorable, but the way he does it is unforgettable.

Early in his show, Rob makes an announcement: "Tonight is a very special occasion. It's my grandfather's ninety-third birthday, and he is here for this performance. So would you all put your hands together as I escort out my grandfather, the blessed Reverend Doctor Ivan Zabrecky." Rob calmly walks to the wing and returns, slowly, holding an urn. He opens it and peers in at the ashes. "Happy birthday," he says. Then he sets a conical birthday party hat on the urn, tosses a handful of confetti into the air, and moves on.

Rob is surrealist theater, avant-garde at every stage, and entirely surprising. Watching him work is watching the magic genre bend before your eyes, the way Andy Kaufman did with comedy. His pacing is his most distinctive feature. Often the biggest laughs come from the *absence* of words. It's a slow gaze from the audience over to a hapless spectator, or an uncomfortable pause after a cryptic line of dialogue.

You won't find Rob Zabrecky on a Las Vegas stage or on *America's Got Talent*. You have to look in smaller venues—where the burlesques perform and the freaks and geeks hang out. It's an alternate universe, a place for jokes without punch lines and magic that is creepy and campy, too. In Rob's alt-universe, every night is his dead grandpa's birthday.

———◆———

DAVID WILLIAMSON
1961-

I love the moment in the movie *The Princess Bride* when Inigo Montoya, a great swordsman, is locked in an intense duel with the Man in Black, another great swordsman. "I admit it. You are better than I am," Inigo says.

"Then why are you smiling?" replies the Man in Black.

"Because I know something you don't know."

"And what is that?"

Inigo Montoya smiles and flicks his sword from his left hand into his right. "I am not left-handed."

David Williamson isn't left-handed, either, but his shocking reveal is on par with Inigo Montoya's. If you see David, an Ohio native like me, in the huge theaters he now tours, you will laugh until your sides hurt at his antics. He is six feet, six inches tall, so he towers above the small children he frequently invites onstage and then organizes, playing them hilariously off each other. I could watch him all day every day.

David's material is undeniably wacky: He pulls coins from people's hair, makes a stuffed raccoon catch a card in midair, and swaps two people's underwear. But if you sat across a table from David after his show, that's when you'd *really* get your jaw-dropping moment.

He has enormous gorilla-sized hands that dwarf the cards and coins when he holds them. And yet when David manipulates these objects, his hands *dance*. I've tried to be careful with my superlatives in these pages, but David Williamson is the finest sleight-of-hand magician I've ever encountered. There are young gunslingers doing more difficult material, but they're developing moves nobody would dare use in a show under fire. David's sleight of hand is old-school fundamental. You hear golfers deify Ben Hogan for his beautiful golf swing. But you can't quantify the beauty of someone's swing the way you can their score. I'm talking about "The Touch." And very, very, very few magicians have it.

David has it.

What does The Touch really mean? When David does the classic moves, they just look better. It's in his timing, his fluidity, the hand pressure, and the coordination between his shoulders, feet, and hands. It's not just that you won't see the sleights—you won't even know when to look.

I went to Ohio State University, an hour's drive from Yellow Springs, Ohio, where David and his family live in a two-hundred-year-old converted schoolhouse. We would meet often at a dairy farm restaurant in Yellow Springs, where they served soup and sandwiches. And there I would sit across the table from, undisputedly, the finest magic technician I have ever seen. He would share techniques, but also tease me with others he wouldn't explain ... until the next time. Often during those meetings, I would pause to actually pinch myself, thinking about how lucky I was to sit at that restaurant countertop, all the people around us clueless to the virtuosity of the tall man in their midst. It's the same for the thousands who watch him, crying with laughter, on several of the leading cruise lines for which he works. They'll never know David's hidden genius. They're not supposed to.

But I know.

———◆———

TOMMY WONDER
(1953-2006)

If I had to list my five favorite close-up magicians, Tommy Wonder would be on the list. If you asked me for my favorite stage performers, Tommy Wonder's name would be on that list. If you wanted my opinion on the greatest magic book ever written, it would be Tommy Wonder's (and coauthor Stephen Minch's) two-volume *The Books of Wonder*. If you asked me about my favorite parlor magic trick, it would be a tie: Tommy Wonder's "The Ring, the Watch, and the Wallet" and Tommy Wonder's Cups and Balls.

My choices are a product of my life. Someone my parents' age would pack a favorites list with the older greats. But magic is like music: You're imprinted for life by whatever is happening when you're fifteen years old. Tommy Wonder was the magic of my youth.

When I was fifteen, *The Books of Wonder* appeared on the last night of Hanukkah. Most of the magic books I had read up to that point were recipe books: Put your right pinky here, turn twenty degrees to the left, vanish the coin using your favorite method. Magic books provided the script or "patter" you would say when you performed. I rarely felt a connection to the author.

Tommy Wonder reached out from the pages of his books and pulled me away from a tough freshman year of high school. He was a temporary escape from an awkward time. His books were personal, filled with humility about his worst ideas and shows. They were also filled with ingenious explanations for how he accomplished his tricks, and essays about why he created them in the first place. For me, Tommy was a master.

When I was nineteen, we performed at the same event in Argentina. It was my very first time working outside the United States, and Tommy was the headliner. He opened with "The Ring, the Watch, and the Wallet."

The trick goes like this: Tommy walks onstage and announces, jarringly, that just before the performance, he was mugged. Recounting the story, he explains that the thief demanded his ring, his watch, and all his money. In turn, Tommy removes a large signet ring, visible even from the back of a theater, and places it inside an envelope. He does the same with his wristwatch and then removes a wad of cash from his wallet. "Then this thief did something pretty clever," Tommy explains, as if in casual conversation. "He had this envelope with his name and address on it, even a stamp. In case the cops approached him, he placed everything inside the envelope so he could drop it in a postbox." By now, Tommy has clearly put all the objects inside the envelope. "But he was a bit disappointed, because I am a magician. . . ."

Tommy rips up the envelope, and the torn pieces flutter to the ground like confetti—the objects are gone. An impressive trick, and nobody sees the ending coming.

"Because I still had my ring, my watch, and all my money!" Without a single movement out of step, Tommy displays the ring *back* on his finger, the watch *back* on his wrist, and his wallet again full of money. And that was just his opener.

The trick works so well for a variety of reasons: There's an engaging story to grab your attention, an unusual but dramatic premise for the trick, and an ending nobody expects. It has every element in harmony, every detail worked out. I can't tell you how "The Ring, the Watch, and the Wallet" works, but I wish I could. The method is right out of Q's lab in a James Bond film. Beneath the surface, there are pulleys and fulcrum points. Nothing is what it seems. I studied the complex drawings in *The Books of Wonder* and read the nearly thirty pages dedicated to this trick—and in ninety seconds on that Argentina stage, it was all over. Ninety seconds of pure astonishment.

Magicians tend to make and publish variations on tricks that are interesting. I've published dozens of variations on other people's work, and other magicians have published their takes on my routines. It's hard to swallow someone "improving" on my work. You almost never see anyone publish an improvement on a Tommy Wonder trick. It's that hard to find flaws in his magic.

I don't know how it works at big music festivals like Lollapalooza or Bonnaroo, but the big headliners at magic festivals typically don't go to the shows or lectures of the newbies. I paid my dues in those early days, performing off-times at FLOSOMA, an Argentinian festival of magic. But when I started my show, I spotted Tommy Wonder near the front, watching *me*. I was stupefied.

After the show, he found me and offered some encouraging words about my work (he clearly hadn't taken Jerry Andrus's vow of truth telling). Still, his words were pivotal. A little encouragement at the right time from the right person warms the soul. Magic is lonelier than most people realize. A life in magic is one in which you're surrounded by people but isolated by the secrets you keep. Tommy was a friend in that moment, a voice of affirmation. He had a suggestion for me, too. He thought that producing a spoon at a particular moment would be thematic for a routine I was doing with a coffee cup. I thanked him, wrote it down, and promised myself I'd think about it later.

The next day, Tommy found me in a corridor and removed from his pocket a twisted wire gimmick. "I made this for you," he said. "It's for the spoon production. It goes under the jacket." He had, in his hotel room, I presume, fashioned a delicate, beautiful piece of equipment. Tommy's father was a watchmaker, and Tommy had inherited his breathtaking craftsmanship. Where he got the materials and soldering iron I don't know, but this object was *custom-made* for me. By my childhood magic hero.

Tommy died of lung cancer in 2006. He emailed me when he was sick and mentioned that he had smoked from the time he was thirteen. I've long since abandoned the coffee cup routine, along with the spoon production Tommy suggested. But I saved the little gimmick he fashioned for me—because Tommy Wonder *made* that thing, for me. It's bent upward now, from years of being pinned and repinned inside my performing jackets, and then more years being moved from one shelf to another. It doesn't resemble anything familiar and has been mistaken for an abstract sculpture by curious houseguests. "What's that?" someone asked, holding it up at different angles.

"That," I told her, "is the magic of my youth."

THE THREE INDISPENSABLES OF GENIUS ARE: UNDERSTANDING, FEELING, AND PERSEVERANCE; THE THREE THINGS THAT ENRICH GENIUS ARE: CONTENTMENT OF MIND, THE CHERISHING OF GOOD THOUGHTS, AND EXERCISING THE MEMORY.

—ROBERT SOUTHEY, POET

If I could snap my fingers and see any magician in the world perform, I would be spirited away to Juan Tamariz.

There's a word of Arabic origin—*baraka*—with no exact English translation, but it relates to a person's spiritual energy. It describes someone whose very presence affects you, alters you, and realigns you. I didn't understand the word when I first heard it.

But I get it now.

To see Juan live is to have a nonreligious awakening. If you search for online clips of him, you'll be impressed, but you won't fully understand how fresh, funny, smart, and amazing his material is. However, if you leave yourself open to it when you see Juan live, you will feel *baraka*. Juan is extraordinarily gifted and supremely dazzling. Nothing I have ever seen approximates watching him do close-up magic.

Juan hails from Spain, where he is beloved and a household name. The magicians there call him Maestro, a term of reverence reserved for masters of music. But in Juan's case, the title is apt. He speaks often of music—classical and flamenco, mostly—and has written about the correlations between the movements and pacing of music and magic.

One of Juan's calling cards is that after all of his pieces—his tricks often exceed ten minutes—he plays an air violin, shouting the first measure of *Carmen. Yaaaa! Ya-da-da-da-da-daaaaaaaaa!* His fans love and expect this and go wild when he does it. As with everything Juan does, it looks innocent, even silly. But Juan is eight moves ahead, always. The air violin is an indication that the piece has finished. It's an applause cue, a message to the audience that something is ending and something else is about to begin. Rodney Dangerfield quipped, "I don't get no respect." George Burns took a drag from his cigar. Juan plays the air violin.

Juan is short, has crooked teeth, and wears mismatched, ill-fitting clothes. He is in his late seventies, but has been partially bald since he was a young man, with an unruly gray ponytail falling from beneath a colorful top hat. His voice is nails on a chalkboard, and since he shouts often when he performs, he is always halfway hoarse, like a sports fan after a close game.

But give Juan a shuffled deck of cards—this is how nearly all of his performances begin, with an audience-shuffled pack—and let him take you to church. The best way to see Juan is not on a huge stage, though even approaching eighty years old, he sells out large venues in his native Spain. The only way to experience Juan in his purest form is to be lucky enough to see him up close, with a dozen or so people surrounding him.

When the shuffled deck is handed back to him, the trick begins innocently enough. Juan starts with low energy and seems indecisive about exactly what to perform. But I've seen Juan enough to know better. He's laying a foundation. In a few minutes he will be jumping, screaming, and pounding the table. He is plotting his first mark low on the graph so he can later send the needle off the chart.

One noteworthy difference between average card tricks and a Juan Tamariz card trick is that most magicians ask you to pick a card, whereas Juan often asks you to *think* of a card. The difference is subtle for a muggle, but magicians understand the complexity of adding this wrinkle. A *picked* card can be forced or influenced. You can use marked cards or sleight of hand to know in advance what card is chosen, or where it goes. But when you ask someone merely to *think* of a card, you're not just doing a card trick. You're reading minds.

Last summer, Juan asked me to shuffle my own deck and think of a card. Then he drew a line on the floor with his foot. In his muddy English he said, "I don't cross this line." We were five feet apart. He rearranged the other onlookers on my side of the line in a semicircle around me.

"What was your card?" he asked me.

"The five of spades."

He instructed me to take a group of cards from my deck and go through them. No five of spades. He asked me to take another group and look through. Again, no five of spades. Then I searched the last group. No five of spades.

"Not there?" Juan asked. "Check again!" Minutes earlier, Juan was calm, even somber, but now he was locked in. He stood up straighter and performed with authority.

"The one you think is gone!" he shouted, poor grammar and all, while laughing, posing for applause. Then, a pause. A long pause. Long enough for me to contemplate the sheer impossibility of what he had already done. And yet I knew he wasn't finished. I had no choice but to surrender to his effect.

He looked as confused as the rest of us. Then something in the air caught his eye. He said nothing but reached into the empty space and pretended to pluck out what I thought to be an imaginary card. He then slapped his chest with the card. With two fingers, he slowly reached into his shirt pocket and removed a card. The design on the back of the card matched my pack of cards. He turned it around. The five of spades. *Yaaaa! Ya-da-da-da-da-daaaaaaaaa!*

He never crossed the line to come near me or my cards. He couldn't have known what card I would think of—I *almost* thought of the seven of hearts. The back design of my cards that day was unusual, so he couldn't have had a duplicate deck.

How did he do it? I have no fucking idea.

I was once hired to perform for one of America's wealthiest individuals, a finance guy and art collector whose net worth is listed at more than a billion dollars. After I'd performed for his guests, he invited me to sit with him and some friends looking out over the New York City skyline. He offered me a glass of wine, which I sipped while he asked several of the questions I have tried to answer in these pages. "How do you create magic?" "Do magicians insure their hands?" "Do you cheat at cards?" I remember the wine being very good, but the view was spectacular.

Later, with a twinge of disgust, one of the man's assistants pointed out to me that I had been sipping a 1990 *Romanée-Conti*, considered by many to be the finest (and most expensive) wine in the world. There have been bottles sold for more money, but those are *collected*. The 1990 *Romanée-Conti* is a wine people buy to drink. And because it's $20,000 a bottle, many who spend a lifetime appreciating wines will never taste a drop.

I knew the wine was good, but the fact that it was the *best* was lost on me. I didn't know enough about wines to appreciate its intensity, its fullness, its purity. Books have been written about this wine.

I've introduced a handful of friends to the magic of Juan Tamariz. Some get it and some just sip their wine. Everybody loves the guy, but I do think it takes a thorough understanding of magic to appreciate how brilliant he is. True appreciation requires a deep understanding. That is to say, what *we* bring to Juan Tamariz is as important as what he gives to us.

I'm biased, of course. I've had the great pleasure of sharing a stage with him, and I've periodically studied with him at his home. The impact of this opportunity isn't lost on me. If I were a visual artist, I would *never* realistically be able to share a studio with Jeff Koons at his summer home, or open an exhibition with Damien Hirst, or call up Banksy to ask his opinion on a new piece. In magic we get to meet our heroes, often in meaningful ways. Juan is our Picasso, talented at a young age and famous in his own lifetime.

———◆———

Juan is always on the move. Everywhere he goes he attracts magician disciples. In the cooler months, he's usually at his home in Madrid, but he also spends a month every year in Argentina. In the sweltering Spanish summers, he resides at his sprawling complex in San Fernando, on the Andalusian coast.

It was there that Juan invited me to join him for "a few days." He'd seen me do my original piece "Hitchcock," and I think he wanted to discuss it. That's my guess. Either way, the invitation changed my life forever.

I arrived at Juan's home in the late afternoon. Once buzzed inside his gate, I saw Juan seated at a table for one in his front yard, sipping tea under a lemon tree, writing in a notebook. He greeted me, but it was brief. The late afternoon is Juan's time for working alone, and he seldom lets anything disrupt his habits.

The grounds were filled with lemon trees and fragrant herbs. Juan loves to cook and eat fine food. He mentioned the jasmine plants, which were everywhere. "I like the smell when I am practicing," he said.

My bedroom was barren of any art or furnishings except a small postcard of—what else?—a Picasso painting: *Old Man with Guitar*. It depicts an expressionless man looking down, concentrating, as he plays his instrument. The shutters in the room, which could be found in *every* room, were heavy and thick, the kind that block out all light. They were the first indication of the upside-down hours we would keep in the company of Maestro Tamariz.

Juan wakes up in the late afternoon to early evening. His first hours are spent alone, making notes on his previous night's work, or perhaps the magic he imagined in his dreams. He begins his day at a table that has room only for a teacup, a deck of cards, and a notebook. He writes constantly in notebooks—feverishly if the inspiration has struck him, but more often at a contemplative pace, taking breaks to watch the olive trees waving in the wind. Even though I often passed Juan in a corridor in his first few hours of the day, I got nothing more than a nod. This is his alone time. He is creating magic.

At some point in the early evening, Juan will move from one of his solo tables to his patio. It has mosquito netting around it, which is convenient since we convene each evening at twilight, when the bugs are prowling. As soon as he sits down, there is life in the house. The cooking starts, pots clanging by those who work for him, and guests are welcome to join Juan at the table.

Some years ago I was one of a dozen guests at that table—all of them packed into the many simple bedrooms of his cavernous home. At other times—unforgettable ones—I have been the only guest at that table. Just the Maestro and me.

We sit and jam, the way a band does in a studio. Some nights Juan is all business, eager to share a work in progress and break every aspect down, just to stack it back up another way. A guest might offer him a different move to substitute or a suggestion on what to say there. But I'm careful about this—I know my place. We all do. There's a burning desire to be able to claim, even if just to ourselves, that we "helped" Juan with a trick. But nobody wants to volunteer something stupid in the presence of such greatness.

Other times, Juan barely touches his cards. On those nights it might be me sharing a work in progress, with the group commenting on what they like and don't like. I take notes and stock of my tricks. Juan never talks the most at the table, which is odd, given his station. He never—not once in my presence—has proclaimed any rules or ideas as genius, or even correct. His humility is his most surprising and endearing feature.

One night I was at a crossroads with a new piece. I had two options: Reveal a chosen card with a written prediction or look into the eyes of the person I was performing for—another magician-guest—and announce the card. A prediction is a stronger trick. How could I know in advance the card she would choose? But telling someone a chosen card is theatrically stronger. These may sound like small details to you, but these details are the subject of hour-long debates on Juan's patio.

When it was finally his turn to speak, Juan told me to look into her eyes and reveal it in the moment. When faced with the choice, Juan always goes for the heart before the head: "You can't erase emotion." His words brought clarity to my confusion, and my trick was ready to go into the world. *Baraka.*

That's another thing about Juan that only his friends realize. His English is *much* better than he lets on. In his shows, his sentences are riddled with grammatical errors, and he often asks the audience for words that escape him: "How do you say, *put* the cards to the table?"

Someone will fill it in for him: "You mean, *deal*?"

"Yes! *Deal* the cards." But in that exchange, you have missed the sleight. His words are often his strongest misdirection.

But under a rising Andalusian moon, his English, though imperfect, is more than enough to fascinate and inspire his many guests. He is an avid reader, and not just of magic. He loves and quotes the titans of literature and art: Cervantes, Shakespeare, Borges, Dalí, Velázquez. And most of all, Picasso. "Inspiration exists," Juan says, paraphrasing Picasso, "but it has to find you working."

The work often goes late into the night. There will be a break for a great meal at midnight. Sometimes, depending on the size of the gathering, we walk to the local town, where restaurant owners set up a prime table for Juan and his guests. Juan points to the fish he wants, and we choose after Juan. When dinner is over, we return to our work, doing tricks and talking theory of magic until, quite literally, I can't do it anymore. During the last hours of the session, our cards and coffee cups are bathed in the early morning light.

I find that my mind gives way before my body. At some point after seven or eight in the morning, I just have to be *away* from that table, so my muscles and mind can decompress. Juan is always the last to leave. When everyone has finally departed, he returns to one of his solo stations and fills more pages of his notebooks with the fruits of that night's offerings. Once, when I did manage to stay awake the whole night, I took a picture of him silhouetted by the rising sun, jotting in his notebook. It's my favorite image of him but one I cannot share here, as Juan has only one rule in San Fernando. For reasons of privacy, he doesn't allow any photos or videos inside his home.

Juan might have a bite of breakfast before heading off to bed, and the house is silent in slumber from 8:00 a.m. until as late as 5:00 p.m. Only after my very first night in San Fernando did I understand the importance of those thick bedroom shades. When you're going down as the rest of the world is waking up, there is a pressing need for darkness.

———◆———

On the last day of my last visit to San Fernando, I stayed up with Juan until I had to leave for the airport. We had, it seemed, run out of material to work on in the moment. I asked him a loaded question: "What is the role of the magician?"

We talked about it for a while, and eventually he crystallized his thoughts. "To be fascinating, and to do the impossible." He took a sip of his tea and then told me that doing the impossible has taken him a lifetime to learn. But it was the other part, being fascinating, that kept him awake each night.

✦ ✦ ✦

43

DO MAGICIANS INSURE THEIR HANDS?

I AM NOT WHAT I AM.
I AM WHAT I DO WITH MY HANDS.

—LOUISE BOURGEOIS, SCULPTOR, PAINTER

✦ ✦ ✦

In the summer of 2009 I was in Ohio visiting my parents, who live on a lake. While tubing behind our speedboat, I collided with a metal buoy at fifty-five miles per hour. I don't remember immediate pain or the impact of the collision. I remember only gasping for air and breathing in water, then passing out.

When I came to and was helped into the boat, I looked down at my arm, horrified. My entire left forearm was misshapen into a backward S, the whole appendage seemingly made of rubber. On the way to the hospital, I reluctantly canceled a show I had in Vegas two days later.

At the first hospital they suggested immediate corrective surgery, which failed. I was then taken to the Cleveland Clinic. If there is *any* bright side to an accident like this, it's the fact that it took place less than an hour from one of the most prestigious hospitals in the world. I have been told by everyone familiar with my case that if the accident had happened in any other location, I would likely not have use of my left hand today. Timing is everything, even offstage.

I also sustained injuries to my hip, ribs, and elbow, in addition to breaking two bones in my left arm in two places. But my wrist bore the brunt of the injury. Of the eight bones in the wrist, six were shattered. Worst of all, my ulnar nerve was damaged. I lost feeling in two of my fingertips. The first surgeon who looked at X-rays of my hand held them into the light and shook his head.

"Look," he explained, "you've had a very serious injury."

"Will I be able to use my hand again?" I asked, cutting straight to the point.

"I'm not even sure you'll have use of your arm."

My mom, sitting next to me, wept. I was on a morphine drip and didn't feel anything at all; it was like the whole thing was happening to someone else and I was just watching. Apparently, this is a common feeling for people in traumatic accidents. This surgeon's plan was to replace my wrist with titanium joints and fuse them to my arm. I would have no mobility, and would have use of only my thumb and first two fingers. I would be disabled, he told me, but I would "still be able to drive a car."

The second surgeon we spoke with, Dr. Peter Evans, had a more optimistic take. He made no promises but asked if we were open to a flexible plan. He wanted to open up my arm and make several judgment calls as he went along. I went with Dr. Evans.

The surgery lasted four hours. He installed a plate, two pins, and four screws in my wrist. Within five days, I was out of a cast and rehabbing my hand. I wondered, for a moment, if magic insurance would have covered the surgery. Probably not.

I spent almost half of 2009 in bed recovering from my accident. Dr. Evans asked me to spend at least three hours per day stretching, moving, and working on my left-hand muscles. So I spent almost *every* waking hour working on my hand muscles. I couldn't *wait* to get my hand back so I could start performing again. My therapists were astounded by the regeneration of the muscle strength and tissue. But this was no miracle. My secret was an intense regimen of cards and coins.

After six months, I began performing again. My range of motion was severely limited. I still wore a sling whenever I wasn't onstage. In some ways this was a dark time in my career, but as I look back, I realize it was also a transformative moment. I was no longer capable of the extreme sleight-of-hand maneuvers I had relied on before the accident. So my work had to change. I had to rely on subtlety and storytelling more than technique. It was during this time that I developed some of the pieces of which I'm most proud.

I eventually recovered full use of my hand and 80 percent of my wrist motion. The only things holding me back—and this was quite a hurdle—were my left fingertips. These were still numb— not *totally* numb, but they felt the way your fingers feel if you fall asleep on your hand, like someone else's fingers were attached to my hand.

I had to invent workarounds for every move that involved tactile precision in my left fingertips. The pinky count—a move where the little finger imperceptibly flicks the very corner of a pack of cards and counts downward—was no longer a possibility. If you have no feeling in your pinky, well, you're not going to count very far. So I created an alternative for this move and others that allowed me to revisit many of the tricks I had lost the ability to perform.

One day, two years after my accident, I woke up and the feeling in my fingers was back. *It was back!* I had given up all hope of performing serious sleight of hand, and the feeling was back. They call it nerve regeneration, and in some cases the nerve networks grow *around* obstacles or scar tissue. After two years of what felt like a thick glove over my hand, I now had acute feeling in my fingertips. I was whole again.

When I was a kid, there were ads for magician's insurance in the back of *The Linking Ring* magazine, one of magic's monthly magazines. I bought coverage for a few years, but a fellow magician told me he tried to make a claim when he accidentally set someone's house on fire after a trick went wrong, and they denied his claim. Perhaps the whole thing was a scam.

As magicians, our hands are our instruments. Noah Levine, a fine New York sleight-of-hand artist, has observed that in all instructive magic books, hands are treated like inanimate surgical devices: "The hands are placed around the deck in Biddle grip. The left third finger applies slight upward pressure on the bottom of the deck . . ."

I'm *extremely* careful with my hands since my accident—no chopping, no ice-skating, no rock climbing, and definitely no water tubing. Although the ordeal is a defining moment in my life, I don't speak of my accident in detail at my shows or with the press. It's genuinely too traumatic to relive over and over.

I still get flashbacks of the accident itself; it makes me spasm in a seizure-like reaction. If someone starts to describe a bad hand injury, or one is shown on TV, it brings me back to the accident. I shut my eyes and block out everything until it passes.

I roll my eyes when magicians speak of the "real magic" in the universe. But the idea of a magician losing use of his hands is almost operatic in its tragedy. I glimpsed life without a left hand— a life without magic. Then, in fairy-tale fashion, I got it all back. How's that for magic?

44

IS DAVID BLAINE FOR REAL?

IF YOU TAKE ANY ACTIVITY, ANY ART, ANY DISCIPLINE, ANY SKILL, TAKE IT AND PUSH IT AS FAR AS IT WILL GO, PUSH IT BEYOND WHERE IT HAS EVER BEEN BEFORE, PUSH IT TO THE WILDEST EDGE OF EDGES, THEN YOU FORCE IT INTO THE REALM OF MAGIC.

—TOM ROBBINS, AUTHOR

✦ ✦ ✦

David Blaine's Lower Manhattan office is always consumed by his latest obsession. For a time, there was a baby alligator in a terrarium near the entryway—it once swam in a tank with David during an underwater stunt. On another visit, all the tables were covered in playing cards, hundreds of them stacked to eye level. On a visit in 2016, I walked in and asked David what was up.

"Learning to become a human aquarium," he said. Then, before I could process the words, he opened his mouth and stuck out his tongue. His mouth was empty. He closed his lips for a moment. When he parted them again, a three-inch-long frog was perched on his tongue. He popped the frog into its enclosure and abruptly left the room.

David Blaine's magic blurs the line between what's real and what's a trick. You simply never know. "It's one of the best illusions I've ever seen," said comedian Ricky Gervais when he watched David stick a skewer through his biceps, "or you're a maniac."

This is a book of questions about magic, so it wouldn't be complete without considering one that I get asked perhaps more than any other: "Is David Blaine for real?" And that, by itself, is something. People—intelligent, discerning, thoughtful people—ask me about him all the time: "Can David Blaine actually levitate?" "Is he really eating those frogs?" "Does that ice pick go through his hand or is it fake?" David has cultivated a generation of believers and skeptics by sandwiching his sleight-of-hand magic with feats that are *exactly* what they appear to be. "I think what it does," Blaine says, "is make the tricks more believable. It becomes something more engaging to the audience."

━━━━━━ ✦ ━━━━━━

David Blaine appeared, seemingly from nowhere, in living rooms around the world with his first network special, *Street Magic*. It was 1997, and David was just twenty-three years old. *Street Magic* was like nothing anyone had ever seen before. It wasn't that David broke any particular rule—he broke them all. Penn Jillette says that *Street Magic* "was the biggest breakthrough [in television magic] in our lifetime."

David flipped fifty years of television magic on its head. Suddenly, the magician took a back seat to both the material *and* the audience. Blaine was understated in appearance and personality. He wore solid-color T-shirts and spoke as little as possible. "Watch," "Look," he would repeat, over and over. The material Blaine performed on *Street Magic* was a mixture of classics and understated tricks—which enraged magic's old guard. Here was a guy who didn't script his material or dress the part. They didn't get it. But it didn't matter. The special was a wild success and launched David's career.

A coterie of magicians and illusion inventors surround David, spending their days concocting material the same way sitcom writers develop episodes. "People can feel when someone isn't authentic," says Daniel Garcia, one of Blaine's closest collaborators and a fellow magician. "Magic is already such a combative artform. Many magicians almost make fun of people's intelligence through their material. The genius of David is that he left the narrative to the viewer. By not talking, they convince themselves [of] whatever they want."

David's major innovation was the way his magic was filmed. Rather than focusing on himself or the magic, the focus was flipped almost entirely to the audience's reactions. In one segment, David begins with a command to a group of people. "Here," he says, monotone. "Gimme a quarter." He puts the borrowed coin between his lips and proceeds to bite off half the coin. He chews on it for a moment, then *spits* it visually back onto the half-coin piece, fully restoring it. Blaine positions his head just inches from the woman's eyes. When he bites off half the coin, she actually *shrieks* and runs away from him. Her friends are laughing, but she's clearly affected by what she's just witnessed. Throughout David's television work, the camera zooms in close—sometimes uncomfortably so—to give us an intimate view of what our faces do when we're amazed.

My favorite part of *Street Magic* is one of its quieter moments, one that had a huge impact on me as a kid and still gives me chills when I watch it now. David approaches a teenager in ill-fitting clothes. The scene looks to be a trailer park, and David is directing a cameraman to shoot it from a different angle. Everything about the segment is raw and unpolished. Blaine places a coin on the boy's outstretched hand and asks him to examine it. He then waves his hand over the coin but doesn't touch it. The coin disappears. It's a beautiful moment, but the trick is just a trick. The boy doesn't react or look up. He stares at his now empty hand, holding perfectly still. "Cool," he says with no inflection at all. This isn't someone who has been entertained or diverted. A mysterious stranger walked up to him and performed a *miracle*, and it caused a magnificent system overload to his brain.

That segment was initially cut by the studio, David explains. "I had to fight to put that back in. They thought reactions had to be big and over the top." But David recognized how people actually react when they see something they can't explain. He fought to keep these rough, natural segments in the show.

David also performed outside, on the street, for real people. In *Street Magic*, he performed for finance guys and skateboard goths and everybody in between. It didn't matter if they were A-list actors or street sweepers, we watched as they became giddy children again. *Street Magic* was a tribute to why we love magic in the first place.

Since those early specials, David's magic has evolved. "When I was doing my first TV special, YouTube had just come out," he explains. "People were putting my secrets on there. And suddenly nonmagicians were walking up to me, doing tricks for me from my first special. And that's when I started to think that maybe I should do things that are real, that are almost impossible or at least look impossible, and combine that with magic, because by doing that, if they do research . . . it's actually more interesting than the trick itself." David evolved his approach to include magic that looks so authentic, you're forced to ask yourself, *Is it real?*

So . . . is it? "I think a lot of people think that because I'm a magician, there must be a trick to it," David says. "But I think, ironically, it's actually easier to do it than it is to fake it."

◆

Artist and critic David Salle writes that a style can be judged successful if it influences other artists. By this measure, David Blaine is wildly successful, and peerless amid his copycats. Since *Street Magic*'s sea-change moment, most of the magic shown on television has followed this guerilla-style, on-the-street approach that David pioneered.

When we evaluate his contribution to magic's landscape, we do so by method of subtraction. David dispensed with everything magicians are taught to put in their shows: humor, context, a point of view. His absence of showmanship has become, in a strange way, the best kind of showmanship. He is a revisionist magician.

"I always thought that if a magician could really do things, they wouldn't present magic," Blaine told me. "They would just do things and let the things speak for themselves."

Street Magic and the specials that followed always featured a stunt. The stunts were a smart format decision, since they could be teased throughout the special, leading up to a live feed of David on top of a tower (standing without restraints on a hundred-foot tower for thirty-five hours) or hanging upside down (for sixty hours, in the middle of Central Park) or encased in a freezing, ice-lined block (for sixty-three hours). David loves Hermann Hesse's *Siddhartha* and was inspired by the main character's endurance through long periods of starvation and deprivation. This novel, he says, was the genesis of his early stunts. "Everyone can perform magic," Hesse admonishes us, "everyone can reach his goals, if he is able to think, if he is able to wait, if he is able to fast."

But not everyone, I assure you, can do what David Blaine does. He alone is crazy enough to regularly flirt with death.

"Buried Alive" was David's first stunt: He entombed himself in a clear coffin for seven days, buried beneath three tons of water. Seventy-five thousand people waited in line outside for the chance to gaze at him as he stared back from inside his box. To prepare, Blaine placed a coffin in his apartment and slept in it at night. He then tried to remain inside for long periods of time without food, peeing into tubes as necessary.

In 2012, he sent one million volts through his body in an endurance stunt he called "Electrified." The performance was as interesting to scientists as it was to our own dark curiosities, the primordial question being "Can he even live through that?"

Each of David's stunts was enormously popular, and the best of them were pop-culture signposts. I distinctly remember where I was and who I was with as a kid watching "Buried Alive," "Vertigo" (where he stood on a hundred-foot-high pillar for thirty-five hours straight), and his Guinness World Record–attempt at holding his breath underwater for seventeen minutes and four seconds. (He failed on that attempt, then set the record months later on *The Oprah Winfrey Show*.)

To be clear, these stunts aren't magic tricks. They're something else, but deciding exactly what they are divides people. At first, his feats of endurance might seem like made-for-television gimmicks, a way of luring media glare and keeping viewers glued to their sets until the end. But what's most remarkable to me about David Blaine is his deep understanding of his own work. As his career progresses, David's stunts have morphed into a kind of performance art. Nobody since Houdini has had an understanding of the power of metaphor in magic like David. When considering his tricks and stunts individually, it isn't easy to see. But twenty years into a storied career, David has amassed a staggering body of work that includes all manner of life-threatening endurance stunts.

In 2003, in "Above the Below," David placed himself in a 3' × 7' × 7' Plexiglas box suspended thirty feet in the air alongside the Thames River. And then fasted for forty-four days (roughly the time needed to grow a carrot from seed to harvest), drinking only enough water to survive. At the end of the stunt, he'd lost twenty-four pounds and had developed hypophosphatemia, a by-product of starvation.

Everyone on Blaine's team tries to talk him out of his stunts: doctors, assistants, management. "I listen to all the doctors, all my friends, and then just try to override their theories of why it can't be done," David says.

In 2016, David performed a new twist on "The Bullet Catch." This is magic's deadliest stunt—at least twelve people have died while performing it (see page 206). A recent example happened in 2007, when a Ghanaian magician named Zamba Powers was accidentally shot in the stomach by an audience member who partook in the stunt. David's wrinkle was to perform it on himself . . . and to do it *for real*. Others have used blanks, wax bullets, or doctored guns, but David's defining theme is believability. In his version, a gun was positioned twenty feet away and pointed at his face with a length of cord attached to the trigger so that he himself could fire it. In this suicidal setup, no marksman could be at fault if the stunt failed.

"We practiced it just one time before we put it onstage," recalls Asi Wind, one of David's magician collaborators. "Then we moved it to the stage at the MGM Arena in front of sixteen thousand people." David asked Tim Moore, a professional dentist and amateur magician, to construct a conical mouthpiece that would, if all went according to plan, absorb the blow of the bullet in the recess of David's open mouth. During the rehearsal, the bullet cracked his mouthpiece, and Moore had to construct a second one for the performance.

In front of a packed arena, the stunt proved impossible to set up. "When we rehearsed it," says Daniel Garcia, "there was nobody onstage except David. At the show, there were other people around, and the weight on the wooden stage caused alignment issues with the laser scope." After an hour of scrambling, David finally pulled the string. *Bvvvvvvmm.*

David's head snapped back, and after five seconds of shock, he reached into his mouth to remove bloody shards of his mouthpiece. "I was sure the bullet went right through my head and that I was dead," Blaine recalls. "Suddenly I became aware of the pain and it brought me back. At that moment I realized that the mouth guard had shattered again, and I was alive."

David survived the ordeal, but sustained lacerations on the tissue lining of his throat. Wind was furious that it had gone wrong, and also terrified. "I looked at David at the hospital and said, 'If you're doing this in your live show, I'm not in.'" In this rare instance, David listened. He hasn't performed "The Bullet Catch" since 2016.

Viewers haven't always been sure *why* David is doing these stunts, and that includes the celebrities who are ever-present eye candy in his television work. Chris Rock, a Blaine admirer and friend, joked about Blaine's motivations in 2004. "Are we so desperate that we fall for a trickless magician?" he asked in his *Never Scared* special. "Where the fuck's the trick? . . . I'm in a box and I ain't gonna eat. That ain't no trick. That's called living in the projects."

———◆———

A criticism is sometimes leveled at David Blaine that he's the most famous magician in the world . . . who doesn't perform live. That isn't true. Throughout his career, David has maintained a busy performing schedule for oligarchs, presidents, and distinguished celebrities—Harrison Ford, Stephen Hawking, and Kanye West were featured in his most recent special. But until recently, the only place the public could see David's magic was every few years, when a special aired on television. In 2017, after two decades in magic and at forty-four years old, he finally announced his first North American tour. When I asked why it took him so long to launch a live show, he replied, "I needed to understand what my show would be—and it took me that long to figure it out."

Waiting twenty years to perform a touring show is its own endurance stunt. David's contemporaries have clocked thousands of shows onstage and spent years developing and perfecting their material. Before 2017, David made a career of designing and performing magic for cameras. Once the segment was captured, he moved on. Then there was the issue of his signature stunts. Surely David couldn't cheat death every night, in one city after the other, on a tour.

It turns out he can. David Blaine's live show is unexpectedly every bit as disruptive and brilliant as his early forays into television. The result is the most modern, engaging magic show in our industry. Quite simply, it's something you must see.

Like his approach to television, the show is raw. I never get the feeling that David is reciting a script or trying to influence his audience with charisma or energy. Instead, he walks onstage and does an even mix of amazing close-up magic (projected with cameras) and inexplicable, highly dangerous stunts. On the night I attended his show, he sewed his lips shut with a needle and thread, then tossed a deck of cards into the air. A chosen card was eventually revealed in his mouth, trapped behind his sewn-shut lips. He also swallowed four liters of water and regurgitated them in a controlled stream that is every bit as impressive and disgusting as it sounds. Then, near the end of his show he pushes an ice pick through his hand. After removing it, he gives the ice pick to an audience member to take home. It's an eclectic and inspired set list, especially from the perspective of a magician. In David's capable presentation his sleight-of-hand magic looks real, though of course it's not. And the stunts—mostly adapted from the world of carnivals and freak shows—are so outrageous that they look fake. But—I'm telling you— they're *real*.

The show is so intense, it can be run only once every few days. "In simple terms," Blaine says, "it's torture. I'm stabbing myself, not eating for twenty-four hours, putting a gallon of water in my stomach, swallowing gasoline, spitting out fire, eating frogs, and then doing a breath-hold for more than ten minutes." Clearly exhausted, he adds, "I'm just trying to make sure I don't kill myself onstage."

At one moment in the show, David swallows a spectator's ring. He then fashions a wire coat hanger into a long, thin ring and inserts it down his throat. When he withdraws it, the spectator's ring is looped on the hanger.

All of these moments build toward the marquee attraction of the evening, when David holds his breath in excess of ten minutes. During that time, audience members can see him floating in a Plexiglas enclosure. He smokes an underwater cigar, and kids are allowed onstage to interact with him. After ten excruciating, suspenseful minutes, he emerges from the water to an ovation unlike any I've ever heard in a magic show. Because people are applauding his survival.

What all the magicians in this book have in common is that their onstage personas are inflated, exaggerated, theatricalized versions of their offstage personalities. But that's not the case with David Blaine. What you see on television is the real David Blaine.

In person he's monotone, to the point, and notoriously stubborn about even the smallest details of his work. Unlike many famous magicians, David is also generous with his time and energy. He encourages young magicians—and not just when the cameras are rolling. His adviser, Danny Garcia, related a recent experience in which he and David were on the New York subway going toward Queens, the train car empty aside from the two magicians and a little boy and his mother. The boy, an aspiring magician, recognized David, who insisted on performing for him, even after they missed their stop. "David wouldn't quit," Garcia recalls. "He just kept doing tricks until, literally, the last stop on the train. So finally we say goodbye to this kid and his mom, and David turns to me and says, 'Okay, now where's the train back into Manhattan?'"

David is often unable or unwilling to be practical. He has finished television specials a year late, turned down million-dollar sponsorships because they didn't align with his tastes or beliefs, and offered particularly, well, David-like financial advice. At the World Economic Forum in Switzerland, he said, "Whenever I make a decision, I always try to decide: Would I do this for one dollar? The idea is if I'm offered a gig or something, if the answer is no, then I won't do it for any amount of money; and if the answer is yes, then I'll do it for whatever the deal is." And David lives his own advice. He does magic wherever he goes—yet he might turn down a lucrative trade show or appearance because it doesn't interest him. Which means that anyone could be at the receiving end of a David Blaine card trick. His advisers pointed out to me that he always flies in coach class, and invariably ends up doing magic for whoever is sitting around him.

But David's only major prop is his body, and the focus has always been on new ways to punish it. At forty-seven years old, he faces a challenge similar to Houdini, who died too young: How much longer can he put his body through these stunts? At what point will his faculties diminish? What will he do then? When I asked him this, he demurred. He has no plans to slow down. In fact, he said he was training for his most elaborate stunt, which is rumored to involve a midair escape. When I pressed him, he was elusive, unsurprisingly. "We can always be amazed at the human body and what it does," he said. He was somewhere noisy, the reception cutting in and out. "But I have to go now," he explained. "I'm about to jump out of a plane."

❖ ❖ ❖

45

CAN A
MAGIC TRICK BE
TOO GOOD?

ELEMENTS OMITTED
FROM A WORK OF ART
ARE AS MUCH A PART
OF THAT WORK
AS THOSE INCLUDED.

—SCOTT MCCLOUD, CARTOONIST

The hottest magician in the United Kingdom is a guy who goes by the name Dynamo. He performs to packed stadiums, and his television shows have shattered all network records in the UK. He has the great luxury (and responsibility) of filling his show with the most outrageous, expensive, and whimsical effects money can buy. Dynamo has reached a level where he can afford a team of consultants. His team's approach is that they ought to perform whatever they can dream up, regardless of development costs or resources. At one point in his show, he walks across a barren stage—no set, no props, just Dynamo—and without warning or explanation floats ten feet into the air, slowly somersaults as he hovers above the stage, then descends back to the ground. Blackout.

On paper, at least, it is the perfect illusion. Simple, striking, and utterly baffling. And I know just how hard his team worked to essentially invent a propless illusion. Yet somehow this sequence is the weakest in his show. When people leave, they are buzzing about the part where Dynamo causes a borrowed cell phone to appear in a bottle. This trick is great, too, though it is unequivocally smaller and less impressive than human levitation.

There are countless examples of astounding magic tricks that are somehow less than the sum of their parts. Curiously, some of the strongest tricks are the most forgettable. Why? Because the best magic contains an element of *conflict*. I've mentioned that great magic and stories are governed by the same principles (see page 37): conflict, rising tension, and more often than not, resolution. Dynamo first performed a borrowed-cell-phone-to-bottle sequence on his TV show, and the clip went viral. There was grumbling that he couldn't do it live, that it was a setup, that he used camera tricks. There is innate conflict in causing a borrowed, valued object to disappear and then reappear in an unexpected place. There is further conflict (and humor) when Dynamo sends the spectator back to her seat with the bottle, her phone impossibly imprisoned inside. Will she have to break the bottle to get her texts? What happens if someone calls her? The trick delivers conflict *and* leaves us with a good story (and leaves her with a *great* story). Dynamo's levitation trick, for all its attributes, leaves us cold because it lacks conflict.

This is one of those counterintuitive principles that even magicians overlook. Screenwriters often fall prey to it. *Now You See Me*, a magic caper film released in 2013, grossed $350 million at the box office. The film is full of bombastic tricks dreamed up by nonmagicians and then rendered in vivid, digitized detail. Humans are teleported into bank vaults with a zap of lightning, and yet the illusions (and the plot) fall flat. The mistake the filmmakers made (assuming they cared about the magic as much as they cared about profits) is rendering the magic *too* perfectly. It simply isn't believable.

The magic industry, like the worlds of science and philosophy, has theories and theorists who help us magicians understand the way things work. One of those theorists, Rick Johnsson, offered his "too-perfect theory" in 1970. The best minds in magic have been furiously debating it ever since. Put simply, the idea is that by virtue of their perfection, some tricks become imperfect. Conversely, by virtue of their imperfection, some tricks become perfect. Wait. Huh?

The too-perfect theory posits that if a trick looks too good to be true, it will be perceived as such and ultimately lead the audience directly back to the method. If you saw a floating giraffe illusion and determined that, based on what you saw, the only possible solution was wires, chances are you'd be right.

As of last year, the too-perfect theory seems to have scientific support to back it up. Cyril Thomas and Gustav Kuhn designed an experiment in which a viewer chooses one card from a shuffled pack. The facilitator looks into the viewer's eyes and apparently reads her mind: "eight of diamonds!" The facilitator correctly divines the chosen card. How did he do it?

Every card in the pack is the eight of diamonds. And in the test, 75 percent of the viewers correctly guessed this method. It's fairly obvious because it is, to use magicians' jargon, too perfect. But when the facilitator simply guessed wrong first, and then correctly, less than 30 percent figured out the method of the experiment. The facilitator looked the viewer in the eyes and said, "I see the eight of clubs."

"Wrong."

"Look at me again. Ah, I did make a mistake. Concentrate on your card. . . . Eight of diamonds!"

It's the same trick, the same method. But by adding in a tiny weakness—a little grit—the effect becomes stronger in the eye of the beholder.

There are times when seeing less means believing more. "Coins Across" is a classic magic effect where coins travel invisibly from one hand to the other. In the last decade, several resourceful magicians found ways to cause the coins to *visibly* travel from one hand to the other. The coin actually floats from one hand and lands in the other hand. Surely this would be an improvement on the classic "Coins Across," since nothing is left to the imagination.

As it turns out, that is a problem. When the coin travels invisibly, we are forced to imagine how and when and what actually happened. The audience creates most of the illusion because they fill in what it might look like when the coin disappears and reappears somewhere else. The same holds true in horror films—the less you see of the monster, the scarier it is. It's the shark's fin in *Jaws*, emerging from the water. *Da-na, da-na, da-na.* The way we imagine the great white in *Jaws* is far scarier than the mechanical shark.

I like to think of the phases of magic tricks as comic book panels. Each panel shows a moment of a trick. But in comics, the "gutter"—that small, white space between panels—is where most of the action takes place in our imagination, an idea best described by cartoonist Scott McCloud. We use the gutter to connect these moments into a fluid mind movie, adding our own embellishments along the way. The sensation of magic is actually weakened when every vivid detail is laid bare before our eyes. When nothing is left to the imagination, there is nothing left to imagine.

46

WHAT ARE THE MAGIC OLYMPICS?

I HAVE BEEN UP AGAINST
TOUGH COMPETITION ALL MY LIFE.
I WOULDN'T KNOW HOW
TO GET ALONG WITHOUT IT.

—WALT DISNEY, ENTERTAINMENT ICON

We've already asked and answered the impossible question, "Who's the greatest magician in the world?" But in practice, that question is answered every three years, at an event called FISM.

In 1948, the Fédération Internationale des Sociétés Magiques (FISM) was founded, and every three years since, magicians have convened in a different city around the world for magic's version of the Olympics. And yes, it's as nerdy as it sounds.

In 2015, FISM was held in Rimini, Italy. For one week, the most influential magicians in the world huddled together in this seaside resort town known for, among other things, being the birthplace of famous Italian film director Federico Fellini. In one of the great honors of my life, I was invited to judge at FISM in 2015. There are different categories: close-up, stage, grand illusion, and mentalism. Each country holds its own national competition, and the champions from each place compete at FISM for various titles.

The best part about being a judge at FISM is the front-row seat. There are so many people watching the competition that in past years I had to see it from the back of the theater. In Stockholm in 2006, I watched from another room on a screen. But in 2015, I was in the front row. Each competitor has eight minutes. At seven minutes, a red light begins to blink. That's a signal to wrap things up quickly, because when the red light goes solid, the act is disqualified.

Woody Aragon, a sensational magician, fell victim to the red light, going over by a mere six seconds. He would have been a finalist, certainly, and I had to sit through endless backroom debates about whether we could rob someone of such an opportunity over six seconds. But the timekeeper, from Switzerland, was unsurprisingly rigid about the rules. Woody was disqualified.

If an act is of extremely poor quality, we can signal a buzzer. If all the judges buzz out, the performer is stopped midact and pulled from the stage. This strikes me as unnecessarily cruel, and I've seen it done only once: Alex Stone, an American, was pulled from the stage midact and later wrote about it in *Fooling Houdini*. His performance was undeniably awful and unworthy of the FISM standard—but, I mean, it's only eight minutes.

The year I judged, the competition level was strong. We are instructed to judge based on three criteria: technical skill, performance skill, and originality. My pick to win was Shin Lim, who would go on to win *America's Got Talent* in 2018. I scored Shin the highest because his act featured completely original concepts presented in a way that was, to me, unique.

In the jury room, I discovered that four of the six other judges hadn't even scored him in the upper half of the competition.

"His music was too loud and modern," said one guy.

"He's using the same concept over and over," said another.

"It's not his time yet. I think he needs a few more years."

The old guard always has trouble accepting change. I was stunned and lobbied for Shin to be scored high enough to make it to the next round. Then at least he would be judged against five other finalists. Eventually the other jurors relented, and Shin was in the finals.

This mattered to me because, like the Olympics, people dedicate years of their lives to be on that stage, and they get *eight minutes* to prove their worth. Careers are made (or not) on the FISM stage.

Shin Lim won his division, but not the Grand Prix. Instead, Switzerland's Pierric stole the show in the final round. His act starts a little slow for my taste yet has an ending that compels you to your feet. Pierric's act is meta, a frenetic medley of comedic false starts that become increasingly hurried. As he begins his act, something goes magically, amazingly awry, and he starts again. He attempts to find the four aces, but they keep vanishing from his hands. Each time he starts over, the "problems" compound: His watch jumps from one arm to the other, coins appear where the cards are supposed to be, and the coins keep disappearing. The act becomes more and more absurd, and at the end the playing cards float, his necktie changes, and coins appear on a table without him even touching the table's surface. The whole thing is presented by a neurotic character who keeps having to start over because he demands perfection.

In the film *Adaptation,* the screenwriting guru Robert McKee (played by actor Brian Cox) offers a great admission to his student, which is true in magic as well: "You can have flaws, problems," he says, "but wow them in the end, and you've got a hit."

We unanimously chose Pierric as the 2015 Grand Prix winner.

47

WHY DO MAGICIANS PULL RABBITS OUT OF HATS?

IDEAS ARE LIKE RABBITS.
YOU GET A COUPLE AND LEARN
HOW TO HANDLE THEM,
AND PRETTY SOON YOU HAVE A DOZEN.

—JOHN STEINBECK, AUTHOR

In 1726 the *Mist's Weekly Journal* in London reported that Mary Toft, a young married "servant girl," went into labor and gave birth to nine rabbits. The rabbits, the story noted, were stillborn.

By eighteenth-century standards the story went viral, attracting the attention of several of Britain's finest surgeons, including Nathaniel St André, the Royal Family's official surgeon. Upon examination of Mary Toft and her unusual birth, St André declared the incident genuine.

At the time, it was widely believed that a woman's thoughts and experiences could influence her offspring. A loud noise, for example, might cause a baby to be born deaf. A cut on a mother's arm might explain a baby born without arms. Toft worked the fields for the estate of her employer in Godalming, and she told authorities that she gave chase to a rabbit for no reason. Hence, that would explain her rabbit offspring, she believed. Toft first attracted attention because it was reported that she gave birth to several animal *parts*: a rabbit heart, foot, and head. Only afterward did she give birth to full rabbits, nine in total.

Lest you think I'm kidding, all the prominent news journals of the time reported on the unusual birth. As the saying goes, you can't make this stuff up. But of course, Toft *did* make it up. With help from at least one accomplice, she had inserted dead cat parts and rabbit heads into her uterus, and passed them off as her progeny. Why? We may never know.

Toft was imprisoned briefly for fraud but ultimately never charged with a crime. It was a humiliating embarrassment for the surgeons involved, as well as the journalists who reported on it, and became a news story that stood as a cultural reference point for a hundred years.

Whether or not her story was inspiration for the iconic trick of pulling a rabbit from a top hat is disputed. Magic scholars credit Louis Comte as the first magician to reach into a top hat and produce a rabbit, but the idea that he referenced Toft during the presentation is an assumption at best. Comte, who lived in Paris, performed decades *after* the Toft scandal, so it's plausible the trick was inspired by it. But it's impossible to say for sure. What looks today like a fluffy bunny coming out of a velvet top hat may be inspired by this awkward and disturbing story.

The genesis of the trick aside, the production of a live animal is always compelling theater, and rabbits are both cheap to get and easy to find, whether you're living in eighteenth-century England or twenty-first-century New York. Also, they are most often white, which contrasts nicely with the magician's traditional black tuxedo. As is sometimes the case in magic, a simple illusion may have a sinister past.

———————◆———————

Pulling a rabbit from a hat has become one of the most iconic effects in magic. The other candidates—sawing a person in half and producing a dove—have been mainstays in magic acts since they were invented. But pulling a rabbit from a hat is almost never performed in contemporary magic shows. What these iconic tricks have in common is that they are each high stakes. Producing a dove or a rabbit is about the creation of life. Sawing through a person is about survival, about staying alive.

As a boy I produced a rabbit, "Henry," from a box at the end of my show. Not a hat, but close enough. But I soon learned what I suspect other magicians realized, each in their own time: Onstage, producing a rabbit is about the creation of life. But offstage, taking care of a rabbit is a pain in the ass.

48

IS MAGIC MEMORABILIA VALUABLE?

ARTISTS LIVE THEIR ART;
COLLECTORS LIVE WITH IT.

—PAIGE WILLIAMS, WRITER

✦ ✦ ✦

My apartment in Manhattan is 750 square feet, or about the size of a two-car garage. Most of the stages I perform on have a larger footprint than my living space, but this is life in New York City, where space is precious and the prices are, too. From ceiling to floor, wall to wall, my apartment is a museum of magic. Books line the north wall from floor to ceiling—four thousand of them, many inscribed by the magicians who wrote them. I have Houdini's straitjacket, the white gloves Cardini wore in his act, and Juan Tamariz's purple top hat. On my coffee table is a cheating device confiscated from a cowboy who delivered cards from his sleeve to his hand. I have the Amazing Kreskin's signature thick-rimmed glasses, and the pink tuxedo jacket Doug Henning wore on his first television special. I *love* these things, and I often take them off the shelf to feel their weight, to absorb their power. My apartment isn't practical for hosting guests or doing Pilates, but if you spend fifteen hours every day inventing magic tricks, it's home.

After a tour date in Phoenix years ago, I went antiquing through the Old West town of Tombstone. I entered an old shop and asked if they had anything magic or cheating related, and was greeted with a fast and curt "Nope." But as I turned to exit, I noticed an old framed engraving hanging over the door.

"What's that?" I asked.

"Oh, that's been here longer than I have. I don't think it's for sale." I put my face inches from the piece. On the surface it looked like a poker scene. But upon closer examination, I noticed a secret behind the harmless card game depicted. A couple of players were up to no good. A bystander peered over the shoulder of a player and was signaling the cards to his friend across the table. The reason I collect anything related to cheating is that many card sleights are derived from the gaming table.

"I'll sell it to you for fifty dollars," the woman behind the counter called out.

"Sold," I immediately said.

I had the work appraised in New York and found that, although I bought it out West, its origins were British. It was from the eighteenth century, long before cowboys were cheating at poker in saloons. And it was worth $5,000. The engraving now hangs by my bed.

Houdini ephemera is the most expensive. Potter & Potter Auctions recently sold a Houdini Water Torture Cell poster—the only surviving print of its kind—for $114,000. The buyer was David Blaine.

David Copperfield is the biggest magic collector in this or any era. My admiration for David is great, but I curse his name every time there's a magic auction, because when he bids, he almost never loses. His net worth is estimated at close to a billion dollars. A *billion.* So what David wants, David gets. His secret museum (see page 150) is filled with the choicest magic artifacts on the planet.

The way I have assembled a respectable collection has less to do with money and more to do with an honor code that still exists in pockets of our industry, the kind of secret ritual you almost expect to occur behind closed doors from magician to magician. We gift each other important relics.

In 1999, I performed in Argentina and met Martin Pacheco, who owns an important magic book collection. He had a first edition of *The Discoverie of Witchcraft,* the very first book in the English language to include magic tricks, published in 1584. It was *the* book that clarified the difference between spells and demons—so called "black" magic—and the earliest conjuring feats. Historians later exaggerated the impact of *Discoverie*, saying that it single-handedly saved magicians from being burned at the stake as heretics. That's overstated, perhaps, but it *is* true that the book was published at a time when many people considered magicians powerful, even supernatural. *Discoverie* changed the entire trajectory of magic. I was eighteen when I held that crumbling book in my hands, and I stared at it dumbfounded. It is our bible, and I was holding one of the only surviving originals.

Fast-forward a decade. Martin reached out by phone with a shocking declaration: "The time has come for my *Discoverie* to pass to the next generation. I want to pass it to you."

"What?"

I explained that I couldn't even wrap my head around the $50,000 price tag associated with clean first editions of the book. He explained that many of the finest items in his collection had come to him from older magicians who wanted their magic to fall into the hands of people who would cherish it. He wanted *Discoverie* to pass to me. He named a price that was such a small fraction of the value that, even in my twenties, I could manage it without a second thought. Because of Martin, I'm the new custodian of one of magic's oldest, rarest, and most significant volumes. The pages are delicate and cracked; the book is so old that it's not actually a book, but a "folio" of pages stacked between two covers. I've been advised to keep it at exactly 66 degrees, in darkness, and under special protection. But then I wouldn't be able to pick it up when I'm searching for inspiration, to run my fingers gently across the rough parchment pages, to hold a book that six generations of magicians have held. And although I can enjoy it for now, I know what I have to do. Someday, when I'm finished with it, my charge will be to find a young magician caretaker that I can entrust with my copy of *Discoverie*.

Ken Klosterman was one of magic's most elite and eccentric collectors. He was the owner of Klosterman Baking Company, an enormous Midwest operation that outfits major chains (including McDonald's and all the regional grocery stores) with bread products. He passed away in October 2020, but when we last saw each other Ken was in his late eighties, slow on his feet but with a quick wit that remained.

It was winter 2017 when Ken invited me to his Cincinnati estate. It's set on a sprawling, working farm, and I drove down a mile-long driveway past horses in stables and a small pond, arriving at a stately home far from prying eyes. Ken was a widower and lived alone among his unequaled collection of fine magic. Although Ken had a white-hot enthusiasm for magic and its history, one couldn't escape the obvious comparison to Orson Welles's 1941 film, *Citizen Kane*, which tells the story of a formerly powerful titan wandering around his "Xanadu" alone, surrounded only by his priceless collection.

Ken had his curator on hand when I arrived—Richard Hughes, whom I had met as a child when he still performed. Now Richard's job is to archive and catalogue the items Ken acquired, a Herculean task given the breakneck speed at which Ken bought them.

When I arrived, Richard and Ken were blasting Fox News.

"Come on in!" Ken shouted. "Let's go down to the mine shaft."

Ken was blunt and always in a hurry. He escorted me to an elevator in his home and spun a tale about discovering a mine shaft buried deep beneath his house. We descended via a creaky and rattling elevator into a dark, ancient mine shaft. My ears popped. I sensed we might not be in an actual elevator shaft, but the ruse was airtight.

The doors parted to reveal a lush, astounding display of magic's history. Even the temperature in the rooms was different, adding to the illusion that we were "sixty stories below ground."

Ken had a full theater in his home museum, including chairs repurposed from an old theater known for its magic performances. He had Chung Ling Soo's magic fishing pole, the one Soo (see page

206) used in the early part of the last century, where he would wave the end of the fishing line over the audience and cause a live goldfish to appear on its hook. He had Muhammad Ali's thumb tip (Ali was an amateur magician all his life, and this was the secret to his signature trick). But the jewel of Klosterman's collection was Robert-Houdin's Light and Heavy Chest, the *actual* chest Robert-Houdin used in his most famous illusion (see page 92). Most historians would consider this small, electromagnetic box one of the three most significant objects in the history of magic.

Ken's museum is a labyrinth of hidden entrances and secret bookshelf doors, each perfectly appointed chamber giving way to the next. It felt like a museum of magic, though museums are never quite that lavish. And I could touch *everything*. Ken barked orders at Richard, instructing him to open this cabinet or prepare that prop. He turned a corner and noticed a rabbit production by Dell O'Dell, a prominent female magician in the fifties. His eyes aglow, Ken called me over and proudly lifted off the lid, causing four walls to pop open with a huge bang, panels flying all over the room. There was no rabbit inside, thank God, but I got the idea. "Now clean this shit up," Ken ordered Richard, urging me to follow him to the next room while Richard struggled to reassemble the rabbit production for the next tour.

After seven hours of talking shop and playing with the tools of our past masters, I hinted that I had to go. "But we haven't even gone to the country," Ken said, disappointed. It turned out that once Ken's collection exceeded his estate, he bought another sprawling house an hour away to accommodate the overflow.

"It's getting late, Ken," I explained. His collection was sensory overload, like eating too much ice cream.

"It's okay," Ken said. "Richard'll drive."

An hour later we arrived at a historic mansion in the area, secluded within a sizable spread of farmland. This old country manse was filled with more one-of-a-kind pieces, curated and displayed with great care and taste.

"What's that sword?" I asked, pointing. I had a hunch but wasn't sure.

"Lafayette's sword," Ken replied. It was the sword worn by the esteemed Munich-born illusionist, The Great Lafayette, on the day he died in 1911. He and ten of his company were killed in a fire during the last piece of his show, "The Lion's Bride." Lafayette's body was so badly burned that it could be identified only by the ornamental sword on his hip. This was that sword. I've since asked several collectors to put a value on the sword. I kept getting the same answer: "Priceless."

Some months later, Ken hosted a retreat for magic collectors. David Stahl presented new scholarship on The Great Lafayette, research that took him around the world and half a lifetime to uncover. At the end of David's presentation, spontaneously and in front of everyone, Ken gifted him the sword. It was an astounding gesture. The sword is now exactly where it should be.

At 10:00 p.m. Ken announced that it was time to go to "the mill," which is a third property he bought to house his largest illusions. A century-old gristmill and a historic landmark, it was filled on two levels with illusions from everyone from Herrmann the Great to Siegfried and Roy.

By that point, I was both numb to the endless stream of magic history and beginning to succumb to the question gnawing at me: What was Ken going to do with all of it? A man like Ken Klosterman would surely have connections to a prestigious museum, or perhaps the local university would build a new wing in his name to house his collection upon his death. Or maybe he would donate it to the Society of American Magicians? "Ken," I finally asked, as Richard drove us back to Cincinnati, "what's going to happen to all this stuff?"

"Absolutely no plans," he said. "You want it?"

◆

This is what collecting magic is about, and what few outsiders understand. The allure of collecting magic is its accessibility—almost anyone can own a part of our history. Obviously the Klostermans and Copperfields of the world help themselves to the choicest materials, and we of mortal means barter and trade for the rest. Collecting magic boils down to a combination of deserving it and being in the right place at the time. There's a bigger barrier in sports and rock memorabilia. A Babe Ruth game-worn jersey sold for $4.4 million in 2012. Microsoft cofounder Paul Allen paid $2 million for a Jimi Hendrix Fender Stratocaster guitar.

In magic it's possible to own significant, unique, museum-quality pieces for the same kind of money many of us spend on tickets to basketball games or golf trips or an overnight stay at a spa. I've been given priceless artifacts from magic's history, and I have been privy to outrageous bargains.

All of that is changing, thanks in part to Gabe Fajuri of Potter & Potter Auctions, one of the only magic-dedicated auction houses. Gabe travels the world propositioning collectors (and their surviving spouses) to put their collections on the auction block. His auctions aren't on the level of fine art or musical instruments, but a recent magic auction at Potter & Potter cleared $750,000. Celebrities and billionaire CEOs are getting in on the magic hoard, and suddenly magic is an "investment."

I made such an investment recently, when I purchased Houdini's original "Needles" effect from Potter & Potter Auctions for $18,000. It's a small, velvet-lined leather box, the hinge broken from Houdini's nightly performances. Inside is a wooden spool and a rusted set of sewing needles. This was a considered purchase for me, but I look at it like this: Swallowing and regurgitating needles was one of Houdini's signature effects. There are numerous photos and reviews depicting and describing this very prop. Anything Houdini touched is sold for big money now—canceled checks, telegrams confirming health insurance, membership cards to organizations.

But these things are just stuff. They don't tell a story. Houdini's needles were a feature of his act, and most interestingly, the secret to how he accomplished the trick is evident in the artifact. If you look carefully at scuff marks on the spool of thread and study how the needles have aged, you'll see enough clues for a discerning magician to deduce Houdini's method. I find this not just riveting but historically significant. I could have purchased Apple stock with that money, but you can't hold Apple stock in your hand or display it on a coffee table. When I hold these needles, I'm holding something Houdini held every night of his performing life. The remnants of his saliva—Houdini's DNA—are on those needles.

The investment appears to have paid off. A serious Houdini collector offered me $36,000 a little over a year later, generously doubling what I had paid. By now I hope I don't have to tell you that I declined.

It helps that magic objects are, in my biased opinion, a more fascinating conversation piece than a vase or a gold coin or some Flemish artist's preparatory drawing. Magic props *do* stuff—they pop open or reveal a camouflaged trapdoor. They fall apart on command or change shape, even if they are hundreds of years old.

The most popular magic artifacts are the magic posters. In magic's golden age, the 1870s through the 1930s, the most effective way to advertise an upcoming show was on large, color prints. Like baseball cards or *Star Wars* figures, these posters weren't seen as collectable in their time, and most people discarded them once the shows left town. Which is part of what makes them so rare. Magic posters were made using a process called stone lithography. This process yields smoky, rich pastel colors that feature haunting skin tones and shadowy portraits. Magic posters of this age are filled with whispering imps and beautiful women, fantastic costumes, and puzzling tricks. Most are enormous, since their intended purpose was to hang on barn walls and in alleys en route to the big cities. Alexander Conlin, who performed as "Alexander, the Man Who

Knows" made particularly beautiful posters. The so-called "striped" Alexander hangs in my apartment, a print taller than a man, with Alexander's imposing head staring directly at you, adorned with his signature bejeweled turban. David Copperfield has this poster *and* Conlin's original turban to go with it. (The guy has *everything*.) It's a stunning poster, and not terribly expensive or rare. When people ask about it, I can share that Alexander was, in his prime, the highest-paid entertainer on the vaudeville circuit. He was married at least eleven times and was an admitted murderer. If you ever come to my apartment, I can tell you the whole story.

This poster. The dusty book. The rusty needles. These aren't just antiques—they're conversation pieces. They're history in physical form.

✦ ✦ ✦

49

WHY DO MAGICIANS HAVE SUCH BIG EGOS?

A PROFESSIONAL MAGICIAN NEVER REVEALS HIS TRICKS, OR THE FACT THAT HE STILL LIVES WITH HIS PARENTS.

—PETE FIRMAN, MAGICIAN, COMEDIAN

Magicians are often satirized for outsized egos—and the punishment fits the crime. Seemingly more than their performing arts peers, magicians possess an (over)abundance of self-confidence. Cockiness is so part and parcel of the magic profession that it's written into nearly every fictional magician character in literature. In the eyes of those who write about us, we're egomaniacs bent on being taken seriously, even if the magic underwhelms.

But what if the overconfidence, the arrogance, is part of the equation? I would argue that the reason so many magicians have large egos is that having one is essential to being a magician. I'm not excusing magicians like *Arrested Development*'s Gob Bluth, oblivious to their own cringeworthy narcissism. I'm suggesting that, kept in check, a healthy ego is a necessary tool for a magician.

Many of our greatest innovators had inflated egos. You have to have an against-the-odds belief in yourself to succeed where other magicians fail. The best magicians in history stared down their defining moments, believing they could do what others could not. Every great performer looks at their contemporaries, then at themselves, and has the ego to assert, *"I can do better."* Some part of us must believe we're better than we really are if we ever hope to get better. An inflated ego is an obstacle to progress, but I do think a *little* ego—an I-can-do-better approach—is an essential part of the creative process.

Right before I walk onstage, I convince myself—superficially, perhaps—that I really can do magic. I visualize each trick in my head, but I do it from the audience's perspective as seamless and magical, with the moves omitted. *I can do magic,* I say to myself. This isn't some superficial preshow ritual. In magic, it matters. You can't convincingly ask someone else to suspend their disbelief if you aren't willing to do it first yourself.

On the flip side, vaudeville magician Howard Thurston had a sweet ritual before he went onstage each night. He would, in his words, "get pep," drawing strength from his audience. He would position himself in the wings and, looking at the crowd, say aloud, "I love my audience, I love my audience, I love my audience."

50

IS THERE REAL MAGIC IN THE UNIVERSE?

THOSE WHO DON'T
BELIEVE IN MAGIC
WILL NEVER FIND IT.

—ROALD DAHL, AUTHOR

✦ ✦ ✦

I was performing in Ecuador in 2005 when my hosts asked if they could show me "real magic." I flew to the coast, threw my bags in a local lodge, and found myself hiking along a cliff that overlooked the Pacific Ocean.

Two local boys, both around fifteen years old, stood at a fork in the road. "Turtle magic," they said. They spoke no other English. We paid them a fee and followed them down a dirt path to the edge of a cliff. The wind was so loud, it was hard to hear our mysterious companions. Both boys removed small flutes from their pockets, faced the wind, and dropped to their knees. In unison, they began playing a special tune to summon the turtles. It was weird and exciting.

As the wind carried the music into the air and swirled it around, magic was unfolding below on the surface of the water. A turtle's head popped up, as if responding to the music. Then another turtle, and another, and another. They were assembling, it seemed, summoned magically by the flute. It was, as my host described, *real* magic.

◆

After particularly good shows, I'm often asked this question by people—smart people—who hold on to a glimmer of hope for something more to this world beyond the laws of nature. "Is what you're doing real, or is there a trick?"

In a way, this is the highest compliment a magician can receive, but also a dangerous one. In that moment, we are a "yes" away from becoming gurus and con artists, prophets to an audience of one. But for most magicians there is an inborn attraction to the unexplainable. We're drawn to things we don't understand, to things *nobody* understands. We want to believe in magic that just *happens*.

There are a lot of believers out there. A 2005 survey found that 31 percent of Americans believe in telepathy, 32 percent in ghosts, and 41 percent in extrasensory perception. Despite an abundance of reality television shows that say otherwise, there has never been a shred of evidence supporting any of these phenomena. They are as fake—sorry, as *real*—as a magic trick.

When I heard the turtle song and saw sea turtles emerging from the deep, I was fooled right on cue. I knew those animals were wild and couldn't be trained that way. I knew also that soft flute music couldn't even be heard from such a distance. The atmosphere certainly played a role. Like a magic trick performed within a tight spotlight and musical accompaniment, those boys created a spiritual moment: They said very little, walked ahead of us, then dropped to their knees in ritualistic fashion. It felt otherworldly.

But there's a reason magicians don't want you to watch the same trick twice. After we left the cliff, I hung back for thirty minutes, watching secretly as the boys returned to the path to accept the next group of magic-seeking pilgrims. While they were away, I saw it—some turtles poked their heads up again, almost in unison. No music played. They just popped up, took a gulp of air, and retreated to the depths. The turtles were simply coming up for air, and the boys had created a magic trick around it.

Eventually they returned to their spot and did their ritual for a new audience. I even noticed a turtle or two popping up prematurely, but the misdirection was strong. The boys didn't point out the turtles until after the song played. Why would anyone scrutinize the surface of the water before being directed to do so? They didn't know what was coming.

When the boys pointed out the turtles, I saw a woman cry. For her, it was a spiritual experience on a level I've never seen evoked by a magic trick. For her, what she saw was *real*. For me—the second time, anyway—it was two boys playing flutes as a flotilla of sea turtles naturally came up for air.

In 1973, a young, handsome Israeli named Uri Geller burst into the world's consciousness. Geller bent spoons with his mind, duplicated drawings made by people isolated in other rooms, and could stop borrowed wristwatches with his mental powers. At the time, he claimed that his powers were bestowed on him by aliens from fifty-three thousand light-years away.

Scientists at Stanford Research Institute put Geller's powers to the test in laboratory conditions and concluded that Geller was *real*. The United States government commissioned a report on him, and the term "Geller Effect" was coined, referring to people with telekinesis, who could move things with their minds.

My aunt, a university student at the time, saw Geller speak at a school-sanctioned event. She recalls going to spoon-bending parties, holding hands with her friends and concentrating their energies on the spoons in their laps. "Did it work?" I asked her.

"Depends who you ask," she said. To many, he was real.

But of course he wasn't. James Randi, a magician, escapist, author, and skeptic, thoroughly debunked Geller's claims, and it became increasingly clear that his predictions and feats were easily explained by preparation and sleight of hand. Geller disappeared from public life for more than twenty years, and in recent times has had a renaissance in popularity, this time as an entertainer and reality television host. Geller hasn't officially renounced his claims of genuine power, but he also doesn't claim he's the real deal anymore. Like Farrah Fawcett and pet rocks, Uri Geller is a seventies icon, his "powers" best viewed through the cultural prism of that era.

Many magicians *hate* Uri Geller. They despise the fact that he so blatantly lied to the public, taking credit for what the rest of us know was all deception. Many magicians are horrified at the distorted view of science Geller offered to his fans. Because of him, some say, segments of the public still believe that certain people are imbued with supernatural powers the rest of us lack.

I remain astounded that all this actually happened. It was *War of the Worlds*-level hysteria for the disco age. By 1973, we had microwave ovens and heart transplants, and had sent men to the moon. Yet people—lots and lots of them—believed Uri Geller could bend spoons with his mind. The lack of ethics aside, that alone is something to marvel over. In the bright light of modern day, it's unthinkable that a magician doing tricks would be taken so seriously by so many for so long. I didn't understand it—until September 2012.

Uri Geller called me one day out of the blue and introduced himself. He told me he was in town from Israel, had just purchased my book *MAGIC*, and was flattered that I had featured him in the historical section. "Next time I see you," he said, "I will bend a fork for you."

"Thanks," I said.

Four years later, it happened that we were booked for the same event in Italy and would share the same stage. I reminded him about his generous offer. What happened next I'll never forget.

"You're right! Come with me!" he shouted. He grabbed my hand and pulled me out of my backstage chair, frantically escorting me to the refreshment table. He snatched a fork from the table, and then, before my eyes, it bent.

It *bent*.

I know *for a fact* that what he did wasn't real, but in that moment, in that place, it felt real. This happened because I was able to suspend my hardened, jaded disbelief for a fleeting moment. In that moment the floor fell out from under me, and I finally understood the power he held over the public.

Right after the fork bent, he signed the back of it and gave it to me. I treasured that fork, and it held a place of honor on my bookshelf (in the paranormal section, obviously). Authentic autographed Uri Geller bent forks go for big money on eBay, but I loved mine because of the rare occurrence it represented—a moment when I, the magician, was the participant, experiencing "real" magic. So it sat on my bookshelf as a conversation piece until January 2018.

I came home to find my housekeeper dusting the shelf at the spot once occupied by Uri's bent, signed fork. "Janina," I said, "where did the fork go?"

"Don't worry," she said. "It was all bent up and had black smudges on it. So I straightened it out and wiped off the dirt. It's in your drawer now, with the other forks."

51

WHAT'S THE NEXT BIG THING IN MAGIC?

TOO MANY MAGICIANS ARE STATING THAT MAGIC IS DEAD.

—PAUL MORRIS, MAGICIAN

✦✦✦

Magic has surpassed the age of innovation and graduated to a new era where *curation* is the thing. When it's possible to perform almost every trick you can imagine, the question for magicians becomes "What *should* we perform?" A magician's toughest job is no longer devising the next great illusion. It's deciding which illusion she should pursue. When I sit in rooms brainstorming with creative magicians, we spend far less time than you would think figuring out *how*. Most of our time is spent curating *what*.

Want to make an elephant disappear? There are a dozen ways to do it. Want to change your dog into a cat? No problem. Want to help a guy propose to his girlfriend by floating a ring onto her finger? Give me a week and I can make it happen. A well-known underwear company recently asked if I could make their underwear appear on passersby for a television commercial, with me in a Santa costume. I explained that yes, it would be possible to magically change someone's underwear, but just because you *can* do a trick, it doesn't mean you should. They hired another guy, and the commercial got made (in a surprisingly tasteful way).

The climate in magic right now feels empowering because we practitioners are pushing into new places, unburdened by the limitations of technology and sleight of hand. It's cliché, and probably a slight exaggeration, but if you can dream it, you can perform it.

It's folly to define the era you're in, but it's hard to imagine we won't look back and define this time in magic as one in which accessibility reigned supreme. Wireless technology, nearly invisible wires, and powerful magnets are not products of the twenty-first century, but only now can these things be remade, reshaped, and altered in the comfort of our homes. The greatest methods in magic were once safeguarded only in the most exclusive libraries. Now, thanks to the internet, they're within reach of magicians in Essen, Edinburgh, and everywhere between. The greatest magicians of the last century became the greatest because they apprenticed with talented predecessors. In this generation, a young magician can study the great shows and magicians without even leaving their room. The internet is a great equalizer for aspiring magicians irrespective of where they live or how much money they have. Studying the great magicians isn't the same as studying *with* the great magicians, but being able to study them *all* isn't a bad substitute.

Historically, innovation is what separated the best from everyone else. P. T. Selbit shocked the world when he sawed a person in half (see page 25). David Copperfield went a long way toward establishing his legend when he vanished the Statue of Liberty (see page 207). These magicians were defined by the feats they performed—and continue to perform, in David's case.

Tomorrow's magicians will be defined in different terms. The next great magician will be judged by her approach. Someone will come along not just with a new bag of tricks, but a whole new way to experience magic.

It's happening already. Shin Lim won *America's Got Talent* in 2018, then won *America's Got Talent: Champions* with little more than a deck of cards. As dozens of other magicians went bigger with their tricks, Shin offered stunning, visual, original card magic. No misdirection, no cheesy dialogue. Just elegant, impossible card magic. With a Vegas show and a television deal on the horizon, he's one I'll be watching with great enthusiasm.

Derek DelGaudio created a sensation in New York and Los Angeles with his show, *In & Of Itself* (also viewable in a streaming version on Hulu). It was a raw, story-driven production that weaved sleight of hand with DelGaudio's personal stories about identity and his experience being raised by a single, gay mother. The show was about identity, and as each person entered, they were asked to choose an "I am" card from a wall of hundreds of possibilities: "I am a dreamer," "I am a guru," "I am a cowgirl." Each person self-assigned themselves a card. Derek was able to divine everyone's choices, telling each person the identity they chose. He looked at every single person in attendance each night and told them their choice. It was a stunning piece of mind reading, and the entire process of labeling oneself evoked powerful emotions. *In & Of Itself* was a commercial success and a critical darling.

I wish I could tell you who the most influential writer in magic is right now, but nobody knows who he is. "The Jerx" is an anonymous blogger whose biting criticism about everything wrong with magic is as funny as it is true. The Jerx doesn't care about doing magic on stages. His arena is informal, impromptu magic. He refers to himself as a "professional amateur," and he specializes in creating elaborate, bespoke magic tricks for the people in his life. He has created a trick to do for someone when you're sharing a kayak, and another one you can perform only for your partner while cooking together. He also plays with the timelines of magic in new ways. One of his tricks apparently takes thirty years to perform, as you reveal a borrowed cell phone inside a buried time capsule from the 1980s. My favorite Jerx trick is called "Letting Go," where he asks a friend to tie her ring to a helium balloon and persuades her to let go. The balloon—her ring attached—floats into the clouds. Then he makes it reappear in a drawer in her own apartment. It's not the kind of magic you can picture any other magician doing, and that's the point.

Social media is also changing magic and not entirely for the better. In the same way that radio shaped the way pop songs were written (less than four minutes, catchy hooks), social media is shifting the way magicians create magic: shorter, more visual, less presentation. This pressure to "fit" magic into tight, shareable bursts on social media has, in turn, shaped public tastes for magic.

However, because of platforms like Facebook and Instagram, magicians are now performing for audiences of millions from the comfort of their own bedrooms. Instead of applauding, their audiences hit the Like button. In some cases, "influencer" magicians are sponsored to wear particular brands while they perform their material, or to perform magic with a company's product. Las Vegas magician Justin Flom has created bespoke magic for Airheads candy and Pringles potato chips, and ad agencies offer his services to brands willing to pay. But these platforms have a time limit for their clips. And numbers-driven influencer magicians recognize that any clip longer than two minutes is unlikely to go viral.

The result is a new genre of online magic with two defining features: the visual nature of the magic and the short duration of the tricks. For a magician to get you to stop scrolling through your Instagram feed, he has to make four aces appear within seconds. *Like.* Four silver coins change into copper coins. *Like.* An apple floats to the performer's mouth. *Like.*

Chris Ramsay is an influencer magician with some five million followers on YouTube. He has, on his own, built a viewership bigger than many magic TV shows achieve. He teaches magic, interviews magicians, does giveaways, and demonstrates some interesting original magic. And he does it all in less than five minutes per clip.

For the next generation of magic, mastery of video editing skills is crucial. I confess that, even at thirty-nine, I sometimes feel helpless in my amateur efforts to put my magic online. Until recently, I never had to consider things like color correction or which lens is best suited to capturing a card trick. Along with a lot of magicians like me, I was too busy developing the tricks—we didn't embrace the new technology. I'm nevertheless encouraged by much of what I see online, and I'm often fooled. But for me, the experience isn't fulfilling in the same way as a live magic show.

What you lose in these brief clips—and it's you, the viewer, who loses—are the things we've explored in these pages. You lose context and seamlessness. In other words, when there isn't time to build even a simple narrative in a trick, it's difficult to cultivate a feeling of mystery. We might be impressed enough to stop scrolling and follow a new, clever magician. This is visceral magic, but it's also shallow. I've yet to see a ten-second magic clip that has context. I've seen stunning displays of skill, but I don't feel connected to them. Perhaps the next great magician will find a way to reach through our mobile phones and give us real mystery. That will be a trick hard to mimic.

Those of us who didn't yet specialize in performing magic online had a rude awakening in March 2020, when the coronavirus pandemic brought everything—including magic shows—to an abrupt halt. I was performing in Australia when the world started spiking with cases. The first step, we decided, was to stop bringing spectators onstage. Then we increased the distance between the stage and the audience. But within a week, the remaining shows were canceled and I flew home to ponder my future as a performer.

What are magicians supposed to do in a global pandemic? If there's a pervading theme throughout this book, it's that magicians think through problems differently. Within a week of the global shutdown—when most planes were still grounded and retail stores had shuttered—magicians began to develop "virtual" magic material. I began receiving calls and video files from colleagues with ideas on how to mount magic shows virtually.

I performed more than sixty virtual shows during the pandemic. I'll miss performing in slippers and sweatpants, but I won't miss much else. Performing for a screen of faces just isn't the same as a packed theater, and the logistics of doing a virtual magic show were frustrating; nothing can be chosen or signed or held by anyone other than me. I never felt lonely onstage until the pandemic.

There was a turning point for me, sometime around the holidays. With a packed schedule of virtual holiday shows, something fundamental came into focus for me: *my* purpose in the pandemic. I've never experienced audiences who were more primed for entertainment. Forget wonder—most of my audiences would settle for a momentary escape from their isolated existence.

What had felt like work started to feel like a privilege. Here were families who couldn't be together to open presents, but they could congregate online as part of a magic show. As magicians, we deliver experiences. It didn't matter that the card tricks were hard to see on the screen, or that the lag between myself and my spectators made *every* interaction a chore. What mattered in the end was the shared experience of wonder.

Magicians aren't first responders, and we played no role in developing the vaccine. But what's significant about our craft's tiny role in the pandemic is that we kept going. In the face of adversity, magicians fulfilled their purpose. We did what we always do: we kept performing.

I have few expectations for the future of magic, but I do have wishes—three, in fact. It has been said that the world will embrace only one magician at a time, and though I can't prove that with math, it checks out. Houdini to Blackstone to Henning to Copperfield—the most famous magicians come one at a time in a given country. My first wish is that the next great magician will be a woman, ideally one of color. It's time.

My second wish is that you, the public, will come to view magic as you do comedy or music or slam poetry—and judge each artist on her own merits. No one hears a bad song and complains, "I hate music." But every time I walk onstage, I'm fighting a percentage of the crowd who dislike what I do based on what others have done. I hope that someday soon, you'll have a list of favorite magicians, and you'll argue about that list over burgers with friends, the same way we argue over burgers about our favorite films.

My third wish is that magicians will become braver. Most of my contemporaries make their living doing strolling magic, roving around corporate functions and bar mitzvahs, asking guests to pick cards. In season two of *The Marvelous Mrs. Maisel*, a resort magician approaches Abe Weissman, a principal character, with a fan of cards and a big grin. "Get the fuck away from us!" Weissman shouts, and then calmly continues his dialogue. Magicians have settled for being paid distractions. My wish—my hope—is that one day we'll be seen as something more. With the amount of work and sacrifice required to become a professional magician, we at least deserve that.

MYSTERY IS THE CATALYST
FOR IMAGINATION. . . .
MAYBE THERE ARE TIMES
WHEN MYSTERY IS MORE
IMPORTANT THAN KNOWLEDGE.

—J. J. ABRAMS, FILM DIRECTOR

We live in the age of answers. I grew up in a time when too many conversations ended with unanswered questions. ("How old is the current president?" "What's the capital of Paraguay?") Nobody knew, and the nearest encyclopedia was in the basement. But thanks to our phones, answers to questions like these are at our fingertips, and videos of unknowable acts are now searchable in seconds on YouTube.

But magic is one of the few things that invokes a question, not an answer. Whether you see a magician online or in your local coffee shop, you're often left asking, "How did he do that?" You have an experience but not an answer. I wonder sometimes how magic fits into our age of answers: as a pleasant counterbalance or as a challenge to the status quo?

There's a pervasive idea that magic is slowly going extinct. The theory is that, as technology evolves and the culture expands, magic is decreasingly impressive. After all, how can magic compete with the incredible effects of Marvel movies or the phone in your pocket right now? Fifty years ago those things would have seemed like magic—now they're real life. So is there room for magic now that our reality is so crowded?

I'd argue that the role of the magician is more important now than at any point in our history precisely *because* what we do remains cloaked in mystery. We have become the last metaphor for the unexplainable. When we see a great magician, it's a shock to the brain, one we can't typically explain with an online search. "Wonder is unknowing, experienced as pleasure," says author David James Duncan. There's nothing like being fooled by a magician.

"When we see a magic trick," writes Jim Steinmeyer, one of magic's most inventive creators, "when something happens that appears to be impossible, we are forced to realize the limits of our views, our doubts, and our expectations." In other words, the experience of magic is one of humility. We see a coin vanish, but what we feel is cosmic. The magician reminds us that there are things beyond our comprehension that we can still enjoy.

If I have learned one thing about people as a magician it is this: They are, by nature, unfocused. They are easily influenced and alarmingly easy to fool. Too often they give up almost immediately on trying to figure things out. That isn't to say people are stupid. But when faced with a mystery, a puzzle, anything they can't comprehend, they are often content in their ignorance. A gasp, a shrug, and on to the next. I see it every night, over and over and over again. If people were more curious, if they thought more critically, the world would be a more interesting place. But my job would be harder.

Occasionally, I encounter a spectator who wants to know more. They track me down after shows to ask questions like those I've answered in these pages: "How often do magicians screw up tricks?" "Can a magic trick be too good?" "Was Houdini the greatest magician ever?" These are the people for whom I most enjoy performing magic. They're engaged not only with the material, but with the thinking behind it.

There are basically two kinds of people who watch magic: those who watch passively, and those who want to know more. Most of my audiences watch magic as it rolls off my fingertips. They enjoy it.

Then they leave it behind. We do this all the time. We hit the buttons on the microwave and thirty seconds later, *abracadabra*, our food is hot. But most of us never pause to consider the microwave.

You are different. You picked up this book because you aren't content to live in mystery. I haven't exposed any critical secrets in these pages, but between the lines I've drawn a map outlining how to see magic. Only the most curious among us care for such details. Magic is for them. Magic is for you.

NOTES & SOURCES

For a more complete listing of credits and sources, please visit *howmagiciansthinkbook.com*.

1: WHY MAGIC? (PART 1)

"Max Maven was the first person I encountered who expressed the idea that we have to evolve from whatever got us into magic in the first place." Michael Close, *Paradigm Shift: Volume Two* (self-pub., 2018), EPUB.

7: SERIOUSLY, HOW DO YOU SAW SOMEONE IN HALF?

For a fascinating play-by-play on the development of this trick, read Steinmeyer's thoughtful account, which was helpful in writing this piece. Jim Steinmeyer, *Hiding the Elephant: How Magicians Invented the Impossible and Learned to Disappear* (Boston: Da Capo Press, 2004).

To learn more about Goldin's lawsuit, see Gary R. Brown, "Sawing a Woman in Half," *Invention & Technology 9*, Issue 3 (Winter 1994), https://www.inventionandtech.com/content /sawing-woman-half-1.

8: WHAT HAPPENS IF A MAGICIAN REVEALS A SECRET?

Thanks to Michael Weber, who provided the quote to open this essay in a personal correspondence.

Jacob Loshin, "Secrets Revealed: How Magicians Protect Intellectual Property Without Law" (JD diss., Yale Law School, 2007), http://dx.doi.org/10.2139/ssrn.1005564.

10: HOW ARE WE FOOLED EXACTLY?

For more on frisson, see Mitchell Colver, "An orgasm for the skin: The strange science behind 'aesthetic chills,'" Salon.com, May 29, 2016, https://www.salon.com/2016/05/29/an _orgasm_for_the_skin_partner/.

The Paul Schrader quote was as told to Eliana Dockterman, "Ethan Hawke Refuses to Complain About Getting Older," *Time*, August 20, 2018, https://time.com/5362184/ethan -hawke-blaze/.

For more on how we process the unexpected, see Ed Catull, *Creativity, Inc.: Overcoming the Unseen Forces That Stand in the Way of True Inspiration* (New York: Random House, 2014). Catull, a co-founder of Pixar Animation Studios, talks about how neuroscientists say we only see 40 percent of reality with our eyes. The rest is filled in by our brains.

11: WHO ARE YOUR FAVORITE MAGICIANS? (PART 1)

The René Lavand quote ("That's why I've come here—to stimulate your sense of wonder") comes from Richard Kaufman and René Lavand, *Mysteries of My Life* (Kaufman and Company, 2013).

15: WHY IS MAGIC STILL SO MALE-DOMINATED?

For more on Ding Yang's act, see "Ding Yang Performing at the Greg Frewin Theatre," uploaded July 10, 2018, YouTube video, https://www.youtube.com/watch?v=tPEnoMTwGCM.

Details about the gender-based experiment were drawn from Gustav Kuhn, *Experiencing the Impossible: The Science of Magic* (Cambridge, MA: MIT Press, 2019).

Suzanne Sauvage, Christian Vachon, and Marc H. Choko, eds., *Illusions: The Art of Magic* (Milan: 5 Continents Editions and Montreal: McCord Museum, 2017).

Ersy Contogouris, "More than a Lovely Assistant: Representations of women in magic posters during the golden age of magic," (working paper, Université de Montréal): 127–131.

16: WHY ISN'T HOUDINI CONSIDERED THE GREATEST MAGICIAN EVER?

Steinmeyer, *Hiding the Elephant*.

The Bernard Shaw quote comes from Sauvage, *Illusions*.

17: HOW DO YOU BUILD A MAGIC SHOW?

The story about passing through towns was told to me by Andi Gladwin, as told to him by David Jones.

The Gene Wolfe quote ("You never learn to write a novel. You just learn to write the novel you're writing") came to me via Neil Gaiman.

The Jorge Luis Borges quote ("The secret is not as important as the paths that led me to it") comes from his short story "The Ethnographer."

18: HOW DO MAGICIANS USE TECHNOLOGY?

Robert-Houdin likely didn't stop a major war with a demonstration of a magic trick. Jim Steinmeyer and Peter Lamont dissect and correct this error, one of magic's gospels, in their book *The Secret History of Magic* (New York, TarcherPerigee, 2018).

19: HOW ARE *YOU* USING TECHNOLOGY?

For a great comparison between science and magic, see Noel Daniel, ed., *The Magic Book* (Cologne: Taschen, 2019): 334.

21: WHO ARE YOUR FAVORITE MAGICIANS? (PART 2)

The "flight time" reference in the Jeff McBride profile should be attributed to Penn Jillette, who used it to refer to a magician's stage time.

22: DO MAGICIANS GET FOOLED?

The Teller quote that opens this chapter is from Teller, "Teller Reveals His Secrets," *Smithsonian Magazine*, March 2012, https://www.smithsonianmag.com/arts-culture/teller-reveals-his -secrets-100744801/. (Michael Close has expressed a similar sentiment in print and verbally.)

The Teller quote ("My job is to leave you with a beautiful question, not an ugly answer") comes from a program from a New York City show by Teller.

23: WHY DO SOME PEOPLE HATE MAGIC?

"Believe it When You Need It" is a phrase I borrowed and adapted from a Grateful Dead album (The Grateful Dead, *Pacific Northwest '73–'74: Believe It If You Need It*, recorded in 1973 and 1974, Rhino Records, September 7, 2018, compact disc).

27: WHAT MAKES DAVID COPPERFIELD SO ICONIC?

I refer to Chris Kenner as David Copperfield's consigliere, but Kenner is also one of the most influential magic creators of his era. He invented a seminal coin effect called "ThreeFly" and helped pioneer the "cardistry" movement (see pages 70–71).

36: WHAT MAKES PENN & TELLER SO DYNAMIC?

Penn & Teller's "The Red Ball" trick is based on David P. Abbott's floating ball trick. In 2005, Teller carefully studied, annotated, and co-authored a two-volume account of Abbott's work: David P. Abbott, *House of Mystery: The Magic Science of David P. Abbott*, ed. Teller and Todd Karr, (Los Angeles: The Miracle Factory, 2005).

The John Lovick quote is from Nicky Ramos-Beban and David Cox, "Asparagus Valley Cultural Society," *MAGIC Magazine*, September 2015.

Penn & Teller Souvenir Booklet, undated. Profile pieces written by each.

37: WHAT'S YOUR FAVORITE MAGIC TRICK?

Additional thanks to John Lovick, who corresponded with me on the details of "Honor System" and provided great insight.

38: WHAT DO MAGICIANS DO IN SECRET?

The Michael Ondaatje quote ("What is interesting and important happens mostly in secret") comes from Michael Ondaatje, *The Cat's Table* (New York: Knopf, 2011).

39: DO YOU HAVE MAGIC STUDENTS?

At Rafiel's request, I've changed details of his story and, in two cases, I've merged details with another prison pen pal, to help protect their identities.

41: WHO ARE YOUR FAVORITE MAGICIANS? (PART 3)

The idea that Tommy Wonder would make a list of best stage *and* close-up magicians was originally a Max Maven observation, and I heartily agree.

49: WHY DO MAGICIANS HAVE SUCH BIG EGOS?

For more on this, see "Introducing the Dumb Houdini Store," *The Jerx* (blog), November 26, 2018, https://www.thejerx.com/blog/2018/11/25/introducing-the-dumb-houdini-store.

52: WHY MAGIC? (PART 2)

The J. J. Abrams quote ("Maybe there are times when mystery is more important than knowledge") comes from J. J. Abrams, "The Mystery Box," March 15, 2007, TED video, https://www.ted.com/talks/j_j_abrams_the_mystery_box?language=gl.

The David James Duncan quote ("Wonder is unknowing, experienced as pleasure") comes from David James Duncan, *My Story as Told by Water* (San Francisco: Sierra Club Books, 2001).

The Jim Steinmeyer quote ("When we see a magic trick, when something happens that appears to be impossible, we are forced to realize the limits of our views, our doubts, and our expectations.") comes from Steinmeyer, *The Secret History of Magic*.

ACKNOWLEDGMENTS

Neil Gaiman said that writing a book is like wrestling a bear. And that's how much of the last four years have felt while writing *How Magicians Think*. For all sorts of reasons, this book was a unique challenge that tested me in ways I didn't expect. I'm indebted to the kind people in my life who have made space in their lives for me and my words. To my parents, Trish and Rocco, thanks for believing in this project.

Thanks to Eli Bosnick, Michael Close, Rod Doiron, Trisha Ferruccio, Andi Gladwin, Michael Kardos, John Lovick, Jamy Ian Swiss, Teller, Peter Turchi, Michael Vance, and Gabriel Zucker for reading various drafts of the manuscript.

Thanks to Jim Levine for staying with this project and for believing in me. Thanks to Workman Publishing—you're family. Thanks to John Meils, my editor. John: you understood exactly what I wanted this project to be when nobody else did. Thanks for getting us here. Kass Copeland synthesized the chapters in this book into stunning visuals, and I'm grateful for her contribution. And to Lisa Hollander, Hillary Leary, Barbara Peragine, and Anna Cooperberg at Workman, among many others. I am in your debt.

Thanks to the many magicians who sat for multiple interviews and provided information for *How Magicians Think*. In particular David Blaine, David Copperfield, Rune Klan, and Teller allowed me into their lives for extended periods of time, which was intrusive and inconvenient, I'm sure. All the same, thank you, friends.

The most important thanks is for my best friend, Andi Gladwin. Andi is two years my junior, but I look up to him in all things except his fashion sense. Every show, trick, and idea I've had is better because of his guidance, and this book owes much to his extensive wisdom.